Sakyadhītā: Daughters of the Buddha

Sakyadhītā: Daughters of the Buddha

Edited by Karma Lekshe Tsomo

Snow Lion Publications
Ithaca, New York

Snow Lion Publications, Inc.
P.O. Box 6483
Ithaca, New York 14851
USA

Copyright © 1988 Karma Lekshe Tsomo

All rights reserved. No part of this book may be reproduced by any means without prior written permission from the publisher. Printed in the USA.

ISBN 0-937938-72-6

Library of Congress Cataloging-in-Publication Data

Sakyadhītā: Daughters of the Buddha / compiled and edited by Bhikṣuṇī Karma Lekshe
Tsomo.
p. cm.
Report of the International Conference on Buddhist Nuns held Feb. 1987 in Bodhgaya, India.
Bibliography: p.
Includes index.
ISBN 0-937938-72-6
1. Buddhist nuns—Congresses. 2. Monasticism and religious orders for women, Buddhist—Congresses. I. International Conference on Buddhist Nuns (1987: Buddh Gaya, India) II. Series: Karamm Lekshe Tsomo, Bhiksuni, 1944-
BQ6150.D38 1989 88-31948
294.3'657—c19 CIP

Dedicated to removing the sufferings of beings everywhere, especially the sufferings of women.

Contents

Preface

This book is essentially an abridgement of the proceedings of the International Conference on Buddhist Nuns, the first worldwide gathering of its kind ever to be held in history. The talks, discussions, and personal exchanges were taped during the conference in Bodhgaya, India. They were then transcribed, typed, and edited in Dharamsala, a small hill station and Tibetan refugee settlement in the Himalayas where His Holiness the Dalai Lama resides.

Nuns, monks, and laypeople from many different countries took an interest in this project, contributing their energy and talents with warmhearted enthusiasm. The transcripts of the talks presented at the conference as well as a composite of the ideas that emerged in response to those talks were written first in longhand. I, an American nun from Honolulu and one of the three organizers of the conference, then typed them out on a manual typewriter while sitting cross-legged in a forest hut. The work was completed in this pleasant ambience in good time, despite the humidity of the monsoon season and the rather primitive working conditions.

Buddhists often say that hindrances attend most worthwhile endeavors. This may be so, considering the number of disruptions that arose in relation to this publication. From the moment plans for the conference began, through completion of the book, obstacles cropped up with astonishing regularity: illness ranging from amoebas to hepatitis, thefts of typewriters, tape recorders and tapes, four unsuccessful attempts to tape His Holiness the Dalai Lama's talk at the opening ceremony, lapses in water and power supplies, monsoon floods and leakage, rodents, scorpions, accidents, and many other interruptions of dazzling variety. Yet innumerable blessings and small miracles also came our way. From these humble beginnings, the participants at the conference and other contributors to this book aim at nothing less than the spiritual awakening of half the human race—women's liberation in the truest sense—so a few stumbling blocks can no doubt be expected.

Under the circumstances, the reader is asked to excuse any errors or flaws in presentation. Since this book is a composite of many people's viewpoints, there is a wide range of style and tone. While some of the pieces included were carefully formulated papers, the majority were totally extemporaneous talks. Speakers included laypeople as well as nuns, arriving from many countries and representing various religious traditions. Many were experiencing their primal landing on the mysterious Indian subcontinent, and were in the process of adjusting to all its wonders and inconveniences. Their approaches may differ, but the conference served a definite purpose in allowing Buddhist nuns a chance to meet and freely discuss their views. The discussions that took place revealed the need for further thought and action on issues of vital concern to Buddhist women.

Female mendicants at the end of the twentieth century find themselves literally in No Man's Land, seeking to gain their spiritual footing. Exploration of women's spiritual potential is an adventure in vaguely charted territory, on a path which transcends territoriality. As I look at the well-read books upon the window sill just now—*Monastic Discipline for Buddhist Nuns*, *Gyn/Ecology*, *Meditation on Emptiness*, *Nepalese Women*, *Aikido: The Way of Harmony*—it is clear that I and many of this generation are attempting to synthesize a multitude of seemingly divergent ideas and methods to apply in our personal development. My prayer beads are perched upon a Sony Walkman, prayer book atop the typewriter—classic dichotomies, yet each item serves its function in a larger scenario. People in the modern world concerned with non-material goals have more tools and knowledge than ever before. Although we are advancing headlong into a multitude of unknowns, if we proceed with positive motivation, our potential for effecting good in the world is greater than at any previous point in history.

The flowers seen from my window were in bloom when the idea of the conference first took shape and are in full bloom again as the words documenting it take shape—the life cycle of a dahlia, a brief but significant cycle in the life of a Buddhist nun. Writing by candlelight, sipping tea prepared on a kerosene stove, momentarily relishing the quietude of this forest retreat, I rejoice in the opportunity to share experiences born of a visionary concept—a universal congregation of spiritual friends drawn together to celebrate the potentials of Buddhist women. I hope that some of the attendant joy will reach the reader.

Bhikṣuṇī Karma Lekshe Tsomo
Dharamsala, 1987

Acknowledgements

All the friends who have helped on this book have been people who love the *Dharma* and believe in the potential for realizing spiritual perfection which lies within all living beings—human and non-human, embodied and disembodied, female and male. All of them are in the process of receiving and practicing the Buddhist teachings and have brought with them to the task the blessings of their practice and of the great spiritual masters from whom they receive guidance.

Deep appreciation for help with transcribing goes to Wendy Barzetovic (U.K.), Lobsang Shastri (Tibet), Sallie Davenport (U.S.), Clara Luque (France), and Quee Josayma (U.S.). For translation assistance, thanks are due to Bhikṣu Thubten Jinpa (Tibet), Bhikṣu Tenzin Wangdak (Tibet), Bhikṣuṇī Jampa Tsedroen (West Germany), Śrāmaṇerikā Thubten Dekyong (Nepal), and Khandro Rinpoche (Tibet). Valuable editorial assistance was rendered by Cynthia Berman (U.S.), Robyn Brentano (U.S.), Michael Harrington (U.S.), Karon Kehoe (U.S.), Gabriele Küstermann (West Germany), Barbara Makransky (U.S.), Andrew Marcus (U.S.), Daniel Purdue (U.S.), Gary Tow (Australia), and Richard Weingarten (U.S.). Sincere gratitude for typing and calligraphy goes to Bhikṣu Gendun Tenzin (Tibet), Śrāmaṇera Thubten Kunga (Tibet),

Śrāmaṇerikā Yeshe Gyatso (Tibet), and Joyce Neves (Brazil).

Thanks go to all those who have made efforts to improve conditions for their ordained sisters, especially to the nuns of the Mahayana Buddhist Nunnery (Tilokpur), to the members of the Tibetisches Zentrum (Hamburg), and to the monks of the Institute of Buddhist Dialectics (Dharamsala).

This book is a tribute to women working together, to nations working together, to religious traditions working together, to women and men, nuns and monks, ordained and lay practitioners working together harmoniously and creatively. It is hoped that this work will be an auspicious beginning for the global progress of Buddhist nuns and a step toward human understanding.

Introduction

It is a tremendous honor and at the same time an immense responsibility to address the powerful topic of women in religion. Having spent most of the past twenty years in Asia, I admit to being somewhat out of touch with both feminist thought and Western Buddhism. Living continuously in an Asian culture, one faces a different everyday reality.

Life in an Asian village is often feared, often glamorized, but in truth it contains both the awesome and the ordinary. The age-old pleasures and struggles of humanity are enjoyed and endured, tempered by mutual social agreements and blending into the larger collage of universal joys and sorrows. As a woman, I am more in touch with the women of my community. As a nun, I am most in touch with the religious life of the community. As a foreigner, I have space, time, and a special perspective. The experience is demanding and frustrating as well as enriching and instructive.

Even after living for more than ten years as a Buddhist nun in Buddhist communities, I cannot presume to make a comprehensive survey of women in Buddhism. Nevertheless, since there are many Buddhist women these days who are seeking spiritual inspiration and encouragement, the conference proceedings and a blend of ideas formulated during and subsequent to the conference are being presented here in the hope that women on the spiritual path can learn from each other's experiences.

If ever there has been a silent minority among Buddhist practitioners, it is the nuns. Many people do not realize they exist. Even in traditionally Buddhist countries, nuns seem more or less invisible. There is a strong likelihood that they would remain that way, except that Buddhist women in Western countries have begun to take an interest in them. Increased attention has been called to the auxiliary, often second-rate position that nuns hold in relation to the monks. Now, emboldened by feminist thought, both Asian and Western Buddhist sisters gradually are beginning to see themselves in a new light.

The present volume collects the ideas and experiences of women who attended or contributed in other ways to the conference on Buddhist nuns in Bodhgaya. Here are women with new-found voices speaking from their hearts on issues that concern them deeply and immediately. These issues primarily relate to the spiritual development of ordained Buddhist women and their role in both Buddhist and secular society, but these issues have relevance for monks and laypeople also, in that they are concerned with important aspects of Buddhist life both in the East and the West. We explore the meaning and value of celibacy in spiritual development and discuss the role of women in religion during times of social and cultural change.

It is significant that the first international gathering of Buddhist nuns was held in India, the birthplace of Buddhism and a land central to religious thought. At the time of the Buddha, innumerable women braved poverty, danger, and loneliness, leaving their homes to follow the path of the Enlightened One. Since that time, the goal of liberation has inspired generations of women, both in India and beyond, to lives of renunciation. Today there are barely a dozen ethnic Indian nuns practicing Buddhism, and they are scattered widely, lacking monasteries, instruction, and support. Yet communities of Buddhist nuns can be found throughout Asia, and individual nuns live in such unpredictable places as Poland, New Zealand, Norway, and Brazil.

Considering the scope of material covered, it may be helpful to set forth at the very outset the major premises upon which the ideas in this book are formulated. One supposition is that since human beings are interested in achieving happiness, naturally they should be interested in gaining enlightenment, the liberating awakened state of mind that is free of suffering and is capable of leading others out of suffering. The next supposition is that women are equally destined, perhaps especially gifted (judging from the relative numbers of women drawn to religion and the contemplative life), to realize this enlightened mode of being. Recognizing that beings assume myriad forms in the course of their evolution, it is also important to recognize that in different lifetimes a person may make progress toward enlightenment as either a woman or a man. Another supposition is that, whether a person interested in enlightenment is a woman or a man, it generally is more efficient to work toward this goal unencumbered by the distractions of family life. Last is the supposition that those women and men who choose to lead the homeless life are entitled to full ordination, and that society as a whole will gain from their appearing in the aspect of *bhikṣuṇīs* and *bhikṣus*, meaning fully ordained nuns and monks. At present, women everywhere do not have this right, though the Buddha originally granted it.

To reiterate, the viewpoint presented here is that beings will gain happiness through seeking enlightenment, that female and male beings should have an equal opportunity to seek that goal, that the homeless state is desirable for many beings seeking that goal, and that homeless ones have a right to seek full ordination, whether they be female or male. Each of these suppositions will be addressed in subsequent chapters.

These days there are many good basic, intermediate, and advanced books on Buddhist thought and practice. This volume assumes a certain degree of familiarity with the field on the reader's part. We shall proceed to dive headlong into the topic at hand, namely, the role and future of women, especially ordained women, within Buddhist and secular society. This topic has relevance not only for Buddhist women, but for all Buddhists and for all women following the spiritual path.

Buddhism is broad enough to accommodate a wide range of ideas and attitudes. If people do not find what they are looking for in one tradition, they are free to explore others. The specter of people forsaking the Buddhist teachings on the grounds that they are sexist is alarming and dismaying. The impulse may be understandable but, especially in the West today, a vast array of approaches is available and certainly not all these approaches are sexist. Those that are sexist can be changed.

New Buddhists are not bound to one tradition by birth, but may freely choose the teacher or vehicle they wish to follow. This fact will exert an influence upon existing schools to liberalize their attitudes and their estimation of women's capacity for spiritual achievement. Those traditions that are open-minded and egalitarian will thrive. Those that cling to gender prejudices will have difficulty surviving.

The key point here is that spiritual development is essentially an individual affair. Institutions may limit women's participation in the outer sphere, but no one can limit their inner development. Spiritual transformation occurs within. This inner transformation is an intensely personal experience and does not depend exclusively on external conditions. No one can stop a person from meditating, even in prison. Many supposed limitations, both inner and outer, are of our own creation.

Nevertheless, one characteristic of the female form is often pointed out as the major disadvantage of a female rebirth: its vulnerability to pregnancy and the responsibilities of parenting which fall largely upon the mother. It cannot be denied that if a woman has children and family duties to attend to, her formal meditation practice will be curtailed, at least to some extent, for fifteen to twenty years or longer. This is true for responsible fathers, too. Real life is full of examples of women and men who have virtually had to put their spiritual life "on hold" due to these responsibilities in their personal life.

Time and freedom for spiritual practice are the chief advantages of the ordained life. When we consider that in most cultures women play the greater part in the upbringing of children, we see that ordination is even more advantageous for women than for men. Asian Buddhist nuns are well aware of this and candidly say, "We are so lucky to be nuns. We don't have to have babies."

Luckily, for sensible women in this day and age, motherhood has become a choice rather than an obligation. It is a choice that spiritually inclined women need to face squarely and realistically. In practicing *Dharma* after having children, one runs up against many choiceless situations. However much such situations may contribute to one's spiritual growth, there is no denying that family life is both time and energy consuming. It is not merely a monastic prejudice to say that one's range of options is broader before childbearing than after. The choices we make with regard to lifestyle are an individual matter; the important thing is to be clear about our choices.

One beauty of modern education is the attempt to link history and theory with contemporary social reality. And one social reality that intensely affects fully half the world's population is that of being female. It is time to deal straightforwardly with the gender issue as it relates to all facets of human experience. The topic of women's religious experience is particularly fascinating and deserves meaningful investigation, especially by those who are directly involved in it. Here we hope to explore women's past, present, and future in the Buddhist context, particularly looking at what the place of ordained women has been and could be in terms of their own personal spiritual growth and their potential to benefit others.

There is no need either to exaggerate or deny the problems and challenges faced in the modern day by nuns of an ancient order. There are staunchly conservative elements within the religious hierarchies of many Buddhist countries that have not allowed women maximum participation in the system. The exclusion of women from religious institutions stands out most starkly in the case of ordained women who have dedicated their entire lives to Buddhist practice and yet may have no access to the basic tools of their profession, such as knowledge of the scriptures and conditions for meditation. Placed as they are outside the religious power structure and often humble to a fault, it is difficult for them to make genuine improvements in their spiritual life.

In theory, there are no limitations set on women's spiritual potential. The Buddha made no gender distinctions when discussing the goal of human perfection. In fact, he specifically stated that women are fully capable of attaining *nirvāna*. Liberated women and men were plentiful in his day. Only after his passing did patriarchal ideas and structures become dominant. The Buddha's initial reluctance to admit women to the order had to do with prevailing social conditions and not with women's potential for enlightenment. Social strictures prevailing at that time were also responsible for the rules requiring nuns to demur to monks. The fact that nuns are required to observe a greater number of precepts than monks, often cited as evidence of gender bias, can be easily explained. When the order of nuns began five years later, it inherited the precepts that had already been laid down for the order of monks. The number of precepts formulated on the basis of a nun's misbehavior are only about half the number of precepts formulated on the basis of a monk's misbehavior.

When investigating feminine imagery in Buddhist literature, it is important to keep in mind the social and cultural setting within which the teachings were given. The original texts themselves present a range of variant images, not contradictory in an absolute sense, but speaking to different audiences and to beings of different propensities. One point to be noted, for example, is that many of the discourses in these early texts were aimed at helping celibate males break through attachments to the female form. Had the Buddha been addressing celibate females, the defects of the male form would have ben similarly elaborated. Thus the gender bias would have appeared exactly the opposite.

It would seem that passages in early Buddhist texts that display gender bias have been rather exhaustively dealt with in previous works.[1] To account for evidence of such bias, the blatantly male-dominated cultural and social context within which the discourses were originally delivered needs to be understood. The prevailing social system was thoroughly patriarchal and caste conscious.

We also need to take into consideration the possibility of interpolations by later writers, all male. A period of perhaps five centuries elapsed between the time that the discourses were given and the time that they were committed to writing. The possibility of misogynist elements slipping in during the interim cannot be entirely discounted. Taking these factors into account, we can appreciate the Buddha's radical egalitarianism in asserting women's equal capabilities and establishing an independent religious order for nuns. These innovations contrasted markedly with the pervasive institutionalized sexism of his day. Out of compassion, the Buddha created an alternative community for women which freed them from familial constraints and encouraged their spiritual pursuits.

It is very important that women are now gaining a sense of their identity and dignity as women. At the same time, we need to understand that in the Buddhist view beings take on different forms in different lifetimes. Even though we have assumed a female form or a male form in this particular rebirth, it is by no means a permanent condition. Intensely identifying oneself with one particular gender or another may have as its basis a sense of familiarity from past life experience or may be justifiable in relation to certain experiences in early childhood, but it is nevertheless ultimately just another example of ego exerting its territoriality. To get caught up in female chauvinism or male chauvinism is not a great deal different in essence from getting bound up in racism or nationalism. All these preoccupations are based on mistaken perceptions. One misunderstands the basis of identification as being permanent when it is actually impermanent. Mistaken identifications such as these lead to countless problems.

A growing number of women, and also some men, feel a

need to identify enlightenment in the feminine mode. I reject the notion, however, that enlightenment can be categorized or identified with gender at all. To set up a male/female dualism with regard to the ultimate of human experience seems superficial and limiting. It is also logically untenable. Enlightenment is an awareness and not a form at all. It is a consciousness free of delusions and free of unknowing. How can such an awareness be male or female? We need no sooner get enmeshed in feminine preconceptions than male preconceptions. To trade one bias for another serves no purpose. Let us instead attempt to unfold the mystery of gender and spirituality to see a bit beyond the level of appearances.

We need to question whether and to what extent male/female identification is relevant in the spiritual quest. Is not ego identification, in the sense of a personal image which exists in reality, quite thoroughly rejected in the Buddhist view? Although each one of us certainly has an individual mindstream capable of becoming enlightened, where is the need to identify this mindstream with a particular gender? Why should a mind become so intensely linked with a form, such as the genitals? Is this philosophically accurate? Is it psychologically healthy?

In searching for some basis for the concept of an "I," the Buddha taught us to check through all five *skandhas*[2] to see if the "I" can be identified with any one of them. Investigation shows that the "I" is, in fact, none of them. Nor is it a composite of all of them. Thus, by analyzing logically, we see that it is a mistake to identify oneself with a particular part of the body.

Similarly, we can analyze the notion of male and female mentality. In Buddhist theory, which denies concepts such as soul and spirit, we are concerned basically with the mind. Spiritual development is essentially mental development. Perfect awareness is gained through purifying the mind and becoming free of confusion and delusion. Spiritual mastery is mastery of one's own mind. Realizations are gained naturally in the process of mental purification. Enlightenment is not an experience where all phenomena are heaped together in a great indistinguishable mass or erased in some huge cosmic vacuum. Enlightened mind not only perceives forms and distinguishes forms, it perceives and distinguishes them perfectly as they are. This awakened awareness, being pure and undiluted, is, however, beyond attachment and aversion to forms, and therefore is beyond attachment and aversion to differences of race, sex, and so on. Following this trend of thought, we can definitively say that enlightened mind transcends the gender issue.

There is a point where Buddhism can legitimately be called into question on the gender issue, however, and that is the disparity that exists between the theoretical spiritual equality of men and women presented in the Buddhist texts and the institutionalized inequalities existing within certain Buddhist societies. Even here, though, we must be careful not to overstate the case or to regard such inequalities as immutable. Once inequalities are identified, they can be rectified quite rapidly through the implementation of constructive, well-considered changes. Now is the perfect time to gain support for such changes.

Certain disparities and inequalities in the Buddhist religious hierarchies naturally came up for discussion at the conference, and various proposals and ideas were put forth to serve as solutions to these problems. If some of these ideas and proposals sound rather conservative to the Western reader, it may be well to remember that the overwhelming majority of Buddhist women are Asian. Out of over sixty thousand Buddhist nuns today, for example, only a few hundred are Western.[3] Consequently, we are concerned to find solutions that will also benefit our Asian sisters. In Asia, there are advantages to working in accordance with existing institutions and with awareness of local sensibilities. This methodology is compatible with the Buddhist ideal of promoting social harmony and may be most effective in the long run. What is a skillful and appropriate action in New York or London may not be ideally suited or enthusiastically received in Chittagong or Rangoon. In Asian settings, demands and protests, for example, far from benefiting the feminist cause, may seriously undermine it. Antagonizing people in the existing religious power structure by agitating for too many changes too fast may, in fact, delay the process. Such methods have been tried by a few Western nuns with unfortunate results.

Eliciting the approval and backing of Asian Buddhists, particularly the monks, for a strong and organized order of nuns is of paramount importance. For reforms to be made effectively, it is important to maintain perspective and proceed steadily and patiently toward improving conditions. We need to take care in formulating our goals, basing them on sound scholarship and an understanding of the nuns' actual present situation. Then we should skillfully work toward these goals, presenting them openly so that everyone may become familiar with the issues. At the same time, it is important to involve the nuns themselves and train them to work for their own development.

Some of the issues presented in the following pages are potentially controversial. For example, there are countries in which the very concept of full ordination for women is highly volatile. Even though the goal of the International Conference on Buddhist Nuns was simply to establish communications links between Buddhist nuns and laywomen to improve their facilities and educational opportunities, one sensationalized report in *India Today* magazine, replete with misinformation and internal contradictions, portrayed the event as if the Buddhist nuns were drawing their battle lines against the male Buddhist clergy! As if that were not enough, this same report was further distorted and reprinted in the Sri Lankan press, causing serious misunderstandings and setting off a whole chain of unpleasant reactions among the *Bhikṣu Sangha* there. The question of equality with monks was not even an issue at the conference, but this false and malicious reportage was enough to seriously strain rapport between monks and nuns on the *bhikṣuṇī* issue.

One writer in Sri Lanka charged that creating a *Bhikṣuṇī Sangha* is equivalent to causing a schism in the *Sangha*, a serious offense. If this were so, it would mean that the Buddha himself was guilty of a heinous crime, since he was the first to create the order! In any event, the texts point out very clearly that dissension caused by nuns is never equivalent to creating a schism,[4] so the whole charge merely amounts to intimidation. The fact remains, as these incidents testify, that the prospect of full ordination for women is an emotionally charged issue in certain countries and needs to be handled sensitively and responsibly.

To provide factual information and encourage a reasoned approach to the *bhikṣuṇī* issue was one of the underlying aims of the conference in Bodhgaya. Far from causing any disruption, the conference served the cause of international Buddhist harmony by providing a meeting ground for Buddhist women—and men—from around the world. Mahāyāna Buddhists happily discovered that Theravāda practitioners do not spend all day thinking of their own welfare alone, and Theravāda Buddhist were delighted to find that Mahāyānists do not have horns and tails. Buddhist women can serve a valuable role by furthering ecumenical understanding among the diverse traditions that have grown up and by seeking to emphasize the essential unity that unites all Buddhists. Since monastic discipline is fundamental and common to all the Buddhist traditions, the *Bhikṣuṇī Sangha* can play an important role in broadening the base of communication between these traditions through promoting the proper practice of the *Vinaya* code of conduct.

That the order of nuns can serve as a unifying force for the world's Buddhists became clearer as the conference progressed. Still, while focusing on Buddhist nuns, the gathering was in no way meant to exclude laywomen or men. For some time in the planning stage, the organizers considered the possibility of broadening the forum to discuss Buddhist women or the spirituality of women as a whole. Eventually, however, we recognized that while there have been any number of conferences on women and spirituality, women and Buddhism, Buddhist monks, and Buddhists as a whole, there has never before been a conference on Buddhist nuns. Was this an oversight or was something amiss?

Although we identify ourselves as Buddhist women in the inclusive sense and feel great commitment to achieving the welfare of humanity in general, we consciously took up the topic of nuns because we felt that they have been overlooked, misunderstood, and underrated for too long. In larger gatherings, nuns tend to shun the spotlight and disappear into the shadows. Since they seldom find a chance to speak up on topics that concern them, we felt it was time to give them special consideration. Now is a time for women to be heard.

Certain features of Buddhism make Buddhists open-minded on the question of women in spiritual practice. First, Buddhism is a logical religion. If correct reasoning is used to press for equivalent opportunities for women in spiritual endeavors, this logic gradually will be understood and accepted. Documentation verifying the equal capabilities and attainments of women in the field of religion will help us state the case and attract support for our worthwhile goals.

Buddhism is also a pragmatic religion. If the practical usefulness of recognizing equal rights and status for women in the religious hierarchy is cogently demonstrated, then these aims will surely gain popular support. To Western women, the need for equal rights and responsibilities may seem self-evident, but to some people such ideas are quite novel. Therefore, we must be prepared to explain and actively demonstrate the benefits of providing facilities and encouragement to women in their spiritual development.

Surely Buddhist monks everywhere, being fond of truth and being dedicated to the welfare of all living beings, will be able to see both the logic and practical benefits of allowing women greater access to the Buddha's teachings. They must recognize that for *Dharma* to flourish in the modern world, particularly in the West, it needs the active participation of both women and men.

That changes in existing institutions are warranted will become apparent as we go along. Reports from some countries clearly show the need for greater participation by women in existing Buddhist institutions and the need for facilities to prepare them for such participation. Having recognized how important it is to assure women a place in the religious structure, a variety of ideas were proposed at the conference as to how changes can best be accomplished. Some people voiced the opinion that while it is important to guarantee a place for women in existing institutions, it is equally important to create independent facilities which are specifically designed to meet the spiritual needs of women. They raised the point that women cannot, and should not, rely on men to provide improved educational facilities, monasteries, and practice conditions for women, contending that it is basically women's own responsibility to do so. The facilities and institutions that women themselves create are likely to be more closely attuned with their own particular needs.

The transformation of Buddhist institutions needs to begin with the transformation of ideas. Society tends to judge women more harshly than men. This partially explains the incidence of a poor self-image in women. The tendency of many women to rely upon men to improve conditions for them results from a habit of dependency which is often rooted in feelings of inferiority. Nuns in particular tend to be humble, retiring, and self-effacing to the point of self-deprecation. A lack of confidence in their own abilities often prevents them from achieving things of which they are fully capable. Any effort to help nuns needs to solicit the backing of the nuns themselves; for this, efforts must be made to improve the nuns' own sense of worth by encouraging their abilities and increasing their self-confidence. Self-deprecating habits and attitudes do not change overnight, but require sensitive handling and great patience on all sides. Once we see that there is no choice but for women to take up the work of improving their own conditions, we see the importance of eliciting the support of other women in the task.

The concept of impermanence, a central Buddhist teaching, denotes all composite phenomena as perishable and subject to change. The good news is that they can change for the better. As women learn to appreciate their own good qualities, they can enhance these qualities and use them for the sake of others. Right now, during this time of strife and degeneration, women can be a virtuous force to stem the tide of corruption, negativity, shameless amassing of wealth, and other sub-standard behavior.

Women can take the lead by steadfastly holding to humanitarian principles of truthfulness, purity of heart, and loving kindness, and by their example, encourage others to do the same. Let us now turn on a positive tack and see what Buddhist philosophy, psychology, and contemplative practice have to offer women.

NOTES

1. See, for example, Diana Paul's two books, *Women in Buddhism: Images of the Feminine in Mahayana Tradition* and *The Buddhist Feminine Ideal.*

2. The five *skandhas*, or aggregates, are form (*rūpa*), feeling (*vedanā*), discrimination (*samjñā*), compositional factor (*samskāra*), and consciousness (*vijñāna*).

3. Estimate does not include nuns in the People's Republic of China or Vietnam today, since statistics are unavailable for these countries.

4. The precise conditions required for creating a schism in the order are explained in I. B. Horner's translation of the *Vinaya-pitaka*, Vol. V, pp. 285-87. A schism in the *bhikṣu* order cannot be created by anyone except a "regular monk," i.e., a *bhikṣu*: "Upali, a nun does not split an Order even if she goes forward with a schism. . .a probationer. . .a novice. . .a woman novice. . .a layfollower. . .a woman layfollower does not split an Order even if she goes forward with a schism. Only a regular monk, Upali, belonging to the same communion, staying within the same boundary, splits an Order."

1 *The First International Conference on Buddhist Nuns*

The idea of a conference on Buddhist nuns arose spontaneously in the minds of a few friends in distant places. As we corresponded, we came to feel a need for Buddhist nuns of different countries to come together to meet each other and to share their experiences as women of the *Sangha*. There had never been such a gathering. For centuries Buddhist nuns have remained quite isolated and have lacked opportunities and language skills for international discourse. Proportionate to their numbers, they have been under-represented at worldwide religious convocations and have tended to avoid becoming a public presence, preferring to concentrate on spiritual practice. Spiritual goals are, and should remain, the primary objective of the nun's life. At the same time, we believed that these goals could be nurtured by bringing together women of the Buddhist family to learn from one another. The principal aims of the conference were to promote mutual understanding and to encourage Buddhist women in their efforts to practice the *Dharma*. The discussions fulfilled many other purposes as well.

It is the common goal of all Buddhists to benefit beings and to help lead them out of suffering. Half of the beings in the world are female and we felt that it is the special task of nuns and other Buddhist women to help the women of the world to understand the Buddhist path to human happiness. We hoped that by lending support to one another, we would gain strength and encouragement to serve others better. By gathering our strength together, we hoped that women could begin to take a more active role in preserving the Buddha's teachings, applying them, and adapting them to the needs of modern societies. We wanted the conference to focus on Buddhist nuns, but to have it open to people of various backgrounds and persuasions—from different traditions, women and men, East and West, ordained and lay. The format of the gathering was left open, to evolve naturally in response to the ideas of the participants. Invitations were distributed widely and we watched in amazement as the plan grew into an international event with participants traveling from twenty-six nations. Enthusiastic responses were received from many, many others who, although unable to attend in person, sent their heartfelt support for the aims of the conference.

We chose Bodhgaya as the best location, since it is at the heart of the Buddhist world, with great spiritual and historical significance. As the site of the Buddha's enlightenment, Bodhgaya symbolizes the potential of all living beings to gain liberation. Just as the Buddha's enlightenment represented a beginning, the conference represented the beginning of an increased awareness among ordained and lay Buddhist women. The conference topics were designed to be of interest to a wide range of people. Discussions focused on what it means to be a nun, what it means to be a Buddhist woman, what it means to follow an Asian religion in Western countries, and what it means to follow an ancient spiritual path in the modern world.

Speakers were chosen from those who spontaneously attended not merely on the basis of academic qualifications, reputation, or speaking ability, but also on the basis of real life experience in relation to the topics discussed. We tried our best to give full expression to representatives of various traditions and nationalities from both the ordained and lay communities. A special effort was made to give women a chance to express themselves, including many who had never spoken in public before. Asian Buddhist nuns fluent in English are very rare, and for the most part, due to time limitations, we had to choose panelists who knew English. In the end, a week seemed much too short for all we wanted to say.

The conference opened on February 11, 1987, with a *Sangha dana*. Lunch was offered to over one hundred monks and nuns. These included the abbots and *bhikṣus* of all the temples in Bodhgaya, together with the *bhikṣuṇīs* and other conference delegates from all over the world. Hundreds of well-wishers from many countries gathered to catch a glimpse of His Holiness the Dalai Lama as he arrived for the event and was greeted in traditional Tibetan style with offerings of white scarves, incense, flowers, and the triumphant peal of Tibetan horns (*gya-ling*) played by Tibetan nuns. The luncheon opened with chanting in various languages. While laypeople picnicked happily under canopies in the open air, the monks and nuns partook of the meal in silence. This silence was befitting, symbolizing the common denominator of monastic discipline to which the Buddhist clergy everywhere ascribe. That both *bhikṣuṇīs* and *bhikṣus* attended the *Sangha dana* together was an auspicious portent for future cooperation between the two branches of the Buddhist *Sangha*.

After lunch, the venue shifted to the nearby Kalachakra Temple where Tibetan ceremonial horns again greeted the honored guests for the opening ceremony. Venerable Gyan Jagat, head of the Bodhagaya Temple Management Committee, led a crowd of over fifteen hundred people in the taking of refuge and precepts, chanting in Pāli. Bhikṣuṇī Karma Lekshe Tsomo greeted the assembled guests with a few words explaining the background and goals of the conference. She introduced His Holiness the Dali Lama, the keynote speaker, who delivered an informative and encouraging talk on the role of women in Buddhism. Helen Wilder (now Sister Nyanasiri) read a message from Venerable Nyanaponika sent from Sri Lanka, and Mr. Abhaya Weerakoon, Commissioner of Buddhist Affairs of the Government of Sri Lanka, delivered words of welcome and support. Following tea, we gathered together to hear a talk by Sister Ayya Khema titled "The Significance of Ordination as a Buddhist Nun."

Greatly inspired by the events of the day, we met in the evening beneath the famed *bodhi* tree. A large group of delegates from Sri Lanka had arranged rows and rows of colorful flowers, lamps, and other offerings. The nuns, in orange and brown robes, led the sonorous Pāli chanting and the laypeople, dressed in white, joined in with great devotion. The merits amassed were dedicated for the weal of the world. To gather together at this sacred spot with Buddhist followers of so many nations and traditions was a very moving experience for all.

More than seventy nuns and monks, along with over eighty laypeople, assembled for the activities that were held during the week that followed. All proceedings were translated into Tibetan language for the benefit of the large number of Tibetan nuns who attended. Each morning began with a guided group meditation at the Kalachakra Temple, led by a nun of a different tradition. This provided insight into the various modes of meditative practice. Both morning and afternoon sessions included talks and symposia followed by group discussions on the topics presented, with individuals sharing their personal perspective and experience. In two sessions, presentations were given describing the circumstances of nuns in both Theravāda and Mahāyāna countries. These presentations gave participants a chance to learn firsthand about the lifestyle and practice of women in a rich variety of Buddhist traditions. Each day topical discussions were held on issues of immediate concern such as educational opportunities, moral discipline, community service, and the prospects for introducing full ordination for women into countries where it does not now exist.

After each panel discussion, there were group discussions, fluid and loosely organized, with participants sitting in circles on carpets outdoors. The atmosphere surrounding the discussions and interactions was extremely congenial, with each person respecting and appreciating the traditions of the others.

Everyone was encouraged to contribute, as related ideas led in intriguing directions. The most interesting ideas from each group were jotted down and presented to the whole gathering at the end of each session. Such an assemblage of informed and warmhearted Buddhist followers concerned with women's issues was a tribute to the strength and flexibility of spiritual practice in the modern age.

Each evening at dusk, when we met for chanting and meditation at the Mahabodhi Stupa, the nuns of a different tradition would arrange offerings in their customary way and lead the others in the measured rhythms of *sūtras* and prayers. Curious tourists and pilgrims from around the world stood by, fascinated by the multitude of forms that Buddhist practice assumes. Burmese, Cambodian, Chinese, Japanese, Korean, Nepalese, Thai, Tibetan, and Vietnamese traditions were all represented. The gentle intonation of the Burmese and Nepalese nuns, the melodious chanting of Amitabha's name by the Chinese nuns in procession, the Tibetan nuns playing cymbals, horns, and drums in supplication to Mahakāla—these were unique and impressive sights in Bodhgaya, where normally only monks lead such ceremonies. As we concluded with meditation together, the offering lamps reflected the unity of the Buddhist teachings within all these diverse forms.

Later in the evenings, we caught glimpses of life in the nunneries of different countries through video presentations. We saw Tibetan nuns debating philosophical texts in Dharamsala and hundreds of Chinese nuns receiving full ordination in Taiwan. On other evenings, informal discussions were held on such topics as personal development as a nun, communications between *Sangha* and laity, and the development of monasteries in Western countries. To see women from so many different cultures at last finding an opportunity to open their hearts on matters of spiritual concern was indeed a remarkable experience.

On the full moon night of the twelfth lunar month, ten *bhikṣuṇīs* of different traditions and nationalities gathered for the confession of faults and the recitation of the *Bhikṣuṇī Prāṭimokṣa Sūtra*. Some twelve novice nuns confessed unskillful actions before their fully-ordained sisters. This is presumably the first time that such a ceremony has been conducted in almost a thousand years, since the order of nuns disappeared from India centuries ago.

One goal that emerged vividly at the conference was the ideal of fostering an international Buddhist sisterhood which would unite women of the various Buddhist traditions. This ideal took shape with the formation of Sakyadhītā, the International Association of Buddhist Women, on February 17, the final day of the conference. Sakyadhītā will serve as a network for Buddhist women working together toward world peace and understanding. It will promote the practice of *Dharma* and encourage women to train as teachers, helping to provide education and research facilities. The association will link the nuns of various Buddhist countries who have been separated by long distances and have lacked contact with one another until now. It will assist women who wish to obtain ordination and will work toward establishing full ordination for Buddhist women in countries where it is not currently available.

To be able to hold a spiritual conference with women from such diverse backgrounds, representing so many different nations, professions, age groups, and religious traditions, was in itself a unique and inspiring experience. The journey that followed, of eighty people to the major Buddhist pilgrimage places, further heightened the camaraderie and provided more opportunities to deepen our spiritual experience. The pilgrimage engendered a sense of connection to the *Sangha* at the time of the Buddha, as we wandered in their footsteps. That so many participants were able to meet and travel together in such a wonderful spirit of mutual cooperation, warmth, and harmony, shows how well women can work together and what great potential there is when they unite for higher goals.

The activities that took place at the conference created new patterns of perception, evaluation, and action. History was in the making. Not only was this international gathering of Buddhist nuns an unprecedented event, but we realized that its implications were far-reaching, both on the personal and transpersonal levels. Now, in a time when the equal rights and potentialities of women are being widely recognized, Buddhist women are gaining courage to play a more active role in the flourishing of the Buddha's teachings. Now, when women are taking their rightful place in every area of human society, it is time for Buddhist women to fully exercise their rights and responsibilities for the promotion of spiritual values in the world. We see the need to work honestly, patiently, and diligently, in accordance with Buddhist principles, to encourage the spiritual development of women, as well as men, everywhere.

MESSAGE FROM BIKKHU NYANAPONIKA

Though unable to be with you in person, I wish to send you a few words of greeting and good wishes. In doing so, I speak only for myself as a Theravādin monk, without any special status.

It is to be greatly welcomed that at the International Conference on Buddhist Nuns, Buddhist nuns and Buddhist laywomen of many Buddhist traditions and many countries have met to deliberate as to how Buddhist nuns could best serve the Buddhist *sasana*. By serving the Buddhist *sasana*, you are serving humanity. In grave times like these, we should concentrate on what unites us all. Differences in doctrine, as well as in modes and roles of ordination, should be met with mutual respect, as they derive from saintly teachers of the past. Foremost in our minds is the familial bond of our common dedication to the *Triratna*, the three jewels of Buddha, *Dhamma*, *Sangha*.

This conference is very timely. In the present situation in the world, we cannot afford to be left without the great power for good that exists in Buddhist womanhood, and even more so in the renunciation of Buddhist nuns. This potential has too often been neglected or ignored due to indifference or prejudice. The great and laudable objective is to deliberate on ways and means for improving the situation of Buddhist nuns everywhere, their education, and their spiritual progress.

As a Theravādin monk, I wish to express my full support of these important aims and offer my best wishes for the success of this undertaking. It is my hope that you will not be content with just listening to lectures and formulating declarations, but that you will also decide on action. These are not leisurely times, and we cannot allow ourselves delays, but must be determined.

May the Buddha's message of wisdom and compassion be realized within all of us, and may you carry that word of his everywhere that is in need of it. I send you the blessings of the Triple Gem. May you all be very happy.

OPENING SPEECH OF HIS HOLINESS THE DALAI LAMA

I prostrate to the ever-kind Buddha who,
Clearing away the net of conceptions,
Possessing vast and profound forms,
Illuminates the all-pervasive light of the teachings!

Today, here in the special place of Bodhgaya, we are able to gather to hold the International Conference on Buddhist Nuns, due principally to the efforts of the *bhikṣuṇī* followers of Lord Buddha.

First, I would like to personally welcome all of you with the greeting "Tashi Deleg." Although I am personally conveying this greeting, I think that indirectly our kind teacher Shakyamuni Buddha and many highly realized beings are, in *Dharma* terms, viewing with great delight from the sphere of unmanifest phenomena, the human efforts that have made this conference possible.

I would like to express my thanks to all those who have been actively involved for many months in the preparations for this occasion today. Similarly, I express my thanks to all of you who have gathered here today through great determination regardless of the facilities. Whenever I visit Bodhgaya, I usually catch a bad cold, but this time, as if by the blessing of this conference, I have not caught one.

As mentioned during the introductory remarks, these days there are many conditions in the world which create very real fears, anxieties, and human problems. At the same time, great advancements and great changes are taking place in the world. There have been many developments which we should all heed, such as an increase in the level of human knowledge.

Today we have the opportunity to discuss women's rights and to explore the potentialities of women within Buddhism, one of the world's religions. By and large, numerous problems in the world have been eliminated through tremendous material progress. Yet this is a time of living with great fear, anxiety, and unhappiness. The *Buddhadharma* has a role to play in such a world, and its message has become increasingly relevant and beneficial. Among those who take an interest in this message, there are many women.

In Buddhist practice we speak of the mother as being the main figure visualized when remembering the kindness of all sentient beings. When we speak of mothers, we speak of women, and these mothers play a very valuable role within the family. There are instances when the relationship between a mother and her child takes a different turn as the child grows up, but generally speaking, from the start it is the mother to whom a child naturally feels the closest link. We find the same words, "mama" and "papa," in many languages.

A child's development of both a healthy body and a healthy mind in life is very much dependent upon the love and affection it receives from its mother. Likewise, speaking from the religious point of view, if the mother happens to be a truly spiritual and knowledgeable person, she can become a crucial influence in her child's education as well. Therefore, both in the context of individual personal development and in society at large, the mother is extremely precious.

So we have arrived at an important point: What is to be done in terms of women's rights from the women's side? As has been pointed out, it is correct to struggle for one's rights, not with pride or jealousy, but with a view to taking on one's own share of responsibility in the critical task of improving the quality of human society. In broad terms, we are actually speaking of world peace. I personally have great conviction in world peace and strive to bring it about, explaining that the way to achieve peace in the world is through cultivating mental peace. In this regard, the mother is seen to play an extremely important role.

Next, I would like to speak briefly about the role of women in general in the Buddhist context. The survival of the *sūtra* teachings of the Buddha depends upon whether or not there is proper practice of the rituals of the "three bases" [that is, confession, and commencing and concluding the rainy season retreat] in the *Vinaya* [discipline of the monks and nuns].

In this regard, when we speak of a "central land," there are two ways of interpreting "central." One is geographical and the other is from the religious point of view. In the latter case, a central land is one in which the four categories of disciples exist and a remote area is one in which they do not. There are two ways of interpreting what constitutes the four categories of disciples. One is that they consist of: (1) *bhikṣus*, (2) *bhikṣuṇīs*, (3) *śrāmaṇeras*, and (4) *śrāmaṇerikās*. The second interpretation is that they consist of: (1) *bhikṣus*, (2) *bhikṣuṇīs*, (3) *upāsakās*, and (4) *upāsikās*. Whether we take the first interpretation or the second, in the case of Tibet, since there are no *bhikṣuṇīs*, it cannot be considered a fully qualified central land in religious terms. It has been regarded as a central land in that *bhikṣus* exist there, but to be precise, there must be *bhikṣuṇīs*. Therefore, we see that *bhikṣuṇīs* are a very important element in the Buddhist order.

Speaking in terms of the *bodhisattva* texts, the *bodhisattva* practice, and the practice of the six perfections, there is no discrimination made as to whether the practitioner is male or female. Male and female are equal. For example, in connection with the practice of the *bodhisattva* path, we see that there are male *bodhisattva* deities such as Maitreya, Mañjuśrī and Ārya Avalokiteśvara. Similarly, there are important female *bodhisattva* deities such as Tara and Saraswati.

Speaking with reference to the *tantric* texts, in *yoga tantra*, and more importantly in *anuttarayoga-tantra*, the female practitioner is said to be very important. For instance, it is said to be an infraction if a *tantric* practitioner fails to prostrate to and circumambulate women in his or her usual practice of *yoga*.

There are actual historical references within the various Buddhist schools as well. During the time of the Buddha, many *bhikṣuṇīs* contributed to serving the Buddhist teachings, just as the *bhikṣus* did. There were both *bhikṣu* and *bhikṣuṇī arhats*. Generally they enjoyed equal rights in terms of observing noble conduct. To give an example, among the many *bhikṣus* who caused the creation of the 253 *bhikṣu* rules [as enumerated by the Mūlasarvāstivādin school], there was principally a group of six such as Udāyin and so forth. Among the *bhikṣuṇīs* who caused action to be taken, there was a group of twelve who committed faults, including Sthūlanandā. Thus, equal rights were given. There was a group of six who were said to have been the creators of precedents for the *bhikṣu Vinaya* rules, and a similar group of twelve among the *bhikṣuṇīs*.

In the same way, we always find both men and women among the practitioners of the *bodhisattva* path. Among practitioners of the *tantric* path, it is well known that there were probably four *yoginīs* among the eighty-four *mahasīddas*. Similarly, when we consider the famous lineage of thousand-armed Avalokiteśvara, it originated from a woman—Bhikṣuṇī Kamala. Just as there is the lineage of the six *yogic* practices of Naropa, there is the very precious lineage of the six *yogic* practices of the *yoginī* Niguma, a female relative of his. In the case of Tibet, there arose many natural *yoginīs* like this. Another example is Machik Labdronma, a spontaneously arisen *yoginī* who became very famous in Tibet for her pacifying "cutting" practice. There were many spontaneously arisen *yoginīs* like this. When I was young, there was one called Shungseb Jetsunma living in the vicinity of Lhasa who was said to be more than one hundred years old. There were many such holy practitioners among the women of India and Tibet, both in the explanations given by the various schools and in actuality.

However, in certain Buddhist texts, for example in the *Vinaya* texts, *bhikṣus* are accorded a higher position than the *bhikṣuṇīs*. Similarly, if one has created a certain fruitional *karma* and is sure to remain as a *bodhisattva*, it is taught that one must necessarily take a male body. Many of these explanations came about in relation to the times, the place, and the social conditions, and most probably were not the original thought of the *Dharma* itself. [Applause.]

In the *anuttarayoga-tantra* texts, it is explained that among those who become fully enlightened beings in one lifetime, there are those who become fully enlightened in one lifetime in the body of a woman. These things come about in relation to social conditions. In general, it is totally wrong to discriminate between castes and to speak of some as being innately superior or inferior. However, it is well known that at the time when the Buddha came into this world in the supreme emanation form (*nirmāṇakāya*), there were castes that were revered and those that were despised, so he chose a noble caste in view of the social conditions of that age. At the time when Buddha Shakyamuni took birth, the royal caste was most highly respected, so for that reason, he took birth in that caste. In the future when Lord Maitreya comes into the world, as mentioned in the *sūtras*, it will be the *brahmin* caste that is regarded as superior. Accordingly, Lord Maitreya will be born into the *brahmin* caste. It is clear that such events occur in response to the viewpoints and social norms in particular places, in that it is necessary to bring the greatest benefit to the people.

In some texts, such as *Engaging in the Bodhisattva Deeds* (*Bodhicharyāvatara*) and *Precious Garland* (*Ratnāvalī*), there are some aspirational prayers in which one aspires to not take a female rebirth. These aspirations are only made due to social factors, in that in those societies a female birth was generally considered inferior. If the situation were reversed, if a male birth were considered inferior and a female birth were considered by society to be the best condition, then the prayer would be precisely the opposite, and we would have to say, "May I not be born as a male." This is explained in the *Bodhicharyāvatara* itself. By understanding the conditions of the world, accordingly we should avoid what is unfavorable within society. The reason for this is that practitioners are meant to serve their own societies, and those who serve should do so in harmony with the norms of that particular society. It would not be beneficial to act in contradiction to society, would it? This clearly illustrates the reasoning behind these things.

In the general Buddhist principles very explicitly set forth in the teachings of the Buddha, it is not race or caste that is significant, but the practice of *Dharma* that is significant. This statement of the Buddha about the significance of *Dharma* practice rather than race or caste is naturally one which interests large numbers of people from the lower castes in India even today. Consequently, it is very clear that there is no differentiation between men and women in the practice of *Dharma* whatsoever.

Speaking specifically on today's topic of *bhikṣuṇīs*, there were originally four schools among the Vaibhāṣhikas and these further split into eighteen schools. The lineage of precepts that came into Tibet was the Mūlasarvāstivāda school, according to which the *bhikṣus* follow 253 rules. According to this Mūlasarvāstivādin school, twenty-two people are required to ordain a *bhikṣuṇī*: a preceptor *bhikṣuṇī*, an instructor *bhikṣuṇī*, ten attendant *bhikṣuṇīs*, and in addition, ten *bhikṣus*.

Since the journey was very difficult in early times, *bhikṣuṇīs* were not able to come to Tibet. And since no *bhikṣuṇī* lineage was established in Tibet, there was no danger of transgressing those *bhikṣu* precepts which were incurred in relation to *bhikṣuṇīs*. This is the advantage we *bhikṣus* had in Tibet. These days we find that there are *bhikṣuṇī* lineages in some parts of the world, such as the Chinese lineage. Speaking personally as a Tibetan Buddhist, if an authentic *bhikṣuṇī* lineage like this could be established within the Tibetan tradition, this would truly be something to be welcomed.

From among the many *Vinaya* schools, we find that it is the Theravāda that is practiced in Sri Lanka and Thailand. In this system, the recitation of the *Prātimokṣa Sūtra* is done in Pāli. Therefore, in that there are different schools of *Vinaya* like this, it would seem that there may also be different ways of giving the precepts. It is important for us to conduct research on these matters, and we are already doing so from the Tibetan side. In this way, we can also deal with the matter of lineage. I have been thinking about it and hope that gradually more and more seminars such as this one can be organized so that fully ordained Buddhists from various countries can gather together to discuss these matters.

One point I would like to stress here is that you *bhikṣuṇīs* and other nuns are now showing concern and taking responsibility. Therefore, it is important that you establish relations with those in Sri Lanka, Thailand, and Burma.

Another important thing is that, whether you are a *bhikṣuṇī* or a novice nun, it is essential that you take an active interest in Buddhist studies. In the past in Tibet, there were nunneries with good study programs. Meanwhile, since we have been living as refugees, I have been strongly encouraging and exhorting those staying in the nunneries now re-established in India to definitely take interest in studies.

From the point of view of actually upholding, preserving, and disseminating the teachings of the Buddha, having equal rights in fact means making an equal contribution. This being the case, to study well is to be of service to the transmitted teachings, and to the upholding, preserving, and disseminating of this transmission. After studying the doctrine, to personally practice its inner meaning is to be of service to the upholding, preserving, and disseminating of the teachings of realization.

In conclusion, I pray that during the seminars convened at this conference you will be able to successfully contribute in some measure to the teachings of the kind Lord Buddha. I rejoice in your efforts!

By virtue of these merits,
May we attain the state of the All-seeing One,
Subduing the enemy of faults,
Releasing beings from the tides of old age, sickness, and death
In the turbulent ocean of cyclic existence.

The Buddha has come into the world,
Clearly illuminating the teachings like sunlight,
Bringing sibling harmony among upholders of the doctrine;
May all be favorable for the continuation of the doctrine!

May the ordained upholders of the three
  trainings,
By virtue of their collective merits,
Teach and practice until the end of time;
May all be favorable for the spread of the doctrine in the ten directions!

THE SIGNIFICANCE OF THE CONFERENCE

by Bhikṣuṇī Jampa Tsedroen

Many people are asking why this International Conference on Buddhist Nuns in Bodhgaya has been attracting so much attention. No doubt one reason is the fact that this gathering is the first conference of Buddhist nuns to have taken place in India since the time of Buddha Śakyamuni. It is known that the *bhikṣus* came together for several councils after the Buddha passed into final *nirvāna*, but there is no evidence that *bhikṣuṇīs* played any role at these councils. Nevertheless, Buddha Śakyamuni taught that all sentient beings have the same potential (Buddha nature) to obtain enlightenment, and women today have more freedom than ever before to explore and develop this potential.

Indian society in the Buddha's day was ruled by a very strict system of castes, yet the Buddha rejected such a social hierarchy along with discrimination between men and women. This was quite revolutionary at that time. He instituted an order of nuns invested with rights equal to those of the monks. Nuns were authorized to teach, to have their own administration under an abbess, and to confer ordinations, though these ordinations needed to be confirmed by the order of monks. A bewildering range of opinions is current as to the status of women in early Buddhism, but the most realistic view is that the Buddha's formulations developed against the background of society of that era.

Women in those early centuries were not accustomed to making independent decisions. Influenced by tradition, they derived their orientation from men's attitudes and developed deeply rooted habits of seeking men's protection and guidance. Seen from this perspective, it is natural that women assumed a subordinate role. Immediate and total independence was impractical and would have made the community of nuns extremely vulnerable. Under the circumstances, the nun's life was one of unusual liberties. The order flourished for a long time, often enjoying the patronage of kings' daughters and others of high rank. Throughout the centuries, women unable to join the order yet fiercely determined to dedicate their lives to the *Buddhadharma* also had the option to practice as *upāsikās* (laywomen with five precepts).

The Buddha made provisions for the protection of the order of nuns against attacks from outside. He arranged that nuns maintain regular contact with the order of monks, enabling them to obtain practical knowledge, advice, and inspiration from their ordained brothers. He might also have considered that the monks would gain inspiration from contact with unusually capable and independent women, yet despite the precautions taken, the order of fully ordained nuns did not survive in the Theravāda countries. The order still exists in the Mahāyāna traditions of China, Korea, and Vietnam; in fact, due to political difficulties, nuns sometimes outnumber the monks.

The situation of Tibet is unique among the Buddhist countries. Due to its geographical situation, the overland journey by foot from Tibet to India and back was too difficult for most women. From history books and narratives one can conclude that this prevented the founding of a *bhikṣuṇī* order in Tibet. Some of the nuns who tried to reach India to receive *bhikṣuṇī* ordination died on the way or remained in India after their ordination. There is sporadic mention of Tibetan *bhikṣuṇīs* in the texts, but there were never enough to found a separate order. Nevertheless, many nunneries existed in Tibet, occupied by *śrāmaṇerikās* who received their ordinations from *bhikṣus*. There have been spiritually gifted and highly realized women throughout Tibetan history, sometimes even serving as teachers to monks within the Buddhist *tantra* system.

Since *bhikṣuṇī* ordination can only take place in the presence of *bhikṣuṇīs* and *bhikṣus*, and since in many countries *bhikṣuṇīs* no longer exist, many monks, laypeople, and also a large number of eight- and ten-precept nuns have become resigned to the lack of a *bhikṣuṇī* order. Near the close of the twentieth century, however, we seem to be approaching a turning point.

For some decades Buddhism has been spreading to Western countries. In many cases, Western women have met with great obstacles in their search for instruction and conducive conditions for the practice of *Buddhadharma* in countries where an order of fully ordained nuns does not exist. Some have abandoned their quest, while others persist.

Now, due to the untiring pioneering efforts of a number of dedicated Buddhist women, especially of the chief organizer, Bhikṣuṇī Karma Lekshe Tsomo, and the two co-ordinators, Sister Ayya Kehma and Dr. Chatsumarn Kabilsingh, the first conference of Buddhist nuns has taken place in Bodhgaya, the site of Buddha Śakyamuni's enlightenment. Ayya Khema expressed our heartfelt sentiments during the opening ceremony of the conference: "A dream become reality."

The opening address of His Holiness the 14th Dalai Lama gave many people reassurance regarding the serious objectives of the conference. Some observers had feared that the gathering could be misused as a platform for Western feminists in a blind battle for equal rights that would damage Buddhism. Yet all soon discovered that such fears were unnecessary. The head of the Mahabodhi Temple Management Committee, a highly esteemed monk of the Theravāda tradition, stated with pleasure: "Worries that some people had at the beginning of the conference have obviously not been confirmed. The conference took place in a very harmonious and peaceful atmosphere. The nuns can also count on my support."

The far-reaching long-range benefits of the conference are yet to be seen, but there are already some remarkable indications. Not only did the event have historical importance, it was also a landmark gathering of nuns and laywomen of nearly all traditions, with the support also of many monks and laymen. Those who know of the difficulties of bringing together many different groups all with slightly different opinions and placing them at one table, will recognize the significance of a gathering with 120 officially registered participants. This in itself was a sign of success.

Many nuns attended who have been making their own way with little or no support from an established order, practicing totally on their own for years. Talks, exchanges of experience, discussions, workshops, meditations, and *pūjas* together helped these nuns develop strength, hope, self-confidence, and a sense of community together. The problems facing nuns in some countries also surfaced. Whether there is a direct relationship between the two phenomena or not, it became obvious that in those countries where there is no *bhikṣuṇī* order, nuns face many more difficulties. Where there are no educated *bhikṣuṇīs*, there are no fully qualified women teachers of *Dharma* and no one to take responsibility to give the nuns thorough training. Where there are no highly educated nuns to take the lead, standards of education and training are quite low, and consequently nuns are not taken very seriously. Thus, the opinion prevails that nuns, and women in general, do not have the talent and qualifications necessary for teaching and administration within the religious hierarchy. Under the circumstances, educated women from good families in these countries rarely enter the order.

Now, inspired by the obvious concrete advantages of improved education, disadvantaged nuns are developing a new understanding of their future goals. First, they need to close the gap and remedy their deficient knowledge of the Buddha's teachings. Secondly, they have gained hope for establishing *bhikṣuṇī* orders where they do not currently exist. Upon a foundation of equal education and status, many practical improvements will naturally ensue.

Personal exchanges, video presentations, and some talks by remarkably qualified speakers served as a great source of inspiration for all the nuns, opening their eyes to the tremendous possibilities for advancement that exist. It was very inspiring to see *Dharma* practitioners from various Buddhist countries come together with a common goal of improving conditions for female Buddhists in the world and be able to work together very harmoniously. Not all participants communicated in the same language, but, although translations were necessary, with a wish to ally for the solution of common problems, the participants related to each other with a very benevolent, interested, and tolerant attitude. Through this experience, we saw what could be accomplished if the energy of all women and men who are willing to contribute were concentrated for the achievement of common goals on an international level. To put this idea into reality, on the last day of the conference we founded Sakyadhītā, an international Buddhist women association, which will attempt to translate into reality the theories that were raised during the conference.

It became clear to all of us that a learning exchange among women of various Buddhist traditions is of great significance. For example, participants learned that as a rule, many *bhikṣuṇīs* in Taiwan, Korea, Vietnam, and Western countries become ordained only after completing at least high school. Their educational background allows them to study and practice at a higher standard and eventually to teach others. They are able to contribute substantially to upholding and spreading the *Dharma* teachings in accordance with the Buddha's intentions, side by side with the monks.

In the course of discussions, Western nuns also recognized that after joining the *Sangha* it is their responsibility not only to train thoroughly in all fields of Buddhism, but to prepare the fundamental conditions for establishing nunneries in the West and to help to improve conditions in nunneries in the East that lack support.

These days *śrāmaṇerikās* and also some *bhikṣuṇīs* of the Tibetan tradition study at such institutions as the Institute of Buddhist Dialectics in Dharamsala and the Institute of Higher Tibetan Studies in Sarnath (India). Educational programs in Buddhist philosophy are being set up in the Tibetan nunneries which will be equivalent to those that are found in the monasteries. Thanks to the open-hearted and understanding attitude of the Dalai Lama, the nuns of the Tibetan tradition have begun to make great improvements. Through years of experience, meeting and teaching Western people, he realizes the importance of giving support and vital encouragement to both monks and nuns, particularly with a view toward spreading the *Dharma* in the West. He has pointed out, with his very special sense of humor, that we can only speak of a "central land," and a land where *Dharma* flourishes, if both the *bhikṣu* and *bhikṣuṇī* orders flourish there. Therefore, technically speaking, despite the wide spread of Buddhism there, Tibet has never been a "central land" due to the lack of *bhikṣuṇīs*. His Holiness noted that previously Tibetan monks had no chance to practice those *bhikṣu* rules which relate to *bhikṣuṇīs*, but that now *bhikṣuṇīs* are being welcomed in the Tibetan tradition.

To continue the dialogue that has now begun among nuns and laywomen of various traditions, a second conference is envisioned. Monks, especially *Vinaya* experts of all traditions, would be invited to discuss the possibilities and ramifications of reviving the *Bhikṣuṇī Sangha* throughout the Buddhist world. Nuns expressed their wish that an understanding of the issue be reached that will be congenial to all, such that the order of nuns may grow and function in harmony with the order of monks. The nuns are asking the monks for their support to re-establish the *Bhikṣuṇī Sangha* as it existed during the Buddha's lifetime.

There are a number of obstacles to be faced. Deeply rooted habits and prejudices will confront the nuns on their path. The very nature of their struggle is in many countries circumscribed by cultural and social limitations. All are anxious to proceed by methods that are in harmony with the Buddha's teachings. At the same time, there is a critical need to improve things that have remained unchanged for centuries. Much skillfulness and patience, tolerance and trust, will be required to achieve these worthwhile objectives. Despite the difficulties that loom ahead, the conference evoked hope and optimism in many of us. His Holiness the Dalai Lama assured us that many Buddhas and Bodhisattvas were viewing the conference, and we have faith that they will guide our endeavors in the future. Since our efforts are aimed at spreading the teachings for the benefit of humanity, we are confident that conditions will unfold favorably.

2 *Ordination As a Buddhist Nun*

In exploring the significance of becoming a Buddhist nun, we first need to discuss what a nun is. As any dictionary will tell us, a nun is a woman who lives under a vow of chastity. She is, therefore, celibate by definition. She may hold other vows as well, but the vow of chastity is fundamental to monastic life. Even the term "lay nun," used by Christians to denote someone living outside a convent and wearing conventional clothing, necessarily indicates women eschewing sexual relationships; otherwise, she would be termed a laywoman. To refer to a woman who is not celibate as a nun is confusing both for the woman and the public. The same applies in the case of a monk.

Buddhist nuns formally may be classified into three categories: novice (*śrāmaṇerikā*), probationer (*śikṣamānā*), and fully ordained nun (*bhikṣuṇī*). In addition, due to the extinction of the *bhikṣuṇī* lineage in some countries, there are large numbers of women living the lives of nuns without being classed in any of these three categories. Of the estimated sixty thousand Buddhist nuns in the world today, approximately fifteen thousand are *bhikṣuṇīs*, five thousand are novices, and the remainder are women living as nuns without having received any one of these three ordinations. *Bhikṣuṇīs* are found in the Chinese, Korean, and Vietnamese traditions. *Śrāmaṇerikās* are found in the Chinese, Korean, Tibetan, and Vietnamese traditions. Nuns holding eight, nine, or ten precepts, without formally receiving any of the above ordinations, are found in the Theravāda traditions of Burma, Cambodia, Laos, Nepal, Thailand, and Sri Lanka. The nuns of Japan receive *bodhisattva* precepts, but do not formally receive any of the three abovementioned ordinations. Nuns holding *śikṣamānā* precepts are rarely found in any tradition today.

One becomes a nun by a very precise set of rituals and by undertaking specific commitments that are usually made for life. A nun lives by the precepts of the *Prāṭimokśa*,[1] the Buddhist code of monastic discipline. In some traditions, these precepts are viewed as vows, in the sense of a promise or oath. In other traditions, they are not termed "vows," but rather "training rules," meaning a set of rules that pertain to one by virtue of one's status as an ordained person. The term "precepts" stands midway between the two and can be used in either sense.

Normally, for ordained nuns and monks, the taking of precepts is a lifelong commitment. Thailand is a notable exception in this regard. There are specific conditions under which one may give up the ordination[2] and, by declaring one's intention to a person capable of speech and comprehension, return to lay life, though this is not encouraged. Ordinarily, becoming a nun or monk entails a lifetime commitment; therefore, it is important to consider the matter very carefully before making such a step.

One of the main commitments of ordination is celibacy. The Buddha certainly regarded celibacy as a virtuous and wholesome way of life. He advocated a life of renunciation over and over again. In the Pāli texts, he refers to the celibate life as "the glorious pure life," and in the Mahāyāna *sūtras*, he calls it "the perfect foundation for the Great Vehicle and superior by far."[3] In the Buddha's day and for centuries ever since, untold millions of people have rejected the shackles of family ties and embraced the freedom of the homeless life.

To understand the importance of celibacy, we need to honestly appraise what normally happens in a close relationship. Whether between women and men, women and women, or men and men, the problems of attachment in relationship are basically the same: clinging, unfulfilled expectations, the pain of separation, and so on. A common pattern is initial fascination and subsequent disappointment—what in Buddhist terms is a classic example of the "suffering of change." Ceaseless power struggles, both subtle and overt, also typically attend intimate relationships. Often the longing for a companion is a wish to complement one's missing or underdeveloped qualities. Once in a relationship, one tends to project these qualities onto the partner, which leads to a problematic cycle of expectations and frustrations. Even in the best of cases, there are the energy-consuming tasks of corporate decision making, daily maneuvering, and maintaining appearances.

Celibacy, on the other hand, represents a decision to rely on one's own inner authority. It is an attempt to achieve a balance and wholeness within, independent of the feedback of another person. Being independent, one is released not only from the gross complications of relationship, but also from the dualistic pattern of existence that persists on one level or another twenty-four hours a day. In relationships, there is a tendency to synthesize one's own experience of seeing, hearing, and knowing with that of another. The resulting perception is a synthesis which lacks the freshness of independent perception. There is a certain amount of double-think involved in being one of a pair.

The independent woman makes decisions without the invisible shield of partnership alliance and without the incessant concession-insistence syndrome. Remaining single, she is free to experience life directly, participating wholeheartedly with undivided attention. The resultant unperturbed mental space is very beneficial for meditation and for growth as a whole being.

Singleness is far from implying selfishness, however. As the watchful mind dispassionately observes itself and outer phenomena without being delimited by the dualism of a one-to-one relationship, one becomes free to respond genuinely to animate and inanimate surroundings without restriction. This allows more free leisure time to be devoted to the needs of suffering beings. Instead of devoting one's time and energy exclusively to immediate family members, one can use these resources for worthwhile projects such as attending to the needs of sentient beings as a whole.

Although the central decision entailed in ordained life is celibacy, celibacy is not seen as a matter of repressing a positive natural urge borne of human affection. It has a far deeper implication that is worthy of consideration. The Buddha taught that sexual attachment is the major force that propels beings from one rebirth to the next. To become free from repeated birth in cyclic existence, therefore, it is necessary to overcome sexual attachment. When we realistically reflect on all the problems that intimate relationships and family life bring, we start to see things in a new perspective. Those deeply interested in spiritual development inevitably begin to see romance as overrated. Even for family people, celibacy usually comes as a natural result of spiritual practice. Furthermore, since the advent of AIDS, sexual involvement has even become a life-threatening activity. It is time to begin discussing the merits of celibacy publicly.

The decision to remain celibate is particularly significant for women. It is the ultimate rejection of life as a sex object. It becomes a symbol of independence from the type-casting that sees women only as adjuncts to men or as capable of nothing more worthwhile than partner relationships. For ages women have allowed themselves to be stereotyped in this role, and it requires nearly superhuman effort to step out of the mold. Once taken, the decision to live a celibate life amounts to a positive reversal of repeated, often compulsive, involvement in relationships and signals a new era in independent thinking. It means opting out of the body market and going on to something more meaningful. In the case of an ordained person, this signal is reinforced by the vows and robes, which act both as a protection and as a reminder of one's decision.

Admittedly, such a life entails taking great individual responsibility and is not for the faint-hearted. When we are involved in a relationship, we always have something to pin our deficiencies on: "If only I didn't have a husband and kids, I could really get down to the practice." "All I need is a little space and I could get myself together." It is so human to search outside ourselves for the cause of the problem, but when we are single, it is harder to find something to blame our problems on. Hard as we may try, everything points back inside. We desperately look for a replacement, a scapegoat—food, job, people, the weather. It is astounding how wily the mind can be in trying to evade responsibility for its own well-being. If one faces up to this responsibility, living independently can foster tremendous insight and inner strength.

Women, who normally bear the major portion of familial responsibilities, stand to gain the most by avoiding conjugal relationships in favor of a celibate lifestyle. The life of a nun, or at least a continent lifestyle, is a positive alternative for women who are committed to spiritual development and see relationship as constricting and problematic. Like-minded women have the possibility of creating a real sisterhood united by their common determination to move toward religious goals.

Many people are curious about why a woman would want to become a Buddhist nun. They wonder what motivates such a decision and what conditions have contributed to it. Many imagine that life as a nun is a type of escape and means cutting oneself off from all human contact and from all involvements with "the outside world." There is a mystique and strangeness associated with the idea of renunciation. The notion seems both attractive and grotesque.

People become ordained for different reasons. Many factors may influence the decision. In Buddhist countries, where ordination is viewed as extremely meritorious, it is said that predispositions arising from positive actions created in past lifetimes play a big part in a person's decision to become a nun or monk. In these countries, it is generally believed that without having created certain "roots of merit" in the past, one would never get an opportunity to live the ordained life. It is pointed out that propensities such as a fondness for nuns, monks, and monasteries in small children, for example, are evidence of familiarity with monastic life from past incarnations. Such propensities may be one factor in a person's decision to seek ordination.

Other factors may be more mundane. Illness, poverty, death of a loved one, disappointment in love, failure in school or professional life, and similar frustrations may also play a role in one's decision. In some countries, frankly speaking, ordination is seen as an above-average job opportunity. The life may entail austerities, but there is a certain amount of security in it, at least in the case of monks. For this reason, there are examples of children from poor families being placed in monasteries by their parents. The monasteries sometimes serve as orphanages, too. Nevertheless, the eventual decision to take vows in necessarily a voluntary one, made by the children themselves when they reach a responsible age.[4]

In recent years, as the standard of living in Buddhist countries has improved, economic factors have come to play less of a role in populating the monasteries. In fact, a decline in enrollment correlates to some extent with improved economic conditions. It should be pointed out that nuns generally receive fewer donations than monks. Since ordination is materially less advantageous for them, economic factors accordingly play less of a part in the nuns' decisions to become ordained.

In any case, for most people the decision to lead the homeless life is primarily motivated by a sincere wish to practice the Buddhist teachings full-time. It is a decision which requires courage and thoroughgoing honesty. If one is able to accept the difficulties entailed, the homeless state is said to be the ideal condition for engaging in *Dharma* practice. From the start, for one thing, the decision to become ordained is said to make a very positive impression on the mind. In Buddhist terms, ordination is said to be a virtuous "action" (*karma*) which creates a wholesome imprint upon the mindstream. Those who accept the law of cause and effect believe that virtuous actions like this bring positive results, both in this lifetime and in future lifetimes. Then, to keep the vows purely is considered to be wholesome in itself, accumulating merit moment to moment. It is even supposed to benefit one's relatives for seven past and future generations. Furthermore, having positive vows[5] on the mindstream is said to increase the value of whatever other virtues one may create. For these and other reasons, ordination was taught by the Buddha to be the best condition for *Dharma* practice.

Ordination is also considered a conducive condition from a practical point of view. The precepts that one agrees to live by are very useful guidelines for daily behavior. These guidelines not only prevent one from creating grossly unwholesome actions, they also restrict unnecessary worldly activities which could lead to unwholesome actions. The precepts help to simplify life and serve as constant reminders of the primary purpose for becoming ordained, namely, to practice the *Dharma*. When protected by monastic precepts, there is no longer any need to belabor decisions concerning alcohol, drugs, relationships, and similar involvements. Daily life becomes very simple, and the mind has a chance to become more directed, less dispersed. In this way, precepts help assure conducive conditions for contemplative practice.

Ordination is symbolic of renunciation. When we speak of renunciation here, though, we are not speaking of renouncing chocolate or parties. We are speaking of renouncing the endlessly boring process of repeated birth and death known as cyclic existence (*samsara*). Since unwholesome actions are the causes that involve us in the syndrome of birth and death, ordination directly helps to disentangle us from this process by keeping us on guard against unwholesome actions. By restraining us from creating negative actions, the precepts serve to free us from *samsara*. With this logic in mind, Buddhists regard holding a greater number of precepts as being proportionately more beneficial. The more precepts we have, the less negative *karma* we are tempted to create, hence the less misery we shall have to experience in the future.

Some people feel that ordination is essentially escapist, a cowardly retreat from everyday realities. They view renunciation as seeking an easy way out of the world's problems—a basically self-centered solution. While this may be true for some, it should be made clear that renunciation is not as easy as it looks. It is far easier to constantly occupy one's time with worldly activities than to face the dilemma of human existence head-on. Despite the gnawing sense of dissatisfaction felt by the bulk of humanity, most people prefer to shift their attention from one mundane concern to the next rather than try to tame the mind and search for some deeper meaning in life.

It requires courage to sit down and observe one's own mind even for an instant. It is so much easier to be seduced by worldly ambitions than try to abandon them, since such an abandonment means going against the world's expectations and one's own natural instincts for seeking pleasure. This is not to say that only nuns and monks search for meaning in life. I believe that within each person there is a deep longing for the spiritual life, an earnest wish for inner peace and an uncluttered existence. Perhaps it is the inability to get in touch with this elusive "deeper meaning" that accounts for a great deal of the insanity and despair in the world today.

Again, some people view celibacy and singleness as selfish, and ask what would happen if everyone decided to become a recluse and went off to meditate. There would be no one to cultivate the fields and no one to regenerate the world's population. Human beings would become extinct in a world of celibates and die of starvation.

The answer obviously is that this will never happen. The celibate life has always been an option since the beginning of time, but very few people have availed themselves of the opportunity. Christian cloisters have been functioning for centuries, but have never been swamped with applications for admissions. The huge monk populations of Tibet resulted from a combination of social circumstances (including the fact that the monasteries served as schools), and not solely from the spiritual aspirations of the young monks who were placed there. Life in the monasteries involves hardships on the mundane level as well as in the spiritual journey. Despite the difficulties of life in the world outside the monasteries, it has always been the preferred choice of the vast majority. There is no reason to suppose that this trend should reverse itself, especially in the world today when the media strive ceaselessly to captivate the mind and entice it to worldly pleasures in concerted advertising campaigns.

Sometimes people feel that the clergy are a distinct drain on the economy and criticize them for not contributing materially to society. One response to this is that, although none of the service professions produce anything material, they nevertheless make important contributions to humanity. Moreover, religious practice has always been regarded by many as having its own intrinsic value. Far from being a burden to society, nuns and monks have traditionally been viewed by Buddhists as an asset to the religious life of the broader community. Even a person who is not able to personally follow the religious life finds consolation in the fact that others can. It seems comforting to know that *Sangha* members are devoting themselves full-time to following the Buddha's teachings—studying and teaching them—occupations that are more difficult to find time for when living a household life. Lay Buddhists find it reassuring to call to mind the renunciates who live in quietude pursuing the spiritual life and rejoice in their virtuous efforts. They find it worthwhile to have such people to turn to for counsel when faced with the problems of worldly life. They also find it valuable to have people in society upholding the precepts. In the Buddhist scheme of things, it is important that there be *bhikṣuṇīs* and *bhikṣus* to serve as teachers and to administer ordination to the Buddhist laywoman (*upāsikā*) and layman (*upāsakā*).

Despite all the merits of the ordained life recounted above, these observations are not at all meant to imply that celibacy is the only efficient means to inner growth or that laypeople cannot successfully practice the *Dharma*. There have always been very sincere practitioners who lived within relationships and highly realized beings who were not ordained. Possibilities for practicing as a layperson are better today than ever before. Higher standards of living, increased leisure time, and independent lifestyles can combine to provide fairly ideal conditions for spiritual practice even without joining a monastery.

In modern Western societies, pursuing practice as a single layperson is an attractive option. In traditional Asian societies, by contrast, no feasible middle way existed—one was either married or a recluse. There was virtually no third possibility. Even today in the Asian context, bachelorhood is a dubious status; spinsterhood is worse yet. In such societies, the cloister has always offered a welcome alternative to arranged marriages and tyrannical in-laws. Many Asian nuns become ordained because they do not want to get married. These days, however singleness is becoming a viable alternative to both ordination and family life in the West. It is an increasingly popular lifestyle which is socially accepted and still leaves free time for intensive spiritual practice.

It is possible to be celibate *in cognito*, but one advantage to wearing robes is that it makes one's decision clear to others. While wearing lay clothes, people may still doubt a person's determination to remain celibate, which can lead to some sticky situations. Women seem to be more susceptible to misinterpretation than men in this regard.

Women in most cultures have been stereotyped as more related to "the *eros* principle," more concerned with the body and family life, more prone to romantic love, relationship, and appetites of the flesh, even sexually uncontrollable. I utterly reject all these stereotypes and what they lead to. Nevertheless, it must be admitted that women's image of themselves as women has been profoundly affected by cultural conditioning and the mass media. It will be some time before we see the emergence of a generation of women completely free of such conditioning. Meanwhile, women need to investigate their predilections objectively to assess what is their true nature and what is subtly acquired gender bias. We need a chance to evolve as inwardly balanced individuals without being saddled by sexist conditioning. From the Buddhist point of view, the objective is not merely to avoid male domination, but to avoid being dominated by preconceptions altogether.

Many societies honor the decision to practice *Dharma* as a celibate, but only in men. Why the distinction? The subordinate position given to nuns in patriarchal societies is not only symptomatic of a general devaluing of women's efforts, but seems to reflect societal disapproval of women who reject their customary roles as sex objects. People tend to place a high value on being a Buddhist monk, but the idea of being a nun is often suspect, threatening, laughable, or undeserving of notice. The image of a spiritually committed male mendicant inspires a certain awe and respect, while images of nuns tend to be hazy and ambivalent at best. Some Western women prefer to refer to themselves as monks, though the idea of monks wishing to call themselves nuns is inconceivable. As a child, I very much wanted to become a monk; it was not until years later that I became reconciled to becoming a nun. We need to reflect on why the two words conjure up such different mental responses.

Receiving ordination is an attempt to go beyond personal images and societal prejudices. Still, one has to deal with the image of being ordained! One problem nuns and monks face is that others sometimes have unrealistically high expectations of them. People tend to have a stereotyped image of the ideal *Sangha* member and expect one to conform to it. Even though these expectations usually derive from genuine respect for the *Sangha*, it is hard enough trying to live up to one's own ideals without having to live up to others' expectations as well. People may criticize no matter how hard one tries to live in accordance with the *Dharma*. At times the effort of trying to live up to expectations creates a great deal of stress. Sometimes overestimated, sometimes underestimated, idolized or abused, it is rare that one is seen as an ordinary human being committed full-time to treading the path to awakening. This is partially due to a lack of information on what it means to be ordained. Here, we attempt to fill that gap.

NOTES

1. The term *prāṭimokśa* in its Tibetan translation, *so-so tar-pa*, may be rendered "individual liberation." The *Vinaya* texts enumerate seven levels of *prātimokśa* vows: fully ordained monk (*bhikṣu*), fully ordained nun (*bhikṣuṇī*), probationary nun (*śikṣamāṇā*), male novice (*śrāmaṇera*), female novice (*śrāmaṇerikā*), layman (*upāsakā*), and laywoman (*upāsikā*). The *Abhidharma-kośa* enumerates one additional category, the twenty-four hour fasting vow (*upavasatha*), not included in the *Vinaya* enumeration because it is not a lifetime vow.

Of the three types of nuns, a *śrāmaṇerikā* receives ten precepts (expanded to thirty-six training rules in the Tibetan tradition), a *śikṣamāṇā* usually receives six (twelve in the Mūlasarvāstivāda school and eighteen in the Mahāsānghika). A *bhikṣuṇī* receives 311 precepts according to the Pāli canon of the Theravāda school, 290 in the Mahāsānghika school, 348 in the Dharmagupta school, and 371 according to the Tibetan text of the Mūlasarvāstivāda school, including the seven *adhikaraṇa*.

2. According to the Mūlasarvāstivāda *Vinaya* in Tibetan translation, one is only allowed to give up the robes under certain circumstances, such as during a famine when one cannot get sufficient food, during a war when one is unable to stay in a place, and under threat of death.

3. See Richard Sherburne's translation of *A Lamp for the Path and Commentary*, George Allen and Unwin, Ltd., London, 1983, p. 74.

4. Novice ordination should normally be received after the age of fifteen. In exceptional circumstances, however, it may be received earlier, provided the ordinand is capable of scaring away crows. For full ordination, a person must be at least twenty years old.

5. There is also what is known as a negative vow, such as a vow to kill, made when one joins the police force or the army. This is explained in the *Abhidharma-kośa*.

THE SIGNIFICANCE OF ORDINATION AS A BUDDHIST NUN

by Ayya Khema

To be ordained as a Buddhist nun is such a major step in a woman's life that one should be well aware of its significance before undertaking it.

Up to the moment of ordination, one can, of course, have no idea what being a nun entails, since only lay status has been experienced. Naturally, one will have expectations, hopes, and views, most of which may have to be rectified as one goes along.

One could compare it to getting married; not having known beforehand what it means to be a married woman, many unrealistic ideas are entertained. Because of a strong commitment of love and togetherness, however, one takes the step, regardless of fears and anxieties. Then, as years go by, if love, commitment, understanding, and devotion wane, the marriage suffers, deteriorates, and eventually collapses.

The same applies to becoming and remaining a nun. While at first there may be a flush of excitement and anticipation, if love, devotion, commitment, and understanding are not constantly cultivated until they become intrinsic qualities in one's heart, the nun status will not flourish and will eventually disintegrate, either into disappointments and dissatisfactions or a return to lay life.

There is a significant difference between being a laywoman and being a nun, however, which has great meaning for those who are ordained. I am not talking about status or importance within the community. I am speaking about my own experience, having been a practicing laywoman in the past, and then having become a nun.

It is a matter of priority and commitment. When one practices as a laywoman, one can certainly meditate, live according to the precepts, and practice generosity. One can do many things, but one's daily life is beset with so many other duties and responsibilities that very often, as I have experienced myself, practice comes last. There are only so many hours in a day, and everyone does have to sleep and eat and clean up and wash. And there are so many other items of importance that seem to beset one's mind and also one's time, that the energy allotted for practice becomes minute.

When the time comes that one can see clearly that there is nothing more important to do than to practice the path of the Buddha in order to eliminate *dukkha* (suffering) forever, then comes the moment when ordination seems to be the only possible step. That certainly does not mean that all *dukkha* is eliminated, but it does mean that one should have clearly in mind that the priority, the main objective of daily activity, now is the practice of *Dhamma*. If that is clearly in mind, one must also be careful not to use one's time in a way which will interfere with that priority. In Pāli, we call that *samvega*, "urgency": to remember every single day why we have put on these robes, namely, to practice.

It is also important to determine what it means to practice. In the Theravāda tradition, we say it consists of two things—study and meditation. When we see, for instance, that these are the two most important things to do, that does not mean that we do not sleep at night, eat our meals, or wash our clothes. There are, of course, situations where food needs to be cooked, pathways have to be swept, floors have to be cleaned. We often find women saying, "This is not *Dhamma* work." They only want to do *Dhamma* work. That is a mistaken view. If we practice, then we can do *Dhamma* work in every activity, yet we must not allow the activities to become so overwhelming that we do not have time for study and meditation.

So it means a balancing act, which is often found to be very difficult to maintain. That is why, in the beginning of one's practice as a nun, one needs an experienced teacher to tell one what to do and to follow this instruction with humility.

There is another aspect to being ordained as a nun, namely, to become a professional at it. Wearing the robes should not be wearing some special costume, but it should be a declaration of being a servant to humanity. In our tradition it is *anatta* (non-self). We are not trying to be something. We are trying to become "selfless." So in the last essence, wearing the robes means that one is proclaiming the fact that one is trying to become absolutely nobody.

There are many obstacles in the way, as we all know. One great obstacle is being a teacher! People either love you and think you are wonderful or hate you and think that you are terrible. Another obstacle is building monasteries. Another obstacle is going on trips. And the greatest obstacle of all is the mind itself. But never mind, obstacles are there to be overcome. The only thing that counts is that we know why we are wearing the robes and that we know what we are doing while we are wearing them.

I have often thought of women in robes as *Dhamma* warriors. A successful army has to have the best weapons. What are the most important weapons that this army of *Dhamma* can possibly carry? It is a female prerogative, and sometimes also a female difficulty, that we deal very frequently with our emotions. These emotions can be purified to become real *mettā*, "loving kindness," that the Lord Buddha spoke about. This *mettā* is the most useful and effective weapon that we can have.

The world that we know, the world that we live in, has an enormous amount of fear, hatred, unhappiness, anxiety, and animosity between people. If we want to be true disciples of the Buddha, then it is our privilege to develop within our own hearts that love which is totally non-discriminating. Most people in the world are looking for someone to love them. It is our privilege to learn that this is not meaningful, but that developing loving kindness within our own heart and going out to others with it is the real practice.

Why should one not be able to do that as a laywoman? No reason at all, except that one's own family is always there to grasp at and be attached to. Wearing the robes is the first step of a renunciation process which can and will one day end in *nibbāna* (liberation). Living as a nun in a nunnery, one's own family becomes part of the whole of humanity. So that is one step in the renunciation of one's grasping and attachment. By not being attached in that way, we have the possibility of an expansion of the heart toward all beings, not because they need love, want to be loved, are lovable or otherwise, but because the heart can do nothing else. This practice can be the first step of our renunciation. After having renounced our hair, our clothes, our jewelry, our belongings, the next step is the renunciation of that attachment which especially women know—the attachment to their near and dear ones.

These robes have been called the banner of the *arahants* (liberated ones). Even though we may not all be *arahants*, we are flying their banner. That is one part of making a nun a professional and not an amateur—realizing that we are flying this banner. Another aspect of being a professional, rather than an amateur, is knowing. Knowing here means knowledge—the knowledge of one's own tradition, its history, its implication, and its practice. And the most important aspect is then transferring that knowledge into wisdom. To transfer knowledge into wisdom means to practice through the meditative path, and to experience with the heart that which one knows with the head. I call that "the understood experience."

When we practice in such a way, we find that we, in ourselves, can prove Lord Buddha's words correct. Then comes the time when we can actually *be* the *Dhamma*, rather than simply reading or listening to the *Dhamma*.

So the main difference between wearing ordinary clothes and wearing the robes of a nun is that the greatest priority, the total aspiration, is the *Dhamma* within oneself. Lord Buddha said, "Who sees me sees the *Dhamma*, who sees *Dhamma* sees me." This seeing is the inner vision of the *Dhamma*, which is a different reality from what we live in everyday life. To see that different reality, to listen to a different drummer, gives life a far more profound stability and depth.

Much of the value of being a nun lies in the example given to other women of a female independent of the approval or empowerment of males, being instead totally imbued with spiritual aspirations. If a nun finds peace and happiness in her vocation and is able to impart some of that to others, her contribution toward a better humanity becomes of the greatest value and can, in fact, change the quality of life amongst many people.

PERSONAL DEVELOPMENT AS A NUN
by Śrāmaṇerikā Sangye Khandro

The Buddha's teachings are all about personal development. They are a path to develop ourselves as people, a way to develop all our positive qualities and potentials. This is the essence of Buddhism.

Those of us who have become nuns are so inspired by the Buddha's teachings that we commit our lives to following them, enabling us to develop ourselves as people. That is not to say that it is an easy task. There are many problems along the way.

From my own experience and from the experience of others I know who have taken up the nun's life, one problem we can experience, for example, is being overly idealistic—having very idealistic view and attitudes. We become nuns because we are inspired by others. Sometimes we have met nuns and monks and feel that these people are peaceful and happy and well balanced. We think that is the way we wish to be, the way we wish to live, and so we take vows. Later on we find that it is not as easy as we thought and that it really takes a lot of work to become peaceful.

It is quite an easy matter to change one's clothes and put on robes, to cut one's hair and get a new name. That part is not difficult at all. It is changing the mind that is very difficult. Unfortunately, we do not always realize this before we get ordained. Afterwards, the really hard work begins. Sometimes, being idealistic, being inspired by other nuns and monks that you have met, being inspired by the Buddha and his teachings, can be a little bit dangerous unless you are practical, down-to-earth, and in touch with who you really are.

From my own experience, it came as quite a shock to realize that I was still the same person after I became ordained as before I was ordained. I thought I was going to change, but it did not work like that. We carry with us all of our old habits, problems, and attachments, even after ordination. Pride, anger, selfishness, laziness—all the things we had before remain with us. We have to do a great deal of work on ourselves to eliminate these habits, but that is what the practice is all about.

If you start out idealistic, another problem that can arise is frustration. After taking robes and meditating, studying, and practicing for a few months or a few years, you may feel that nothing is happening. You still have attachments, still get angry, still get irritated, still have problems dealing with people. Some people get so frustrated that they give up and give back their robes, which is quite sad. This is a stage that many people have to go through.

Another problem that can arise is loneliness. Humans are social beings. Most people in the world have a partner and children partly because they do not like being alone. The life of a nun or a monk does not mean that you are alone, but still, you have chosen a path which primarily is working on yourself. You are not living with a partner and you are not living with a family. So loneliness can become a very big problem in an ordained life. Even if you are living in a community with many other nuns, you can still get quite lonely. That is something that we have to deal with.

Conjoined with that is how to relate to other people once we have taken on the vows. Within the context of being a nun, we have to live according to the *Vinaya* rules. So how do we deal with other people—our parents, brothers and sisters, friends and former friends, male and female people—with whom we come in contact? Learning how to deal with others on a practical level is something that every nun must learn. We must find a balance between keeping our vows, being a good nun, being a pure nun, yet still being warm, friendly, and positive when dealing with other people. Sometimes this can be quite difficult.

The idea of balance is very important in our development as people, as women, as nuns. Essentially we must create a balance between the different parts of our being—the intellectual, the emotional, and the intuitive. Some people become very intellectual, learn a lot, read many books, and take many teachings. They know a great deal about Buddhism and can talk about it at length, but they have not really integrated it into their hearts. They have not learned how to really live it.

Other people may be out of balance the other way—by being very emotional. They may be very devoted to their teachers, to the Buddha, to the *Dharma* teachings, and have strong, deep emotions regarding these things, but they are lacking in knowledge and wisdom. Sometimes they cannot even answer when someone asks them a simple *Dharma* question.

So in our development as individuals we have to balance all these different parts of ourselves—our knowledge, our intellect, our feelings, and our emotions.

We also have to balance ourselves in terms of how we spend our time. We need to find a balance between meditation, practice on our own, and dealing with people. Again, some people get out of balance, spending all their time alone until they forget how to talk to people, how to smile, laugh, be friendly and communicate with people. Others may go the other direction and get so involved with people that they forget to meditate. We tend to go back and forth between these extremes. So, in the course of our development as a nun, we need to find a balance between all these different factors.

THE FUNCTION AND MEANING OF VOWS
by Sylvia Wetzel

We blithely say that it is more important to preserve the spirit than the letter of vows, meaning any vows, rules, regulations, or laws. It takes quite some time and experience, however, to discover the spirit of vows. When we as beginners encounter difficulties in keeping vows, we tend to dismiss their literal meaning and pretend to be able to keep their spirit. We should be very careful with this and try to discuss our ideas concerning the interpretation of vows with elder *Sangha* members and teachers. Their experience and explanations are instructive for our understanding of the ordained way of life. A Sri Lankan woman pointed out that the observance of vows and laws is mainly in response to the community and society. It helps create a level of trust and security between people. Rules give a clear outline of what is right and wrong or, put in Buddhist terms, what leads to happiness and what leads to suffering.

It is therefore the task of the individual to check the meaning of vows and rules on a personal level. This is the place for open discussion and interpretation. Without such probing, vows do not begin to create their deepest impact, which is stimulating awareness of one's actions. Once we understand the power and value of vows, we lose the childish fear of external punishment or sanctions. Such mistaken and preconceived fears often lead to deception, pretension, and hypocrisy. Gradually we understand that vows are most efficient tools for the transformation of our minds.

Vows are important at the beginning, the middle, and the end of practice. They are helpful for beings with gross behavior, with dull and unconscious mentalities, and important for beginners on the path to begin taking responsibility for their actions. Once they have gained ever-present awareness of the here and now, vows will no longer be needed to control ignorant and harmful behavior, but will highlight inner development reflected in the external actions of body, speech, and mind. Safeguarding one's physical, verbal, and mental actions in accordance with an agreed-upon moral code is an expression of deep concern and compassion for others and serves as inspiration for achieving greater awareness.

Just as a well-composed poem gains from impeccable adherence to form, in terms of rhyme and rhythm, meter and pitch, so does the mind benefit from observing certain forms and manners of behavior.

The Function and Meaning of Vows

Again and again the question arises of whether it is possible, necessary, or desirable, to change the *Vinaya* rules of moral discipline for Buddhist monks and nuns in order to adapt them to life in modern society. Some want to actually change the minor rules, which the Buddha suggested could be done in certain situations. Some want to rewrite or rephrase them to make them more understandable to people of this age.

Seeing the many different schools and traditions of Buddhism nowadays and the many different Eastern and Western mentalities of the practitioners, this changing of the rules seems to be a formidable task with many attendant dangers. What could be done without damage is to discuss the meaning and context of the vows and study the story behind the creation of each rule. One major objection to outright change in the rules is the fact that the *Vinaya* is one of the three baskets of the teachings (*Tripitaka*), an object in which Buddhists take refuge. Changes in these prescriptions would be equivalent to changing the ten commandments in the Bible.

The aim of the *Vinaya* rules is to transform our whole identity into a purified mode. One could say that the *Vinaya* reflects a pure state of being, in that by trying to keep these rules of conduct we slowly approach a purified state of mind. In other words, a balanced, integrated Buddhist practitioner behaves in accordance with the *Vinaya*—not killing or stealing, not abusing or misusing others, not confusing the mind with drugs and alcohol, harming neither self nor others. This is the main aim of the vows, and living in such a way is in itself of value for both oneself and society.

The psychological function of vows is to direct one's attention to the behavior of body, speech, and mind. In this way, vows help to increase awareness. Awareness of what is happening to ourselves and others is the key to acting appropriately, authentically, and responsibly in accordance with all aspects of a given situation. Such awareness is the key to skillful actions.

We can say that vows are the basis of Buddhist practice, the foundation of the Noble Eight-fold Path, and the ground rules for the Three Higher Trainings (morality, concentration, and wisdom). Only with the help of mindfulness can we control body, speech, and mind in a positive and productive way. Only with reasonably controlled body, speech, and mind can we engage in deep concentration and meditation which lead to the development of higher wisdom.

Rules and precepts point up the primary actions to be cultivated and those to be avoided. To refrain from killing, stealing, and harming helps us to stop acting out thoughts of desire, anger, and jealousy. We become aware that there are other beings to consider, who suffer as much as we do when their life is threatened or their belongings stolen. Rules remind us to be aware of others' welfare. Once we have become thoroughly mindful and considerate, we can dispense with the rules. The awareness entailed in following rules allows us to consider all factors of a situation, rather than simply our own point of view, and helps us determine the right action at the right time.

Through cultivating awareness, rules help us become free from deeply ingrained habitual behavior and the bondage of bodily instincts. There are times when instinct may serve an important function in protecting our life, yet, as awareness grows, instincts become limiting. In time, awareness becomes more acute and instinctive reactions less powerful. Then wisdom becomes the gentle ruler of our lives. Once our energies are less tied to old habits and instinctive unwholesome behavior, they can be used freely for a creative expression of our inner wisdom. These liberated energies also increase our resolution, which is of great benefit for study and practice.

"Never separate from the three circles [the doer, the object, and the action itself]. Never separate from voidness." This prescription helps us to remain ever mindful of the lack of true existence in all objects and experiences. It makes us aware of voidness all the time. "Don't eat untimely food." This precept helps ordained ones to become aware of hunger and thirst, and to distinguish between bodily needs and greed, greed being basically an exaggerated notion that happiness comes from outside objects. Here the awareness evoked helps us become the lord of our body and mind rather than remaining their slave.

Still, there is a danger of getting hooked on the letter of the law. We need to understand the purpose of the vows and their usefulness for the mind. All rules are methods for developing awareness and gaining control over the mind. To let them transform our mind, we must understand their functioning and impact. To insist on a literal interpretation may mean that we miss the point altogether. There is also a danger of using rules to fight against oneself in an oppressive or suppressive way which denies intuition and reasoned choices. We need to strike a balance between being either slack or tense. A good indication of how we are doing is the degree of awareness and control we have gained. The less awareness we have, the more we should strive to be strict; the more control we have over our delusions and emotions, the more emphasis we can put on listening to our inner wisdom.

In this context, it is of interest to understand the psychological effects of understanding. When a question profoundly concerns us, it stirs something deep inside. As we work on the question and gain some understanding of it, the energy bound into the problem is released and we feel refreshed and rejuvenated. The energy is set free and can be used for any purpose. The resulting joyful energy can be channelled into meaningful work of any kind—meditation, service, writing, chanting or whatever.

Once we gain awareness of things as they are, we can follow

our inner wisdom, our intuition. As long as we lack awareness, following our inner drives and instincts may mean acting out of selfish concern, fear, insecurity, or blindness. For these reasons, rules and vows, advice for behavior, and even general standards of politeness are essentially helpful for stimulating awareness of entire situations. Even without understanding the views, they can still stimulate this awareness. Understanding their aim, one discovers their profoundly beneficial impact on the mind and their value in human development.

3 *The Potentialities of Women in Buddhism*

An understanding of the potentialities of women within the various Buddhist schools presupposes an understanding of the process of rebirth. It is a basic Buddhist tenet that beings take birth not just once, but repeatedly, in various states of existence. The Buddhist concept of time is enormous and its concept of space allows for the existence of innumerable world systems. Within this extensive framework, living beings take different forms in different lifetimes. Ordinary beings are said to take birth in one of six states, or "realms," under the force of *karma* and delusions. They may take birth in any of these states at any time, the type of rebirth and circumstances being determined by the positive or negative actions which they have created previously.

Until one becomes liberated, freed from cyclic existence, this pattern continues. As long as a person is under the influence of *karma* and delusions, there is no predictable pattern or guarantee as to what rebirth one will take. The state of rebirth depends solely on one's own actions. In this view, one may take birth in a human realm in one lifetime and, for example, in an animal realm the next. Similarly, one may be born as a female in one incarnation and as a male in the next.

Given the fact that beings take on different forms in different lifetimes, it follows that identification with one life form or another, one gender or another, is somewhat short-sighted. The ideal for Buddhists is to generate loving kindness to all living beings, especially the less fortunate and less lovable, regardless of the form they might assume at the moment. Developing favoritism toward some and rejecting others results from attachment and aversion, habitual unwholesome attitudes which are to be abandoned in the course of spiritual evolution. Identifying exclusively with a particular species, race, nationality, or gender is an extension of self-grasping rooted in ignorance and, we may say, arises from a misunderstanding of the way in which the world turns. Since there is only one moment, literally one breath, between this lifetime and the next, it is rather futile and naive to get bound up in the conception of oneself as either female or male. One's gender could be different tomorrow. Thus, in the larger picture, when striving for spiritual perfection, gender is more or less immaterial.

Among the Buddhist schools, there are various viewpoints concerning the ultimate goal of the Buddhist path. In general, these viewpoints can be summarized into two: those who accept three final goals and those who accept only one final goal, namely, Buddhahood for all. According to the Theravādin viewpoint, there are three possible final goals. One may become an *arhat*, a being who is liberated from cyclic existence: a *pratyekabuddha*, "solitary realizer"; or a *samyaksambuddha*, a perfectly enlightened being who is omniscient, endowed with ten powers, and has a mission to teach. The majority of people, both women and men, aim at becoming *arhats* and achieving the peace of *nirvāna*, rather than striving to become Buddhas. That women and men are equally capable of attaining *nirvāna* is clearly documented by records of the many thousands of women who did so during the lifetime of the Buddha and in subsequent centuries. We can read the inspiring verses composed by some of these female *arhats* collected in the *Psalms of the Sisters* (*Therigāthā*).

In the Mahāyāna tradition, too, there are some who assert three final goals of Buddhist practice. The great Indian master Asaṅga, for instance, maintains that some beings aim only at attaining *nirvāna* and do not achieve full Buddhahood. This means that such beings work to overcome all delusions, such as attachment, hatred, and ignorance, and become free from the cycle of birth and death, but do not aspire to become fully perfected Buddhas (*samyaksambuddhas*). Other followers of the Mahāyāna assert that there is only one final vehicle, meaning that even those beings who become *arhats* or *pratyekabuddhas* eventually enter the Mahāyāna path and become fully perfected Buddhas. All of these states can be achieved by women, that is to say, all women have the capacity to achieve one result or another. Which result will be achieved by whom and when depends on aspirational prayers and diligence on the path, not on a person's present, ephemeral gender.

Of those who accept the Mahāyāna tenets, only those belonging to one branch of the Mind Only school, the Cittamatrins following scripture, do not accept that all beings will become Buddhas. Even this has nothing to do with gender, but is because they believe that some beings lack the roots of merit to do so, namely, those whose "lineage" has been "cut." Otherwise, followers of Mahāyāna tenets accept that all beings, female and male, are capable of becoming Buddhas.

In the Mahāyāna view, all sentient beings are recognized as having Buddha nature, a quality of mind which empowers them to become fully enlightened Buddhas. Both women and men have this quality of mind which is devoid of gender, since it is the emptiness of the mind itself. According to this view, once a being generates the altruistic aspiration to attain enlightenment for the benefit of all sentient beings (*bodhicitta*) and enters the *bodhisattva* path, merits are accumulated for three countless aeons before achieving Buddhahood. This is a very long time indeed, and during the whole process of accumulating merits through the practice of the six perfections, one may practice in the form of either a woman or a man.

Once direct non-conceptual insight into emptiness is gained, which is simultaneous with attainment of the first of the ten *bodhisattva* stages, one not only has the capacity to assume whatever form is considered beneficial to beings, but also may emanate that form one hundred times. On each successive stage, the number of possible emanations increases exponentially, multiplying one's possibilities to benefit others. All the forms emanated may be female if that is felt to be most beneficial.

The Mahāyāna *sūtras* explain that a person aspiring to Buddhahood must train in wisdom and method. Wisdom is likened to the mother. In fact, the *Prajñāpāramitā* (*Perfection of Wisdom*) *Sūtras*, which are central to the Mahāyāna tradition, are known as the "mother of all Buddhas." Method, or skillful means, is likened to the father. Although wisdom is symbolized as female and method is symbolized as male, they are practiced by women and men alike. Both qualities are essential for spiritual development; for enlightenment, both must be perfected.

There are passages in a few Mahāyāna texts to the effect that women cannot attain enlightenment, but their authenticity in terms of being the original thought of the Buddha is doubtful. The enlightened awareness of a Buddha, being totally omniscient, free of any taint of ignorance or afflictive emotion, is surely an awareness that far transcends gender discrimination. To deny the enlightenment potential of women would be seriously at odds with the central ideal of the Mahāyāna, which is achieving the happiness and liberation of all sentient beings without exception. Since the objective is to benefit all limitless living beings, any taint of sexual exclusiveness is clearly contradictory. There is, however, every possibility that a misogynist slant crept in centuries later when the teachings came to be written down.

There is, however, some controversy concerning the gender assumed by a perfectly enlightened being (*samyaksambuddha*) in the final incarnation. The Mahāyāna includes both the perfection vehicle and the *mantra* vehicle, known as the Vajrayāna. Mahāyāna practitioners who do not accept the Vajrayāna teachings assert that in the end a Buddha necessarily takes the form of a male. This is because many texts say that a fully enlightened Buddha manifests in a form complete with thirty-two major and eighty minor marks, one of which is the mark of being a male. In male-dominant cultures, it is not surprising that a Buddha, the epitome of human perfection, should be conceptualized as being a male. Such statements seem to have led to the mistaken assertion that women cannot achieve Buddhahood. On the contrary, however, even if they must appear as a male in their last birth, not only *can* women achieve Buddhahood, they certainly *will*, as will all men and other living creatures.

According to those Mahāyāna practitioners who accept the Vajrayāna teachings, it is possible for beings to attain Buddhahood in one lifetime, in either a female or male body, provided they have a sufficient accumulation of merit. According to the Vajrayāna, to eliminate subtle delusions and achieve Buddhahood, one must train in utilizing the winds, channels, and drops, and for this, a person must practice the *tantric* teachings. That is to say, after storing up merits for three countless aeons, to eliminate the most subtle objects of abandonment, the very subtlest traces of delusion, a tenth-stage *bodhisattva* necessarily attains the final stage of Buddhahood through the practice of *tantra*. Both women and men are equally capable of practicing *tantra* and are capable of achieving Buddhahood in one lifetime through these practices.

To attain Buddhahood in one lifetime, it is prerequisite to have completed the entire general path of the *sūtras* as well as both the generation and completion stages of *tantra*. In the completion stage of highest *yoga tantra*, there are methods which are very powerful for transforming the naturally abiding mind. These teachings, being very subtle, are accessible only to human beings of exceptional capabilities, but they make no discrimination between women and men. No different explanations are given for female and male practitioners, and no differentiation is made in the way the paths are generated. In fact, in the practice of highest *yoga tantra*, particularly in the "mother *tantras*" (which explicitly teach practices related to the clear light), there are occasions where special emphasis and importance are given to women. One of the root *tantric* precepts involves showing respect to women. One reason given for this is that among women there are certainly some who are enlightened beings in female form (*dakinīs*). Since people ordinarily are incapable of recognizing such beings, it is important to respect all women just in case. Therefore, it is taught that women should not be denigrated or vilified.

In the practice of deity *yoga*, the crux of *tantra*, the meditational deity (*yidam*) visualized may be either female or male, regardless of whether the practitioner is a woman or a man. The practice of *tantra* is essentially a process of identifying with the qualities of an enlightened deity (*yidam*) on the basis of realizing emptiness. The meditational deity chosen as the object of visualization may be female or male, emphasizing wisdom or skillful means respectively. Visualization is utilized to enhance particular qualities of enlightened body, speech, and mind, gaining mastery of one's own mind as the central objective. In this, women and men stand an equal chance of success.

There are numerous examples of beings who have achieved Buddhahood in female form, such as Tara, Vajrayoginī, Saraswatī, and so on. Though they appear in aspect different from that of a Buddha like Śakyamuni, they are termed female Buddhas.

Buddhists universally accept that all beings, female and male, are capable of enlightenment. Not only are women shown to be capable of the greatest attainments of Buddhist practice, there are also very positive images of accomplished women to relate to in each Buddhist tradition. There are the countless numbers of women who have achieved the paths and fruits emphasized in Theravādin practice, from stream-enterer to *arhat*. There are the numerous *bodhisattvas* in female form who are revered and emulated by followers of the Mahāyāna teachings. There are the many female meditational deities visualized by both female and male practitioners of the Vajrayāna teachings. In conclusion, there is no shortage of female role models for those on the Buddhist path. All that is required for attainment is diligent practice.

NOTES

1. The six realms spoken of here are the realms of hell beings, hungry ghosts, animals, humans, demi-gods, and gods.

2. In the Theravāda tradition, those who aspire to Buddhahood are termed *bodhisattvas*. They necessarily receive acknowledgement of this great aspiration and there are three types, each emphasizing a different faculty and requiring a specific length of time to attain Buddahood: (1) wisdom, requiring four incalculable and 100,00 great aeons; (2) faith, requiring four incalculable and 100,000 great aeons; and (3) energy, requiring sixteen incalculable and 100,000 great aeons.

3. See Hopkins' discussion in *Meditation on Emptiness*, p. 366 and pp. 393-97.

THE ARAHANT IDEAL FOR WOMEN

by Kusuma Devendra

In its Pāli form the word *arahant* appears in the earliest Buddhist texts, and refers to those who have reached the end of the Eightfold Path and are enjoying the fruits of it (*maggaphala*). The word *arahant* is defined as "a person who has gained insight into the true nature of things (*yathābhuta*)."[1] Everywhere the Pāli canon refers to the *arahant* as having achieved *saupadisesa nibbāna*, which means that, although still suffering physical discomfort due to the presence of the body, one is an enlightened being having destroyed all defilements of the mind. At death such a being attains liberation without remainder (*nirupadhisesa nibbāna*), at which point even bodily discomfort ceases since there is no further rebirth.

The *arahant*'s way of triumphing over "self" constitutes the heart of the Buddha's teaching. All attributes of the *Dhamma* become clear to the *arahant* immediately. He or she knows that greed, hatred, and ignorance were once in the mind, that they are harmful, and that they are not there any longer. Furthermore he or she knows that these defilements have been completely eradicated, uprooted, and will not spring up again, just like a palmyra tree that has been chopped down.[2] He or she is one who has fully accomplished that which is to be accomplished, no longer needs to struggle in maintaining celibacy, has been relieved of the entire burden of defilements, and is now free from rebirth.[3]

Thus the *arahant* being lives in the world yet is not of the world. Such a person is fully established in wisdom, has excellent qualities, and understands the efficacy of the *Dhamma* through personal experience. While still living in the mundane field, an *arahant* enjoys the fruits of the *Dhamma*, such as experiencing immediate results, summoning others to come and see these results, and progressing onwards. Wisdom is directly experienced.[4] This is the *nibbānic* goal as understood in the Pāli tradition.

To pursue this goal, the Buddha recommends the renunciation of household life as a necessary condition. This is evident in many of his discourses. Starting from the practice of generosity, his discourses lead a person toward greater restraint of the senses in reaching for the excellent qualities,[5] then to an understanding of the frustrations of worldly aspirations, and then on toward realization of the Four Noble Truths.

The *arahant* ideal gained ascendancy during early Buddhism and the canon describes the Buddha and the five ascetics as the first *arahants*: "...And there were six *arahants* in the world."[6] With a deeper understanding of suffering, its cause, its cessation, and the path leading to it, the Buddhist disciples withdrew themselves from attachment, learned to turn away from sense pleasures, and naturally proceeded toward the ordained life. Then, as ordained recluses, they adopted the prescribed practices leading to their spiritual goal. The Pāli canon indicates that the goal of *nibbāna* was easily accessible to ordained disciples through the practice of the *Dhamma*.

In his first discourse to the five ascetics, the Buddha described the sensual pleasures of household life as low, vulgar, characteristic of the way of life of unenlightened beings, and conducive to much suffering. He proclaimed the holy life as altogether perfect and pure, and established the ordained *Sangha* living in renunciation (*pabbajjā*).

Even though millions of good men and women living worldly lives regard the going forth into homelessness in renunciation as an unnatural aspiration, unessential for a holy life, the Buddhist standpoint clearly emphasizes it. The Buddha himself said, "Having left parents, wife, son, relations, wealth, land, and all desires of the senses, wander like the rhinoceros."[7] Prince Siddhartha's great renunciation bears out his conviction of the worthiness of the life of a recluse.

In the fifth year after Śakyamuni's attainment of Buddhahood, the *bhikkhunī* order was instituted. The Buddha declared, "Women, Ananda, having gone forth from home to homelessness...are able to realize the fruit of stream-enterer (*sōtapanna*), once-returner (*sakadāgami*), non-returner (*anāgami*), and perfection in sainthood (*arahant*).[8] The beckoning call of sainthood and the prospect of terminating the process of birth and death became so irresistible that women often asked permission from husbands, parents, or next of kin to seek sanctuary in the order. The escape from the crippling harness of the home, custom, and convention was a welcome change for them. In the *Etadaggavagga*, the *Psalms of the Sisters* (*Therigāthā*), as well as in the *Apadāna*, and so on, we see the *arahant bhikkhunīs* expressing exultation about their newly won freedom from the bondage of cyclic existence (*samsāra*). As *bhikkhunīs* they acquired the freedom to go about with shaven heads, clad in saffron robes, gathering alms as did the Buddha and the *bhikkhus*. They were capable of strenuous meditation and miraculous feats, were recognized by the Buddha and the brother *arahants* as perfected beings, and were included in the community of enlightened *Sangha* comprising the eight kinds of saints.[9]

In the *Anguttara Nikāya*, the Buddha refers to the chief female disciples: "Monks, among my female disciples, seniormost is Maha Pajāpati Gotamī, the highest in wisdom is Khema, greatest in supernormal powers is Uppalavannā, supreme in *Vinaya* discipline is Patācārā. The chief of *Dhamma* teachers is Dhammadinā, finest in meditative powers is Nandā, greatest in diligence is Sonā, best in clairvoyance is Sakulā, outstanding in extraordinary powers is Bhaddā...," and so on. Such luminous figures were regarded as the jewel of *Sangha* in the world as much as were the *bhikkhus*.

A person's spiritual attainments are rightly understood as dependent only upon refining the stream of consciousness moment to moment. These attainments have no relevance to age, time period, sex, or social status. For example, the eminent *bhikkhu* Upali was a barber in lay life, Kujjuttarā was a slave, Sopakā was a destitute child of seven years, Sunita was a scavenger, and so on. They attained stages of sainthood and were admitted to the order.

In Sri Lanka the historical chronicles *Dīpavamsa* and *Mahavamsa*, written in the fourth century A.D., refer to many thousands of *bhikkhunīs*, enumerating seventy-two by name and describing their achievements, attainments, and powers. The *Mahavamsa*[10] says that eighteen thousand *bhikkhus* and fourteen thousand *bhikkhunīs* attained *arahantship* during the ceremony of laying the foundation for the great reliquary Maha Thūpa.[11] Unfortunately, with the loss of *bhikkhunī* ordination in the Theravāda countries, the communal protection necessary for pursuing religious goals was lost to women. This advantage is still enjoyed by women in Korea, Taiwan, and so forth, because the *bhikkhunī* ordination is still available in those countries. In Theravāda countries the ten-precept nuns have arisen in the absence of the *bhikkhunī* order. They are seen to hold a marginal status in society, however, and as such are unable to fulfill their spiritual potential. The institution of full ordination is the means to an end, without any divine connotation, yet the order was established by the Buddha for those who are sufficiently motivated to be provided with the tranquil atmosphere, public assistance, and recognition they need to achieve their goal of *arahantship*. It is a heartening fact that in Sri Lanka there is now a move to reintroduce the *bhikkhunī* lineage from the Chinese tradition, where it still exists.

Spiritually advanced women are assets to society whether they be mothers, sisters, wives, daughters, or teachers. *Arahant bhikkhunīs* would be a radiant beacon of light in today's groping world.

NOTES

1. *Encyclopedia of Buddhism*, Vol. 11, Ceylon Government Press, 1966, p. 41.

2. Quoted from the *Anguttara Nikāya*.

3. From the text *Itivuttaka Pāli: "...araham hōti knināsavā vusitavā katakaraniyo ohita-bhāro anuppattasadatto parikkhina bhavasamyojano...."*

4. *From the Anguttara Nikāya*, Vol. IV, p. 453, Pali Text Society edition: *"...sandiṭṭhiko, akāliko, ehipassiko, opanaiko, paccattam veditabho viññuhi...."*

5. The four excellent qualities, or "abodes of Brahma" (*Brahma vihāra*), are loving kindness (*mettā*), compassion (*karunā*), altruistic joy (*muditā*), and equanimity (*upekkhā*).

6. From the *Anattalakkhana Sutta, Vinaya*, Vol. I, pp. 13-14, Pali Text Society.

7. From the *Khaggavisāna Sutta*, third *sutta* of *Uragavagga*, *Sutta Nipāta*, Pali Text Society.

8. *Vinaya*, Vol. V, p. 354, Pali Text Society.

9. The path and fruit of each stage of sainthood, namely, of the stream enterer, once returner, non-returner, and *arahant*, respectively, for a total of eight.

10. Chapter XXVI, Verses 68-69.

11. The Pāli word *thūpa*, or *cetiya*, designates a tumulous cairn, or monument, erected to commemorate the great deeds of worthy beings such as *tathāgatas* and *arahants*, enshrining their ashes.

THE POTENTIALITIES OF WOMEN IN THE MAHĀYĀNA VEHICLE

by Bhikṣuṇī Heng Ching Shih

There is much speculation concerning the rise of Mahāyāna Buddhism. With its emphasis on the Bodhisattva ideal, devotional practices, and its affirmation of the empirical world, it seems logical to assume that Mahāyāna Buddhism developed, at least partly, from the aspirations of lay devotees.[1] Naturally, the positions of both layman and laywoman were elevated in Mahāyāna Buddhism. We shall examine the position of women both in early Buddhism and Mahāyāna Buddhism so as to show that Mahāyāna tradition is indeed a more conducive vehicle for women in general and more favorable for laywomen than for nuns in particular.

In general, the status of ancient Indian women in Brahmanical society was decidedly inferior to that of men. Under Buddhism, the position of women improved significantly. As Horner points out, "during the Buddhist epoch there was a change. Women came to enjoy more equality and greater respect and authority than ever hitherto accorded to them. Although their activities were confined within certain spheres—principally the domestic, social, and religious—their position in general began to improve."[2] True as this was, still we cannot say that women enjoyed complete social and religious equality.

Women in Early Buddhism

Daughter—In ancient India, the birth of a daughter was, if not regarded as a total disaster, at least unwelcome. This attitude resulted from the deep-rooted Brahmanic tradition of regarding a male child as indispensable for performing the parents' funeral ceremonies. A son was considered as ensuring the continuity of the family lineage and the welfare of the departed. Since Buddhism denounced ritualism and advocated a life of ethical responsibility such that each individual strives for liberation, the importance of a son was fast losing ground in Buddhist society.

The new attitude toward female children is best illustrated by the Buddha's consolations to King Pasenadi who was disappointed to hear that Queen Mallika had given birth to a daughter. The Buddha gave the following favorable remarks:

> A woman child, O Lord of Men, may prove
> Even a better offspring than a male.[3]

Although Buddhist society accepted this liberal attitude of the Buddha, it could not entirely eradicate inherited prejudices. The early Buddhist literature does contain evidence of preference for sons to daughters. In the *Kattatari Jataka*, King Brahmadatta said to a young woodcutter: "If you beget a son, bring him to me with this signet ring; but if you give birth to a daughter, then sell this ring and rear her."[4] The preference given to sons is apparent in this passage.

In Hindu tradition the main duties assigned to women were childrearing and housework. Consequently, a single life was seen as a wasted life and unmarried women were subject to scoffs. On the contrary, in Buddhism, married life was viewed as a hindrance to spiritual pursuits and best avoided as if it were a burning pit of coals. Wherever the Buddhist point of view prevailed a woman was no longer compelled to marry to achieve self respect and approval from her family. Once the order of nuns was established, it provided an even better option for women, who were more spiritually and religiously inclined. Sumana, the youngest daughter of Anathapindika did not marry but remained single until she joined the order at an advanced age. There are other instances recorded in the *Therigāthā*.

Even though women in early Buddhist society were freer than before to lead independent lives, there are references in Buddhist literature which indicate the opposite notion. In *Milidanpanha*, it is stated, "There are, O king, these ten sorts of individuals who are despised and condemned in the world, thought shameful, looked down upon, held blameworthy, treated with contumely, not loved. And what are the ten? A woman without a husband, a weak creature, one without friends or relatives."[5] "A woman without a husband" heads the list of the ten most undesirable states. Such references, however, are rare. In general, maidens did enjoy an honored position with the family and in society.

Mothers—The mother has always been the center of the family and revered through the ages of Indian civilization. Motherhood is the most honored phase of a woman's life. In early Buddhism there are accounts of women who were ridiculed and humiliated by society until they bore a son. Both mothers and fathers were honored throughout Buddhist literature. The observance of filial piety is regarded as one of the most imperative obligations of children. It is said that Buddha himself ascended to Tushita heaven to expound the *Dharma* to his mother to repay her. One of the effects of this emphatic instruction to revere one's parents was the great authority which a mother was assured of in the home.

Wives—The ideal relationship between husband and wife is clearly described in the *Sigalovadas Sūtra*:

> In five ways should a wife as western quarter be ministered to by her husband: by respect, by courtesy, by faithfulness, by handing over authority to her, by providing her with adornment.
>
> In these five ways does the wife, ministered to by her husband as the western quarter, love him: her duties are well performed, by hospitality to the kin of both, by faithfulness, by watching over the goods he brings, and by skill and industry in discharging all her business.[6]

The ideal relationship of the husband and wife is thus based on mutual respect and duty rather than subordination to the other. It is also said that just as the sacred fire of the Brahmins which should be honored and treasured, so one's wife and children should be cared for.

The position and duties of the housewife depicted in most early Buddhist literature, however, were not very much different from those of Indian tradition—obedience and devotion to one's husband being the prominent features. Yet, in terms of religious beliefs, we find Buddhist wives were not always passive. Many girls were married to non-Buddhists. In such cases, the wife often converted her husband and his family to her faith. Visākhā Migaramata was married to a family of followers of naked ascetics. She not only rebuked them for their heretical belief, but also was able to convert the whole family to Buddhism.

Women Workers—In Buddhist society, the majority of laywomen played the role either of a daughter or a housewife, who was supported by her children, husband, or father. Still, there were instances of women belonging to the working class, such as maidservants, female musicians, and courtesans. Among them, the case of courtesans deserves our attention. In Buddhist society prostitution was not despised. Perhaps it may be as Horner surmised, "According to the outlook of their own times, it would be thought a woman was a prostitute on account of the working out of her *karma*. It was partly because of the notion of *karma* that the profession was frankly permitted by the social code of the day."[7] Courtesans were not condemned as such, and the Buddhist order was open to any prostitute who was willing to cultivate the path to liberation. Four courtesans—Vimala, Padumavati, Addhakasi and Ambapali—were converted to Buddhism, entered the order, and finally attained *arhatship*. Some verses in the *Therigāthā* are attributed to them. Among them Ambapali was the best known. Once she invited the Buddha for a meal and the Buddha accepted her invitation. Later the Buddha received another invitation for the same day form a wealthy family of the Licchavi clan, but he refused it to keep his promise to Ambapali. Her invitation was not considered inferior.

Female Lay Devotees—Lay devotees constituted one of the greatest assets of the Buddhist *Sangha*. Female lay devotees played no lesser role in supporting the *Sangha* than the male. They shared the responsibility for the *Sangha* and helped it in every way. Because of women's traditional role in the household, female devotees came into close contact with the *Sangha*, for example, by giving alms. Not only their material support was appreciated, but also their opinion was valued. Their suggestions were invited and carried out. No discrimination was made between male and female devotees. In some cases, for the purpose of upholding the Buddhist teachings and discipline and of assuring the spiritual welfare of the *Sangha*, they even offered criticism.

Nuns—Woman did not differ from man in possessing an innate aspiration for spiritual achievement. It was the strong wish for liberation (*mokśa*) that motivated women to renounce the world. The order of Buddhist nuns initially came into existence by the efforts of Mahāpajāpatī who asked the Buddha to admit women to the order. Her request was refused three times until Ānanda pleaded with the Buddha on her behalf. Ānanda asked the Buddha, "Are women not capable of leading the homeless life or realizing the fruit of conversion?" To this the Buddha replied, "No, Ānanda. They are capable." This clearly indicates that the Buddha had no doubts about the innate capabilities and potential greatness of women. If the Buddha did not consider woman inferior to man in terms of religious achievement, then one could ask why he was reluctant to admit women into the order. The Buddha is reported to have said that because of the admission of women into the order, the good law would last for only five hundred years instead of one thousand. At least this is the traditional account of the Buddha's reluctance. Nevertheless, as Horner says, "Again it is possible that he held back, if he did, on account of his already biased, though not culpably prejudiced, view of women. He was born a Hindu, and ancestry, traditions, and education cannot be shaken off simply by the desire to be quit of them."[9]

Another reason for this reluctance is that he was well aware of human weakness. Intercommunication between the two orders would expose both of them to greater temptations. Rather than say that the Buddha underestimated woman, it may be better to say that he did not overestimate his male disciples. The admission was finally granted on the condition of the women's acceptance of eight rules *(gurudharmas)*. According to these rules, the *Bhikṣuṇī Sangha* received instructions and supervision from the *Bhikṣu Sangha* in important matters such as the *upasampadā* (ordination), the *uposatha* (confession), the *vasa* (rainy season retreat), and the study of *Sūtra* and *Vinaya*. Hence, even though the *Bhikṣuṇī Sangha* managed its own internal affairs, the clerical rank of a nun was lower than that of a monk. All the eight rules presupposed the superiority of *bhikṣu* to *bhikṣuṇī*. The Buddha did not doubt the capacity of woman in achieving her religious goal, yet he seems to have considered that her feminine disposition might become an obstacle on her way to liberation. These special rules were seen as safeguards or precautionary measures to ensure the social and spiritual welfare of both *Sanghas*.

Technically, nuns were supposed to be subservient to monks in some respects, yet in the larger perspective, *bhikṣuṇīs* did enjoy the same privileges as *bhikṣus* in terms of spiritual development. They could engage in extensive meditation and strive for enlightenment. They could take an active role in propagating the *Dharma* by delivering sermons to the laity. In spite of restrictions and limitations, women proved that they were as capable as men of realizing their religious goal. The *Therigāthā* vividly records in verse the sublime profundity, serene spirituality, and deep insight that seventy-three *theris* experienced.

We can conclude that the social and religious status of women in the Buddhist era was superior to that of pre-Buddhist times. Even though the *Bhikṣuṇī Sangha* was for practical purposes subordinate to the *Bhikṣu Sangha*, nuns had their own *Sangha* which provided a favorable environment for religious practice, and they enjoyed complete freedom to pursue their spiritual goals. As for laywomen, they enjoyed more security and status at home than before. Nevertheless, due to deep-rooted customs and the male's inherent sense of superiority, women were far from actually being treated equal to men. On numerous occasions in Buddhist literature, women were portrayed as jealous, stupid, passionate, and spiteful. The prototype for the negative attitude toward women was embodied in the daughters of Mara, personified as Lust, Aversion, and Craving. It was thought that women should best be kept at a distance, especially by those men working their way to liberation. Before the Buddha's *parinirvāna*, he gave Ānanda the following instructions with regard to women:

> "How do we conduct ourself, Lord, with regard to women?"
> "Don't see them, Ānanda."
> "But Lord, if we should see them, what are we to do?"
> "Abstain from speech, Ānanda."
> "But what if they should speak to us, Lord, what are we to do?"
> "Keep wide awake, Ānanda."[10]

Women are said to have five obstacles: not being capable of becoming a Brahma King, Sakra, King Mara, Cakravartin, or Buddha. The body of women was considered impure and something to be ashamed of. Such portrayals of women as these appear in early Buddhist literature. It is in Mahāyāna literature that we find positive conceptualizations of women in terms of wisdom and practice.

The Mahāyāna Buddhist Concept of Women

The change in the concept of women in Mahāyāna literature is based on the doctrine and philosophy of Mahāyāna Buddhism. Whereas the pre-Mahāyāna literature represents the traditional views of an established monastic institution dominated by monks, in contrast, the Mahāyāna advocates the ideal of the *bodhisattva* who embodies the highest state of wisdom and compassion in which all sexual and social discrimination has been eliminated. Every being, whether male or female, ordained or lay, is considered a potential Buddha. Nevertheless, Mahāyāna literature, although presenting an egalitarian view, does not present a consistent view concerning the equal status of women. The path of salvation is presented differently from *sūtra* to *sūtra* within the Mahāyāna tradition. Generally speaking, the Mahāyāna *sūtras* which depict women's spiritual progress may be classified into four types, illustrating a gradual elevation in the attitudes toward women.[11]

1. Sūtras That Hold a Negative Attitude Toward Women.

In these *sūtras* women are portrayed as representing the profane world (*samsara*), and thus are potential obstacles to spiritual growth. In the *Udayanayatsaraja-parivartah* (*The Tale of King Udayana of Vastasa*) from the *Maharatnakuta* (T. 11, p. 543), we read,

> Women can destroy pure precepts.
> They retreat from doing merits and honor.
> Preventing one from rebirth in heaven,
> They are the source of hell.

The Mahāyāna *sūtra* on the merits of making images of the Buddha depicts women as narrow-minded, jealous and hateful, unforgiving and ungrateful. Even if they seek enlightenment, they lack determination. It is true that the Mahāyāna vehicle was more sympathetic toward women, but an element of misogyny is still evident in its literature. Extreme prejudice against women, however, is by no means a predominant attitude.

2. Sūtras That Deny Women's Presence in the Buddha Lands

The Pure Land *sūtras* are the most notable in this class. For example, the thirty-fourth vow of the *Larger Sukhayativyuha Sūtra* states,

> O Bhagavan, if after I have obtained Bodhi, women in immeasurable, innumerable, inconceivable, incomparable, immense Buddha countries on all sides after having heard my name, should allow carelessness to arise, should not turn their thoughts toward Bodhi, should, when they are free from birth, not despise their female nature; and if being born again, should assume a second female nature, then may I not obtain the highest perfect knowledge.[12]

The *Smaller Sukhavativyuha* also explicitly declares that there are no women in the Pure Land. Although the possibility of being born in the Pure Land is not denied to women, the implication here is that a male nature is necessary for progress on the *bodhisattva* path in the Buddha land.

3. Sūtras That Accept Women as Lower Stage Bodhisattvas

Most of the Mahāyāna *sūtras* fall into this category. This includes such texts as the *Saddharmapuṇḍarīka*, the *Sumatidarikapariprccha*, and the *Astasaharikaprajñapāramitā*. In these *sūtras* women are acknowledged as "good-knowing advisors" or spiritual "good friends" (*kalyānamitra*), but they are relegated to the lower *bodhisattva* stages. To be consistent with the Mahāyānist egalitarian view toward all sentient beings, the motif of sex transformation was introduced into those *sūtras*. If a woman's virtue, merit, and wisdom are extraordinary, she may, through sexual change become a *bodhisattva* or a Buddha in her present or future life. Transformation of sex symbolizes a transition from the imperfect condition of human beings (represented by the female body) to the mental perfection of *bodhisattvas* and Buddhas (represented by the male body). In response to a challenge from Śāriputra, who represents the traditional attitude toward women, the *naga* princess in the *Lotus Sūtra*, who is depicted as very intelligent and having penetrated into the most profound

Dharma, changes herself into a male *bodhisattva* and at once becomes a Buddha.

Here the transformation of sex from female to male is seen as a prerequisite for the *naga* princess's attainment of Buddhahood. Though the case of the *naga* princess demonstrates the possibility of women's realization of Buddhahood, a dichotomy, namely, the notion of male and female exists.

4. Sūtras That Accept Women as Advanced Bodhisattvas and Imminent Buddhas.

The *Vimalakirti Sūtra* and the *Śrīmālā Sūtra* belong to this category, in which the position of the female culminates. The doctrinal basis for this culmination lies in the Mahāyāna doctrines of emptiness, Buddha nature (*tathagatagarbha*), and non-duality. Instead of seeing *bodhisattvas* and Buddhas as necessarily male, the *sūtras* in the category claim that the notions of duality—of male and female, subject and object—are merely mental constructs and conventionalities. The characteristics of "maleness" and "femaleness" are illusory and irrelevant to spiritual achievement. On this basis, the female *bodhisattva* refuses to undergo sexual change.

When asked to transform her sex by Śāriputra, the goddess in the *Vimalakirti Sūtra* said, "I have been here twelve years and have looked for the innate characteristics of the female sex and haven't been able to find them. How can I change them?"[13] Then the goddess changes Śāriputra into a female. This was to reinforce her assertion that things are neither female nor male when viewed in terms of their essential emptiness. Śāriputra's transformation to female points up his attachment to sexual discrimination.

Conclusion

We have reviewed the development of women's status in terms of wisdom and practice progressing from early Buddhism to Mahāyāna Buddhism. Women are ultimately portrayed as advanced *bodhisattvas* fully capable of obtaining the goal of enlightenment. Let us now examine what particular status the laywoman and the nun hold in Mahāyāna tradition. It is really shocking to see that Mahāyāna literature is almost totally silent with reference to the nuns. No single *sūtra* is devoted to the topic. In contrast to the rather important role they held in the literature of early monastic Buddhism, the role of the nun in the Mahāyāna texts is obscured. This is because of the importance given to laywomen by Mahāyāna Buddhists, who tended to accept familial roles and other lay oriented roles as conducive to religious practice in more concrete and more varied patterns in their scripture than did pre-Mahāyāna Buddhists.[14] In relation to such a lay orientation, the role of nuns, who were disassociated from family life, seems to have been neglected.

While we find few references to nuns, the status of laywomen appears elevated. This is evident from the considerable mention they receive in the Mahāyāna *sūtras* such as the *Maharatnakuta Sūtra*, the *Sumatidarikaparivarta* (T. 11, pp. 547-549), the *Aśokadattvyakarapa* and the *Śrimatibrahmanipariprccha*, among others. In these *sūtras* laywomen, even sometimes girls of eight years old, master the profound doctrine, engage in *bodhisattva* practices, and are portrayed as surpassing great *arhats* in wisdom. Great attention is given to laywomen in the *Sūtra on the Pure Conduct of the Upāsikā*, in which teachings are given by the Buddha to the *upāsikās* (laywomen holding five precepts) exclusively. The importance given to laywomen is also evident in the *Gandavyuha*; only one nun is mentioned as a "good friend," but ten laywomen are mentioned.

Probably no *sūtra* depicts laywomen's wisdom as the *Śrīmālā Sūtra* does. Queen Śrīmālā, the personification of wisdom and practice is capable of the "lion's roar"—teaching the ultimate doctrine of universal salvation. She is straightforwardly accepted as a true teacher of the *Dharma*, and her femaleness is never challenged. At her advanced stage as a lay *bodhisattva*, the idea of sexual transformation is no longer relevant. As a secular woman, a representative of the feminine, she symbolizes the highest development of women's intellectual, spiritual, and religious potentialities. Hence, we may conclude that Mahāyāna Buddhism is a better vehicle for women, particularly for laywomen.

NOTES

1. Hirakawa specifically identifies the rise of Mahāyāna Buddhism with lay stupa-worshippers. See his "The Rise of Mahāyāna Buddhism and Its Relationship to the Worship of Stūpas," *Memoirs of Toyo Bunko*, Vol. 22, 1963, pp. 57-106.

2. I. B. Horner, *Women Under Primitive Buddhism*, Motilal Bararsidass, Delhi, 1975, p. 2.

3. C. A. F. Rhys Davids, *The Book of Kindred Sayings*, Luzac & Co., 1959, Vol. 1, p. 111.

4. Meena Talim, *Women in Early Buddhist Literature*, University of Bombay, 1972, p. 121.

5. Horner, p. 26.

6. Horner, p. 41.

7. Horner, p. 94.

8. T. W. Rhys Davids, *Dialogues of the Buddha*, Part 2, Pali Text Society, London, 1975, pp. 102-105.

9. Horner, p. 109.

10. T. W. Rhys Davids, p. 154.

11. Diana Paul, *Women in Buddhism*, Lancaster Miller, 1980, pp. 169-171.

12. F. Max Muller, tr., *The Bon-so-wa-ei Gappei Jodo Sambukyo*, Taitong Press, 1961, p. 390.

13. Paul, p. 230.

14. Paul, p. 79.

4 *Nuns of the Buddhist Traditions*

Wherever the Buddhist teachings have spread, monastic communities of committed celibate practitioners have developed. And, with the exception of Mongolia, wherever communities of monks have grown up, communities of nuns have developed side by side. As the teachings spread to diverse lands, cultures, and climates, varying interpretations of the *Dharma* arose. The residents of the monastic communities in the new locales also developed their own unique forms of practice and lifestyle by adjusting the regulations of the *Vinaya* to their own particular living conditions. For instance, customs relating to food, clothes, and housing that were viable for monks and nuns in torrid subtropical India were sometimes simply not suitable for monks and nuns in the wild frozen reaches of Tibet.

To allow for adaptations, a certain amount of flexibility was built into the disciplinary system formulated by the Buddha. The *Sangha* was expected to respect the customs and observe the laws of regions where they wandered to benefit beings by spreading the *Dharma*. It stands to reason that these missions were more likely to succeed if the renunciates refrained from transgressing local mores. Thus, considering the many changes that were warranted over the course of time, it is remarkable that the Buddhist traditions resemble each other as closely as they do.

In the process of adaptation over many centuries, special traditions evolved in each land where the *Buddhadharma* took root. Each tradition represents an amalgamation. The styles of discourse, practice, dress, and behavior that originally prevailed among the renunciates of the Buddha's day were combined with adaptations that were deemed necessary for the teachings to gain wide currency in their new environment. This blending process gave rise to the many rich streams of thought which in turn have produced countless generations of realized, creative, and humanitarian women and men. The contributions of Buddhist philosophy and contemplation to world civilization are well known.

In India, the land of its birth, Buddhism flourished throughout fifteen centuries. The first renunciates were instructed to retrieve rags from the trash bin, join them together in a designated pattern, and dye the resultant garments a yellowish hue that was then considered highly unattractive. In addition to the three garments prescribed for monks, the nuns were allowed a vest (or "breast covering") and a bathing cloth as a concession to society's concepts of female modesty. Monks and nuns alike shaved their heads completely and wandered barefoot from place to place, going round to collect alms of food from the faithful each morning. In subsequent centuries, more settled living communities developed and the lifestyle of the homeless wanderers became truly monastic.

At the time of the Buddha, thousands of nuns lived in their own independent communities with their own separate administrative organizations. There is evidence that such communities of *bhikṣuṇīs* existed at least up to the tenth century A.D. It seems likely that the order of nuns died out at about the same time that other Buddhist institutions were eclipsed.[1] At present there are a mere dozen ethnic Indian nuns who have emerged among the new Buddhist communities of Maharashtra State. They live in scattered locations and follow the Theravādin tradition. They have been ordained as *śrāmaṇerikās* by Indian Theravadin *bhikṣus*. There are some five hundred *śrāmaṇerikās* practicing the Tibetan form of Buddhism in Ladakh, in the Kinnaur and Spiti regions of Himachal Pradesh, and among the Mon people of Assam. There are no nuns reported among the Bengali Buddhists or the Buddhist tribes along the eastern border region of India, but recently one hundred nuns of the Chakma people following the Thravādin tradition have settled in the Tripura area as refugees from Bangladesh.

The *bhikṣuṇī* lineage was transmitted to Sri Lanka by Sanghamitta, the daughter of King Aśoka (c. 272-236 B.C.). There are records of *bhikṣuṇīs* in inscriptions dated as late as 885 A.D.[2] The practice and style of dress of the Sri Lankan nuns strongly resemble that of the early Indian nuns. Today there are some four thousand female renunciates in Sri Lanka following the Theravādin school. They are called *dasasil matas* (ten-precept nuns), and dress in saffron or ochre robes. Although they receive ten precepts, they are not called "*śrāmaṇerikās*" nor accorded recognition as members of the *Sangha*, since there are at present no *bhikṣuṇīs* to ordain them.

In Burma, there are some twenty to thirty thousand ten-precept nuns, known as anāgarikās ("homeless ones") or *thila-shin* ("possessors of morality"). They dress in orange and pink-colored robes and practice according to the Theravādin tradition. Stone inscriptions discovered in recent excavations give evidence of *bhikṣuṇīs* existing in the Pagan period (eleventh to thirteenth century), but the order probably died out during the Mongol incursions that brought that period to an end. There are numerous nunneries throughout Burma today, especially in the Mandalay area, maintaining admirable discipline.

Apparently, the *bhikṣuṇī* lineage never reached Thailand, although a Theravādin *bhikṣu* order flourishes there. It is estimated that there are from eight to ten thousand white-robed, shaven-headed *maejis*, women living the religious life, but they are not recognized as being full-fledged nuns. They receive eight precepts and there is a small group who receive ten precepts, but none of them are considered *śrāmaṇerikās* due to the absence of a *bhikṣuṇī* order. Similar orders of Theravādin nuns, dressed in white and holding eight or ten precepts, existed in Laos and Cambodia, but have barely survived recent political events.

The *bhikṣuṇī* order has fared best in the Mahāyāna countries. In 429 A.D. and 433 A.D., two groups of Sri Lankan *bhikṣuṇīs* traveled to China to administer full ordination to hundreds of Chinese nuns. Despite periods of religious oppression and political turmoil, this *bhikṣuṇī* order, which follows the Dharmagupta school of *Vinaya*, has continued uninterruptedly until the present day. Chinese nuns wear either gray, black, or brown robes and don a brown or golden patched outer robe for ceremonies. The Chinese *bhikṣuṇī* order is strongly established in Taiwan and Hong Kong and is making a comeback in mainland China. Chinese *bhikṣuṇīs* are to be found in Malaysia, Singapore, Indonesia, Thailand, the Philippines, and almost every country where there are overseas Chinese communities.

In successive waves, through China, the Buddhist teachings were transmitted to Korea and Japan. The style of monastic practice in Korea today closely mirrors the forms of the Ch'an school as it existed earlier in China.[3] Both the *bhikṣu* and *bhikṣuṇī* lineages became firmly rooted there from early times. The *Bhikṣuṇī Sangha* still flourishes in Korea, with nuns standing side by side and slightly outnumbering their ordained brothers. Both monks and nuns dress in gray robes with pleats and a bow, which are a Korean adaptation of the original Chinese style of robes.

Both forms of practice and styles of dress vary widely among the nuns of Japan. They belong primarily to the Zen, Tendai, Nichiren, Shingon, and Pure Land schools. Neither the *bhikṣuṇī* nor *śrāmaṇerikā* lineages are existent, but Japanese nuns receive *bodhisattva* precepts and live celibate lives. There is also a large number of female priests who are not celibate. Most commonly the robes of the nuns are black or white and closely resemble Chinese robes in styling. Most of the texts and traditions they follow can be traced to Chinese sources, which themselves are traceable to Sanskrit and Indian origins.

Tibetan Buddhist culture also originated principally from India, though in a separate development. The *Bhikṣu Sangha* was established in Tibet in the middle of the eighth century under royal patronage, but a corresponding *bhikṣuṇī* lineage was never transmitted due to the difficulties and dangers of travel. The nuns of Tibet and other Himalayan regions following this tradition receive *śrāmaṇerikā* ordination from *bhikṣus*. They dress in maroon robes, with a yellow outer robe worn for ceremonies. Large numbers of nunneries were built, beginning in the eleventh century, where nuns could practice *Dharma* in isolation and quietude. There were more than eighteen thousand nuns in Tibet prior to the communist invasion; there are less than five hundred Tibetan nuns now settled in exile in India and Nepal.

Similar winds of political change have affected the Vietnamese order of nuns. A *Bhikṣuṇī Sangha* numbering in the thousands previously flourished in Vietnam, but only a small number of them have been able to settle abroad since the advent of communism. Most of these nuns practice in the Mahāyāna tradition and dress in gray or brown robes similar to those of the Chinese *Sangha*. Until recently, there were also Theravādin nuns in Vietnam, dressed in white and upholding ten precepts, but their present circumstances are unknown. Many currents of Buddhist culture flowed into Vietnam—Theravāda, Zen, Pure Land—and blended there to form a unique composite. Nuns both within and without Vietnam now struggle to preserve these traditions.

The diverse forms and practices that have evolved through two and a half millennia of Buddhist history are evidence of the adaptability of the faith and the versatility of human beings in their spiritual quest. Now, in the latter half of the twentieth century, the Buddhist teachings are in the process of being transplanted to a wide range of different countries, many of which are undergoing profound social changes. Undoubtedly novel forms, practices, and outlooks will result from the convergence of Buddhist traditions and contemporary social thought. One of the most fascinating imminent encounters is that of feminist ideology and the Buddhist theory of human perfection. The common denominator in the coming encounter is the value both these views place on truth stripped of preconceptions, prejudices, and delusions.

In addition to seeking the truth in all things, Buddhists add the ideal of effecting the welfare of all beings, human and nonhuman, female and male. In the pursuit of these central ideals, there is scope for the outer forms of Buddhism to adapt in response to the times and to changing social conditions. The current social atmosphere in Western countries, and increasingly in Asian countries, demands that women be given equal access to religious institutions and accomplishments. Such access includes ensuring the rights of women to obtain higher ordination, providing spiritual leadership which will potentially benefit the women of the world in countless ways. Efforts to assure women of these rights will inevitably meet with initial resistance, but since Buddhist practice is a system for achieving the benefit of living beings, when communities of *bhikṣuṇīs* can be shown to promote benefit, this resistance will surely fade. As a consequence, we may see women serving as spiritual role models on an unprecedented scale, working through spiritual insight to benefit beings at an exponential rate.

NOTES

1. N. A. Falk, "The Case of the Vanishing Nuns: The Fruits of Ambivalence in Ancient Indian Buddhism," *Unspoken Worlds*, p. 223.

2. D. K. Barua, *Viharas in Ancient India*, Calcutta, 1969, p. 191.

3. The Ch'an school traditionally dates from the arrival of Bodhidharma in China in the sixth century. One of the five Ch'an schools of China, the Fa-yen, was subsequently transplanted to Korea.

NUNS OF BURMA

by Daw Su Su Sein

All along the range of the Sagaing hills are situated 145 nunneries with a total of 2,229 nuns residing in them. If a woman wishes to be ordained there, she is not allowed to become a nun at once, but must first stay for three months abiding by the eight precepts and engaging in meditation in preparation for the ordination. Parents or guardians of the aspiring nun must apply on her behalf to the dean or administrative body of preceptresses for admission to the nunnery. The candidate herself is required to render a promise that she will do all the duties imposed upon her once she is admitted. All nuns are expected to abide by at least eight precepts perfectly, and they have the option to undertake nine or ten precepts if they choose to do so.

The discipline of the nunnery entails attendance at morning and evening prayers. Nuns are required to wear the robes in uniformity with the others and must conduct themselves with dignity, remaining solemn and taciturn while walking in procession. At 4:00 AM when the conventional call is sounded, the nuns must arise to attend the prayer assembly, to cook rice, and to take breakfast. Then all engage either in *patipatt* (meditation, telling beads, and other practices) or *patiyatt* (study of the Buddha's teachings). These constitute the principal activities of the nuns.

At 10:00 AM they bathe, and at 11:00 AM all have lunch. Between 12:00 noon and 1:00 PM, they take rest or nap. Following this, all must study or recite earnestly. When classes are dismissed, the nuns attend to tasks such as drawing water and changing the offerings of flowers. In the evening again at 6:00 the nuns assemble for prayers, offering lights, flowers, and water, and reciting admonitions and sermons on morality. After the prayers are completed, they repeat the lessons they have learnt.

On the *uposatha* days, the grounds of the nunnery are cleaned and swept thoroughly. On these days of special religious observances, the nuns observe vegetarianism and remain particularly alert while doing helpful deeds for others and in all their other tasks. They pay close attention with respect to "the four materials," that is, the nunnery, garments, meals, and medicines.

The preceptresses are regarded as parents, and the student nuns are regarded as their children. Since the students have left their families and native places to join the order of nuns, they are looked after and provided with all necessities by the preceptresses, who address them with kind and sincere speech. In turn, the students must regard their preceptresses with solicitude and obedience.

Nuns between the ages of thirteen and forty are prohibited from certain activities. They must refrain from approaching any monastery alone, from collecting vegetables, from going outside to bathe, from offering alms to monks, learning from them, or studying with them. Nuns must comport themselves serenely and maintain themselves both mentally and physically. The wearing of dirty or ragged garments is prohibited. They are expected to engage only in religious and beneficial deeds. Speaking loudly, laughing boisterously, and yawning and sneezing loudly are not to be practiced. Whatever activities are unnecessary, such as writing to friends, gossiping, and being over-friendly, are to be avoided.

Nuns are permitted to write to their native village and to go for a ride in the country at the times of harvest. A leave for staying overnight can be obtained from their respective preceptress or abbess. Untimely meals, drinking, and smoking are not allowed. Nuns must be kind, polite, and agreeable in their communications with others and should subdue their minds by means of meditations on loving kindness toward their fellow beings.

The nuns are responsible for sweeping their residences and all areas of the nunnery, including the rest house and *pagodas*. All must follow the required standards of discipline. Those nuns who have individual sponsors live peacefully and enjoy a contemplative religious life. Others generally must visit the neighborhood in their vicinity to collect alms twice a week, spending the whole day to obtain their meals. Kitchen duties and meals are taken in groups of two and three. There are only a few nunneries in which all the nuns can manage to gather together for every meal. For the most part, the nuns are dependent solely upon the generosity of their relatives living in the locality and have no other resources. Occasionally they will be invited to attend a funeral ceremony and be provided with alms.

In spite of the difficulties nuns face with regard to education, livelihood, meditation, and prayer, they manage to attend to all their duties meticulously due to their staunchness in virtue. They serenely and diligently engage in the practice of morality, truthfulness, patience, and gentleness, while pursuing lofty and noble religious deeds. They are frugal with what they have and dwell in contentment.

In the beginning of their religious lives, nuns study the teachings of the Buddha (*patiyatt*) and, as they grow older, they enjoy meditation and other devotional practices (*patipatt*). They have no modern educational facilities. They shun political efforts and civic interests in favor of tranquil recitations, sermons, and studies. They spend time cooking meals themselves and offering alms. They stay aloof from the public and take pride in being nuns apart from the worldly life.

NUNS OF CHINA: PART I—THE MAINLAND
by Dr. Hema Goonatilake

Prior to the Cultural Revolution, there were thousands of Buddhist temples and hundreds of thousands of Buddhist monks and nuns in China. It has been generally accepted that there were 500,000 temples and three million monks and nuns. It is also known that the communist condemnation and suppression of Buddhism as well as of other religions in China began as early as 1920.[1] By 1956, however, the establishment of the Chinese Buddhist Academy, several centers for training of *Sangha*, and the restoration of the Buddhist Publication Society brought a fresh impetus to Buddhism. Before long, though, the Cultural Revolution occurred and many Buddhist temples and nunneries were converted into factories or warehouses. Buddhist monks and nuns were compelled to work in factories or engage in agricultural activities. Since the crushing of the Gang of Four, Buddhist activities have resumed and Buddhist temples, monasteries, and nunneries are being restored with the aid of government grants. Wherever buildings have been restored, religious observances as well as training centers for monks and nuns have started. Provincial Buddhist associations have been reactivated as well.

I was privileged to visit China in September 1984 as part of a study-lecture tour of several countries in Asia. In China, I visited Buddhist temples and nunneries in Beijing, Shanghai, Nanjing, and Canton.[2] The largest nunnery I visited in China was the Zi Xiu Nunnery in Shanghai. The Shanghai Buddhist Association had arranged my visit to this nunnery, and my Chinese guide and interpreter, an associate professor at the Institute of Contemporary International Relations, Beijing, accompanied me. As we arrived, we saw at a distance a crowd of about one hundred men and women who had gathered at the entrance to the temple to welcome us. The abbess of the temple, the senior nuns, and the chairperson and office bearers of the Shanghai Buddhist Association were all in front. I was struck by the deep warmth shown to me. The abbess, her eyes beaming with joy, said to me in Chinese, "We have opened our nunnery to a visitor for the first time in eighteen years."

We were ushered into the main Buddha hall of the temple and then into an assembly hall where we were treated to a grand Chinese tea with a wide variety of sweets. This was followed by a discussion with nuns, office bearers, members of the Shanghai Buddhist Association, and lay devotees.

I gathered that this temple was founded by a nun one hundred years ago and that now four generations of nuns have lived there. During the Cultural Revolution, the nunnery was turned into a warehouse and the nuns were compelled to work in factories or go to the countryside to do farm work. The older ones who have since restored the nunnery said proudly that they had practiced the *Dhamma* while living in their countryside homes and growing their own food. Some others had given up robes. The oldest of the fifteen who had returned was eighty-six years old and was in delicate health. She was being cared for by the younger nuns. The abbess of the temple was seventy-three years old and had become a nun at the age of twenty. The deputy head of the temple was seventy-four years old and had been given to the temple at the age of two years, since her parents had too many children to support. The nun who was a teacher and the head of the training school for nuns was seventy-nine years old.

Of the twenty-six nuns residing in the nunnery, eleven had entered the order after the nunnery was restored in 1982. Their ages ranged from eighteen to twenty-eight years. They all belonged to farming or working-class families. One common characteristic they all shared was that they had been strongly influenced by their deeply religious parents or grandparents. Three among them had even closer connections with the Buddhist clergy: one nun's aunt was a nun; another had two brothers who were monks; the third had been brought up by a nun.

The trainee nuns at the school are given a two-year training course, consisting primarily of Buddhist texts, Chinese language, Chinese history, and meditation. The course began in September 1982 and was scheduled to finish at the end of September 1984. Upon completion of the course, the nuns were to leave for various temples around the country. Another group was scheduled to begin their training at the end of September. Students were recruited for the course after being given a preliminary test in the *Dhamma*.

At the end of the discussion, we were taken upstairs into the teaching-lecture hall where I gave a talk. I described the situation of the Sri Lankan *dasasil matas* (ten-precept nuns) today, different aspects of the controversy over the restoration of the *bhikkhunī* order, and the historical role the Sri Lankan *bhikkhunīs* had played in China with regard to the transmission of higher ordination to Chinese *bhikkhunīs* in 433 A.D.

New interest in the issue was seen after the visit of the Sri Lankan Minister of Cultural Affairs in 1985 to China, where he gained first-hand knowledge of an unbroken lineage of the *bhikkhunī* order, and following his subsequent invitation to *bhikkhus* and scholars to submit their views on the subject. Since then periodic discussions have taken place in the Sri Lankan media focusing on the initial establishment of the higher ordination in China by Sri Lankan nuns, and the possibility of reviving the *bhikkhunī* order in Sri Lanka by having Sri Lankan nuns receive ordination from Chinese *bhikkhunīs*.

During this talk I noticed that some of the members of the audience were deeply moved. Several asked questions concerning ancient Sri Lankan-Chinese Buddhist connections and the possibility of renewing *Bhikkhunī Sangha* links between China and Sri Lanka.

Over the two days I spent at this nunnery, it was interesting to observe the nuns' religious activities and their interactions with the lay community. In the afternoons laypeople occasionally came into the temple, where they chanted or prayed for a few minutes and also spoke with the nuns in a friendly manner. On holidays, the nuns said, the temple was crowded.

Following these two days at Zi Xiu Nunnery in Shanghai,

I next traveled to Nanjing. The nunnery I visited there was in the process of being restored. A large building complex was in the final phase of completing its construction. The nineteen resident nuns and novices were occupying two rooms in a dilapidated building in the meanwhile. Adjoining their living quarters was a shrine room with Buddha images where religious ceremonies were observed.

Here too, we were received warmly and treated to a formal tea, followed by a discussion in which all nuns and novices participated. Over two hours had passed when a bell rang at 3:15 P.M. sharp and all the nuns and novices, except the abbess, moved into the shrine room and began the afternoon service. Walking in procession, they made offerings of food to the Buddhas while chanting. The ritual took about forty-five minutes. We spent the whole afternoon there, some of the time in the company of the abbess who was supervising every detail of the construction work and some of the time observing the novices who swept the sprawling garden, carried pails of water, and cleaned utensils in addition to their religious activities.

The abbess of this nunnery was seventy-two years old. She had been living there from the age of six, when she became a novice. She had to leave the nunnery along with the other nuns in 1966 when the nunnery was converted into a factory. She lived with her sister in the countryside from 1966 to 1972, then went to live with a group of nuns in another nunnery that had been restored. It was only in 1981 that she was able to return to this nunnery and begin the restoration work. Of the nineteen residents in this nunnery, twelve were fully ordained nuns, the others novices. Some novices still had not shaved their heads. They said they would continue with unshaven heads for a bit longer as a test of commitment to see whether they could be lifelong nuns.

The next nunnery I visited was in Beijing. It was also being restored at that time and only six nuns were in residence. The activities and atmosphere of this nunnery were similar to those of the nunnery in Nanjing. One of the major reasons for both boys and girls joining the order, before the communists came to power, was poverty in families with large numbers of children. Circumstances compelled the parents to hand over a child to the temple so that they had one less mouth to feed.[3] Another motivating factor for encouraging the children to enter the order (especially on the part of the parents) may have been the Chinese belief that the ordination of a son or daughter would relieve seven generations of the ordained child's family from suffering, a common belief in many Buddhist countries.[4] An effort is now being made in China to maintain a minimum age requirement of eighteen years for those wishing to enter the order, to ensure that young people are prepared to make a genuine spiritual commitment.

Most of the nuns whom I had the opportunity to meet either had been brought up in a Buddhist environment or had experienced spiritual awakening, even if they had been given to the temple at a young age. I also came across several cases of women joining the order after having lost interest in worldly life following the death of a husband or a child, or after the failure of a marriage or love affair.

In many discussions I had during my three-week stay in China, strong commitment to maintaining ordination was emphasized as a key qualification for a nun or a monk. They categorically stated that theirs is a lifetime commitment, unlike the situation in Thailand, for example, and that those who could not keep the rigorous discipline were discouraged from entering the order.

I noticed deep enthusiasm in all the monks, nuns, and laypeople I met at the temples and nunneries. Although every nunnery I visited had a temple run by the nuns and was patronized by Buddhists in the area, the temples run by monks appeared to be better patronized and organized. Some of the Buddhist temples I visited in Beijing, Nanjing, Shanghai, and Canton were hives of activity, with religious ceremonies well attended by both men and women.[5] The ratio of young devotees to old, however, was low: approximately one to ten.

Since reinstatement of a certain amount of religious freedom, state patronage of Buddhism is evident at several levels. First, government grants are being given for the restoration of Buddhist temples and nunneries. Second, religious faiths are being given representation at major decision-making bodies with the result that monks and nuns are being elected as representatives to the Political Consultative Conference.

The compiling and printing of the Chinese *Tripitaka*, which contains 23,000 volumes of Buddhist texts, has begun and is expected to be completed by 1994. Centers for printing and distributing Buddhist *sūtras* have appeared in different parts of the country. The activities of the Chin Ling Buddhist Text society have resumed, and the publication and distribution of classics of the different Buddhist schools have begun again. Training schools for monks and nuns have also been established in several provinces.[6]

China has had strong cultural ties with countries in the region, especially with India and Sri Lanka, from as early as the first century A.D.[7] My interactions with the heads of Buddhist temples and deans of Buddhist institutions revealed that they are eager to re-establish cultural ties once again, particularly the *Bhikkhunī Sangha* links between China and Sri Lanka.

NOTES

1. Martha Sentnor, "Statistical Figures on the Order of *Bhikkhunīs* in China," New York, 1984.

2. Owing to lack of time, I was not able to visit the provinces better known for Buddhist activity in general and for Buddhist nuns in particular. These include the provinces of Sichuan, Fujian, Hubei, and Shanzi. All those of whom I inquired about *bhikkhunīs* referred to the famous scholar nun, Long Lien, who was seventy-three years old and resided in the Chendo nunnery on Mt. Ome in Sichuan Province. Her book on *Madhyamika* was also mentioned by some of my respondents, and it appeared that she commanded the highest respect in the entire country among contemporary *bhikkhunīs*. I also gathered that Bhikkhunī Long Lien and some of her

colleagues had been permitted to remain behind in the nunnery during the Cultural Revolution, but were compelled to grow their own food.

3. This has also been one of the reasons for joining the order in certain other countries like Sri Lanka.

4. In Sri Lanka, however, it is believed that only a son's ordination will bring this advantage.

5. Exceptions are certain historical Buddhist places, such as the Guang Xiao Temple, abode of Hui Neng, the Sixth Patriarch of Zen Buddhism in China, which have been restored and are being maintained chiefly as museums.

6. Speech delivered at the fourteenth conference of the World Fellowship of Buddhists by Mr. Chao Puchu, head of the Chinese Buddhist delegation, Colombo, 1984.

7. See W. Pachow, "Ancient Cultural Relations Between Ceylon and China," *University of Ceylon Review*, Vol. XI, No. 3 and 4, and Hema Goonatilake, *The Impact of Some Mahāyāna Concepts on Sri Lankan Buddhism*, Ph.D. thesis, University of London, 1974.

NUNS IN CHINA: PART II–TAIWAN
by Bhikṣuṇī Shih Yung Kai

Buddhism is believed to have been introduced to Taiwan with the first Chinese immigrants during the twelfth century. According to early Chinese custom, when the Chinese immigrated to a new place, they usually brought from their homes or temple some statues of deities representing their religious beliefs. In the absence of written records, there is very limited information about Buddhist activities and temples from this period up to the end of the nineteenth century.

During the period from 1895 to 1945, Taiwan was ceded to Japan by the Chinese government, so there was strong influence from the Japanese during this time. According to the Chinese Buddhist tradition, monks and nuns must observe celibacy and vegetarianism strictly, and they are not allowed to live in the same monastery. Under Japanese influence, however, these rules were suspended.

After the Second World War, Taiwan was returned to the Chinese government. Around 1949, when mainland China started to become communist, many senior monks came to Taiwan. Their arrival enriched the traditions of Taiwan and restored the original Buddhist teachings. They helped to clear up the confusion in the Buddhist situation created during the Japanese occupation and encouraged Buddhists to participate in social service work with a positive attitude. They taught traditional Chinese Buddhism and built new Buddhist temples, centers, and colleges.

On April 1, 1912, the Chinese Buddhist Association was established in Shanghai. The name was changed to Chinese Buddhist Society in 1928, but when representatives from throughout the country gathered in Shanghai the following year, they adopted the present name, Chinese Buddhist Association, also known as "Buddhist Association of the Republic of China" or "BAROC" for short. Because of the eight-year war of resistance against Japan (1937-1945), BAROC's First National Congress could not be held until 1947 and this was in Nanking.

The members of the *Sangha* who later moved to Taiwan acted jointly with those born on the island of Taiwan and reactivated BAROC in 1950.

In the past thirty years, Buddhism has flourished in Taiwan. To date approximately 2,000 Buddhist temples and organizations are registered with the Chinese Buddhist Association. Most of these were built after 1950. Thirty-four of these temples or organizations have affiliated institutes for *Sangha* training and over ten of these have Buddhist colleges or study institutions in which advanced Buddhist study courses are being offered.

The first "Triple Altar Ordination" for monks and nuns was initiated in 1952 by BAROC. Since then ordinations for monks and nuns have been given at the end of each year. "Triple Altar Ordination" means that three different kinds of ordinations are given during ordination period. The first is the *śrāmaṇera* and *śrāmaṇerikā* ordination which is usually given after two weeks of training. Then, a week later, the *bhikṣu* and *bhikṣuṇī* ordination is given. The *bodhisattva* ordination is given during the last two days of the proceedings. This *bodhisattva* ordination includes the transmission of the *bodhisattva* precepts contained in the *Brahmajala Sūtra*.

Each year a different temple is selected as the ordination site. It must have facilities to accommodate at least 300 to 500 novice monks and nuns. Novice monks and nuns from around Taiwan and other parts of the world who want to be ordained come together at the temple where the ordination is to be given. The complete ordination lasts for thirty-two days if it is to be administered by *bhikṣus* only.

A dual ordination in which *bhikṣus* and *bhikṣuṇīs* administer ordination to novice nuns lasts for fifty-three days. During this time novices are taught in the correct behavior of a monk or a nun. The *Prāṭimokśa Sūtra* is taught and explained, and the ceremony is rehearsed many times before the actual ordination takes place to ensure that the novices know what to do during the ceremony.

According to the records of BAROC, over 10,000 monks and

nuns have been ordained in Taiwan since 1952. Of these, 6,000 to 7,000 are nuns. The phenomenon of having a much greater number of nuns ordained than monks is something unique to Taiwan and Hong Kong.

There seem to be several reasons for this special phenomenon. First, in earlier days many of the monks came from poor families. At that time a Buddhist temple was the only place where the son of a poor family could get a decent education and sometimes even survive. In the past thirty years, the living standard of an ordinary family in Taiwan and Hong Kong has improved considerably. Now it is not difficult for ordinary families to bring up their sons. Many people feel that it would be a disgrace if they had to send a son to a temple to become a monk, because it would suggest that they were not capable of supporting him. This is one of the reasons why today many Chinese are reluctant to send their son to a temple, even if the son himself would like to make that choice.

Second, the Chinese believe very strongly in the continuity of the family lineage. The oldest son especially is expected to continue the family lineage by marrying and bringing up more sons. It is considered to be a family tragedy if a son wants to renounce lay life and become a monk.

Lastly, I feel that the changing value system of Chinese society as a whole has a lot to do with this special phenomenon. With the introduction of Western culture, people are becoming more materialistic, and as a result, they find less time to look after their spiritual needs. Male dominance is still very much alive in Chinese society. The normal expectation of a man is to have a good education, to be successful in his career, and to raise a family. If a man ignores these expectations of society and his familial obligations, then people will think that something must be wrong with him. Under these societal and familial pressures, fewer and fewer men feel free to choose religious practice as a way of life. Consequently, fewer men are becoming Buddhist monks. I personally feel that this is a very sad and unhealthy situation. Both men and women have their roles to play in Buddhism. Both monks and nuns are needed for the propagation and continuation of Buddha's teachings. I sincerely hope that the number of monks and nuns will soon reach a healthy balance for the benefit of Buddhism and all beings.

Presently, nuns in Taiwan have the same opportunities and responsibilities as monks in terms of learning and teaching the *Dharma*. Of the 6,000 to 7,000 nuns in Taiwan, about half are between twenty and forty years of age, the other half are above forty. They are distributed among the 2,000 temples, most of which have populations of twenty to thirty monks and nuns who live in the same temple but in separate quarters. There are only a few larger temples with more than 200 monks and nuns in residence. Some choose to live in small apartments alone or together with three or four others.

There are more than ten Buddhist colleges in Taiwan, all of which provide education for both monks and nuns. Other institutions of higher education, such as ordinary colleges and universities, do not place any restrictions on the admission of monks and nuns. There are examples of nuns who have successfully completed their studies in medical colleges and law schools.

There are two modes of living for nuns in a temple. The first is for those who choose to study in a Buddhist college, which is usually affiliated with a temple. Those who study here are mostly novices or newly ordained monks and nuns. Their study program normally takes three years and covers various subjects on Buddhism such as history and philosophy. Other non-Buddhist subjects such as English and Japanese are also taught. The students' daily life is very well disciplined.

Those who do not study in the Buddhist colleges live a monastic life in the temple of their choice. Activities and practice differ according to the temple in which they live. The most immediate concern of all temples is economic maintenance. Different temples have different means of achieving this. Some are completely self-reliant, supporting themselves by growing their own food and providing for their own daily necessities. Some perform prayers and chanting for devotees who make offerings for this service, usually in the form of money. Going for alms is not generally accepted in Chinese society.

Some of the nuns do various types of *Dharma* work such as giving public lectures on Buddhism, doing social work, operating kindergartens, organizing retreats, and teaching in high schools, Buddhist colleges, and universities. Some are also involved in cultural activities such as editing and publishing Buddhist books and magazines. Their principal support comes from donations made by devotees. The main religious activity for nuns as a group in a temple is morning and evening chanting. Besides this, nuns do individual practices on their own such as reciting the Buddhas' names, making prostrations, chanting *sūtras*, and doing meditation. Short retreats usually lasting seven days are held at different times of the year. Various *Dharma* functions and *pujas* are also organized on special occasions.

An ordinary *bhikṣuṇī* in Taiwan today has at least a primary education, but most have finished high school and some have also graduated from college or university before entering the *Sangha*. More and more *bhikṣuṇīs* are aware of the importance of education. In recent years, quite a number of them have been going to countries such as Japan, Korea, India, and America to further their education at the undergraduate or graduate level.

From the activities and accomplishments of *bhikṣuṇīs* in Taiwan today, we can see that they are assuming a very important and influential role in the religious sector as well as in society as a whole. As long as the trend of young women entering the *Sangha* continues, adding new talent and energy to the monastic community, we can foretell that the *Bhikṣuṇī Sangha* in Taiwan will become a very powerful force which will contribute to the well-being of the society and to the happiness of all beings.

NUNS OF JAPAN: PART I

by Reverend Tessho Kondo

Japanese Buddhism has maintained the Mahāyāna tradition ever since it was transmitted from China in 552 A.D. There are many schools or orders of both exoteric and esoteric Buddhism in Japan. The two main streams, however, are Zen Buddhism, emphasizing meditation, and Pure Land Buddhism, emphasizing the repetition of the name of Amitabha Buddha. These two streams go their own ways and have not combined in Japan as they have in China. It is difficult to determine the total number of nuns who exist in all the many Buddhist schools in Japan, but I think there are about 2000 nuns in about 1500 temples.

The Pure Land Buddhist tradition to which I belong has about 700 nuns in 500 temples. As you can judge from those numbers, about half of us live alone and carry full responsibility as the head priest of a temple. Many of us are more than sixty years old, and young successors are very few. Why do so few young women enter the monastic path? One reason is that most families have only one or two children, so the parents will not permit their daughters to take the path. (Although Japanese monks often marry and have children, the tradition of celibacy is maintained among the nuns, meaning they do not help carry on the family line.)

Another reason why more women do not become nuns is that we are not supported by our denominations. Rather, each of us must obtain support from our temple members and the community. Since women rarely have temples with large numbers of followers and a good income, they normally must supplement the temple income with fees received through teaching flower arrangement or tea ceremony. During training, of course, no outside activities are permitted, so training expenses must be met by savings, gifts from one's parents, or support from one's master.

Even though we all use the terms "nun" and "monk," the meanings of these terms vary considerably from country to country and from Buddhist school to school. In the case of Japanese Buddhism, we cannot properly be described as "nuns" and "monks," but rather as "priests" or "ministers of religion." Whether male or female, we receive the same precepts, undertake the same training (in principle, at least), and have equal standing within our Buddhist traditions or schools (again, in principle, at least). The precepts we receive are the traditional Mahāyāna precepts from the *Brahmajāla Sūtra* that is conventionally said to have been translated into Chinese by Kumarajiva in 406 A.D., although modern scholarship indicates that actually it was originally compiled in China.

Formal training varies according to Buddhist school and to individual conditions. In the Pure Land Buddhist Nuns' Training Center that I supervise, women undergo two years of training in Buddhist teachings, ceremonies, and living as part of the *Sangha*. In Soto Zen Buddhism, training depends on the amount of prior education. Most men enter their training as graduates of the Buddhist Studies department of one of the Soto universities. The training period then need only be one or two years. Women, on the other hand, often enter training upon graduation from senior high school. Sometimes they even begin training prior to graduation and must continue high school studies at night classes after a full day's activities in the training temple. Such women must complete a two- to three-year course, or sometimes longer.

The formal training program may include many different subjects, but the primary focus is of course placed on that particular Buddhist school's way to enlightenment. For my Pure Land school, this means the practice of *nembutsu* (recitation of the name of Amitabha Buddha). For the Zen school, it is *zazen* (sitting mediation). Other subjects may include Buddhist history and philosophy, *sūtra* study, instruction and practice in ceremonies, sewing of priests' robes, and instruction in the arts of tea ceremony, flower arrangement, and calligraphy.

Upon the completion of training, the nun is certified to perform all the ceremonies of her tradition and to become head priest of a temple. From that time on, either she lives alone or, in the more fortunate cases, as part of a head priest and assistant priest team.

Each temple is, for the most part, an independent legal entity. The livelihood of the head priest depends on the temple supporters. This, in turn, means that the primary duties of the priest are those requested by her supporters. In Japan, this means conducting funerals and memorial services, plus other *sūtra* readings on behalf of the supporters. A second, less defined but often more time-consuming duty is counseling of supporters in all the many problems of everyday life.

Especially in rural areas that are losing population to the cities, there may be few temple supporters left. For this reason, and as a means of propagating the Buddhist teachings, many nuns operate kindergartens or nursery schools or else teach tea ceremony, flower arrangement, or calligraphy. (Monks in similar circumstances are more likely to become civil servants or public school teachers.)

In my own case, I am the head priest of a temple and must maintain that temple and perform its ceremonies. Twice a month I give lectures on *Dharma* to laywomen. Nearly every day I go to the training center that I supervise and where I also teach. The life of a Japanese nun is thus a very busy and fulfilling one, very close to the community of which she is a part, even though she is separated from her fellow nuns.

NUNS OF JAPAN: PART II

by Bhikṣuṇī Karma Lekshe Tsomo

My own experience in Japan began in 1964 when I visited there to go surfing. Since the beaches of California and Hawaii had become very crowded, I took my surfboard by ship to Yokohama and began riding the waves on the coast of Chiba peninsula. During the winter, I went to a temple to do Zen meditation. It was ten years later before I went back again to live in a temple and begin more intensive training in meditation. Still another ten years passed before I returned to Japan as a nun on pilgrimage, which was a very special experience.

During this last trip, just before going to Korea, I spent a month in Japan visiting as many nunneries as I could find. There are a large number of nunneries, but they are scattered throughout the country and it was often difficult to locate them. Although many new Buddhist groups have arisen in Japan since World War II, interest in the traditional schools has declined. Fewer people are joining the monasteries and fewer women are becoming nuns. Many of the exquisite temples in Japan are empty; others have just one or two nuns staying to maintain the temple. These nuns continue with their own prayers and meditation, but many of them are seventy, eighty, or ninety years old. I was deeply saddened to find so few young nuns.

In Kyoto, there is a Nuns' Training Institute belonging to the Pure Land school. At the time of my visit, it had been closed down due to a lack of applicants. I am happy to know that it has now been reopened under the directorship of Reverend Tessho Kondo. The institute offers a three-year course of training for nuns of the Pure Land school. Its curriculum includes training in discipline and deportment, *sūtras*, philosophy, chanting, tea ceremony, and flower arrangement. Nuns of other schools are admitted to the program for a one-year course of study, and foreign nuns are also accepted, provided they are conversant in Japanese.

Just across the street from the institute, I visited a temple with four nuns in residence. The abbess belongs to the lineage of the Japanese imperial family, and wears purple robes as an indication of this. She is in her forties and joined the temple after being orphaned as a young child. The nuns maintain the temple and perform prayers and ceremonies for the laypeople when requested. Temples of this category face few difficulties with support. In addition to the donations of laypeople, they receive stipends from the Japanese imperial household to protect the temples as historical monuments. Some are designated national treasures.

Many of the nunneries found all over the country are in very remote locations. Some of them have also become tourist attractions. One notable nunnery in this category is Jakkoin on the outskirts of Kyoto. The abbess, Reverend Chiko Komatsu, with whom I spoke, is very well known and has taken on some younger disciples. She has also visited India a number of times and has written books on the practical application of Buddhist doctrine in daily life. She is deeply interested in trying to present the teachings in modern language to make them more appealing to young people.

Buddhism came to Japan via Korea in the middle of the sixth century (Nara period), during the reign of the Emperor Kinmei. There are many stories about the initial establishment of the *bhikṣu* lineage, including one fascinating account translated into English by James Araki: *The Roof Tile of Tempyo*. According to this account, controversy arose early on concerning the ordination of Buddhist monks. There were those who opposed the establishment of *Vinaya* procedures for ordination, claiming that self-ordination was permissible. Another faction maintained that ordination could only be considered valid if it were conducted by an assemblage of *bhikṣus* in accordance with the standards of the *Vinaya* texts. Eventually, the Japanese emperor sent a delegation of Japanese monks to invite *Vinaya* masters from China.

Great trials and obstacles beset the mission. Members of the delegation managed to invite the great master Ganjin with an assemblage of monks, but in the attempt to return to Japan the monks were arrested, shipwrecked, and several ships were lost in storms. After they finally arrived in Japan, Ganjin, already blind by this time, directed the first authentic *bhikṣu* ordination on a large platform erected especially for the ceremony. Almost five hundred Japanese monks were ordained and the emperor himself received *bodhisattva* precepts.

During the early part of the ninth century, the master Saicho from Enryakuji on Mt. Hiei taught that receiving *bodhisattva* precepts was equivalent to receiving *bhikṣu* precepts. Due to his influence, *bodhisattva* ordination began to take precedence over *prāṭimokśa* ordination in all schools throughout Japan.

Although the origin of the order of nuns in Japan is less clear than that of the monks, there are frequent references to nuns in historical documents, especially of the Heian period. I have spoken to a Professor Yi of Donguk University in Seoul, who maintains that the first fully ordained nuns in Japan were *bhikṣuṇīs* who were ordained in Korea by Korean masters. In correspondence to me, Professor Akira Hirakawa of Waseda University confirmed that three Japanese women were ordained as *bhikṣuṇīs* in Korea in 590 A.D. Upon their return to Japan, however, they were not able to transmit the precepts to others, since the three did not constitute a requisite *Sangha* of ten *bhikṣuṇīs* required to perform ordination.

When Master Ganjin arrived with a *Bhikṣu Sangha* in Japan in 754 A.D., three Chinese *bhikṣuṇīs* also accompanied him. Again, however, three *bhikṣuṇīs* were an insufficient number to confer the ordination on Japanese nuns, and after that a complete *Sangha* of ten *bhikṣuṇīs* never reached Japan. As a result, although there have been many nuns in Japan holding *śrāmaṇerikā* and *bodhisattva* precepts, a *Bhikṣuṇī Sangha* was never established.

Nuns in Japan today receive the *bodhisattva* precepts set forth in the *Brahmajāla Sūtra*, which closely resemble the ten precepts of a novice, even though they do not receive *śrāmaṇerikā* ordination formally. In contrast to the monks, nuns live closely in accordance with the *Vinaya* rules. They do not marry or drink alcohol, though it is common practice in Japan among those loosely referred to as "monks." According to the people I spoke with, nuns maintain very good discipline; they are strictly vegetarian and live celibate lives in the monastery, rarely giving up their ordination.

In many cases these days the training for nuns is done on a personal basis, with individual masters and nun teachers within the temples. Some nuns also go to universities for higher education. I saw a number of young nuns in full robes on the streets of Kyoto, where they study at Otani University, the Buddhist University (Bukkyo Daigaku), and others. It is a good sign to see young nuns receiving higher education.

The discipline of training under a master in Japan is extremely rigorous. One does not have freedom to leave the nunnery without permission. All activity is strictly governed according to precise rules and regulations, and behavior toward the teacher is very formalized. The result is exemplary deportment.

Overall, however, it appears to me that there is still much work to be done in Japan for women in the *Dharma*. I believe that the time will come when young women will seek an alternative to the hectic materialistic style of life that is common in Japan today. I feel that slowly more and more women will take a strong interest in Buddhism and decide to enter the monastic life. Even now there is a trend of young people beginning to enter monasteries and nunneries again. Many of these have already gone the full cycle of gaining material abundance, seeing the futility of worldly life, and coming back to the *Dharma*. They have a number of advantages in that a Buddhist canon already exists in Japanese, there are still living masters, there is support for the ordained community, and there are thousands of beautiful monasteries and temples where they can study and practice. At this time, clearly, we must try to offer encouragement to all Japanese nuns and to young Japanese women who are interested in entering the monastic life.

NUNS IN KOREA

by Bhikṣuṇī Karma Lekshe Tsomo

Buddhism was originally transmitted from China to Korea during the fourth century. Monasteries and meditation halls were gradually established, first for monks and somewhat later for nuns. It is said that the style of present-day monasteries in Korea is very similar to the ancient style of such monasteries in China and that the monastic traditions of China, particularly with regard to the practice of meditation, are quite authentically preserved in Korea.

Monasteries for monks and nuns are strictly separate. Members live a communal lifestyle, with little privacy or personal property. They have their robes and almost nothing else. They even share soap and toothpaste, though not toothbrushes. Each one has a particular place to sleep each night. When the time comes everyone lies down in a large room to sleep.

Work around the monastery or nunnery is shared on a rotation basis with senior residents usually engaged in administrative responsibilities more than in menial labor. A fairly self-sufficient lifestyle has been established. As in ancient China, the large monasteries in Korea continue the practice of growing their own food. They provide most of their own vegetables, and some grains, although much grain is offered by the lay community. During the autumn, the vegetables, mostly cabbage and large radishes, are harvested, made into pickles, and stored in large jars. These pickles are eaten with rice throughout the winter. All the daily needs of the monks and nuns are taken care of by the monastery, so there is no problem of having to go out to find work or of having to earn a livelihood, though the work around the monastery keeps everyone very busy.

Each year is divided into four seasons: two three-month intensive meditation sessions in the summer and winter and two "free" seasons—the three months of spring and autumn when agricultural work is attended to. During this time the monks and nuns often go on pilgrimage as well. Traveling expenses are provided by the monasteries. It is customary for each monastery to give ordained pilgrims the funds required to reach their next destination. Visiting the many wonderful temples in Korea is encouraged. Although there are many temples in the cities, some of the most beautiful ones are secluded in the mountains and forests of the rural areas. Being quiet and peaceful, they are very conducive to *Dharma* practice.

The practice of meditation is strongly emphasized in the Korean tradition of Buddhism. There are currently 555 nuns meditating intensively in some eighteen meditation halls throughout Korea. In addition, there are forty nuns known to be engaged in three-year retreats. During the summer and winter retreat seasons, the monks and nuns remain in the meditation halls. Once the retreat has begun, one is committed to staying until the end of the three-month session. When it is nearly time for the summer or winter meditation session to begin, a nun goes to the temple of her choice and applies to join the retreat to be held there. Even though she may have originally belonged to a particular temple, she may spend the meditation season in any monastery she likes. Therefore, those monasteries that have especially good meditation teachers become very popular. This is why Song Kwang Sa, a monastery in southern Korea, became so well known: the late master Kusan Sunim was an excellent Zen (Kor: *Soen*) master. He taught widely and showed concern for Western students, establishing the first *Sangha* of Western Buddhists in Korea.

The general schedule of practice is fairly standard. In the cities, the rising time is often 4:00 AM; otherwise, the day begins at 3:00 AM in temples all over Korea. One awakens to the melodious chanting of a single monk or nun who circumambulates the temple complex reciting a *sūtra*. The sound is extremely beautiful, like something from the Pure Land. This is followed by the booming of a huge bell. At 3:30 AM the monks or nuns gather together for a short session of chanting, comprised of reciting the *Heart Sūtra* and a few other texts, and doing prostrations. Breakfast is at 6:00 AM, after which there is time for cleaning the temple. In keeping with the Zen tradition, all actions are considered *Dharma* activity.

Chanting is done at each of the shrines before lunch is served at 11:00 AM. The food in Korean monasteries is simple, consisting primarily of rice and pickles and occasionally soup. Meat, fish, eggs, onions, and garlic are strictly prohibited. Dinner is served at 5:00 PM. Between mealtimes, residents return to their particular activities, depending upon whether they are engaged in work, study, or meditation.

The style of Zen practice in Korea is unique, though it can surely be traced to ancient China. Though there are many different kinds of *koan* practice, a popular one is the questioning: "Who is it?" When asked for meditation instruction, the *bhikṣuṇī* meditation master Hye Chun Sunim calls the student's name. "Yes?" the student replies. "Who is it?" she asks. "Who is it that answers 'Yes' to the name?" This closely resembles the original Buddhist practice of investigating what, and where, is the "I."

In the face of a growing generation gap in Korea, there are attempts these days to make Buddhism more understandable to young people and to give laypeople more opportunity to study the *Dharma*. Since the younger generation is being educated in the public school system, religious education is chiefly a personal matter. Buddhist monks and nuns have set up Sunday schools for children, especially in the cities, and are beginning to work in social service areas. Through such activities, it is hoped that Buddhism will adapt to the changing social conditions of Korea today.

In recent years the numbers of young people being drawn to the monastic life seem to be increasing. There are generally around 200 nuns receiving *bhikṣuṇī* ordination each year. Standards of education of *Sangha* members have also been changing. Now, before ordination all monks and nuns must have completed high school. An increasing percentage are pursuing higher studies, both at universities and at Buddhist institutes and colleges. All monks and nuns attend Buddhist temple school for three to five years where they study chinese and learn various *sūtras*. One well-known institute for nuns is Unmun Sa, located in central Korea. The director is a nun named Myong Seong Sunim, who is highly educated and fluent in Japanese. The nuns at this institute are trained especially in the *sūtras*, using the Chinese texts, and the program of study is four years. Each class concentrates upon the study of a particular *sūtra*—perhaps the *Lotus Sūtra* for a year, then the *Diamond Sūtra* for a year, and so forth. The *Vinaya* texts are also taught.

Another educational facility for nuns is the Buddhist women's college in Seoul. Some of the courses are taught by nuns, some by monks, and others, such as Pāli and Sanskrit, by professors from the universities. Older nuns usually teach Japanese, since many of them were educated under the Japanese occupation. Many also hold doctorates from Japanese universities.

There are about 6000 *bhikṣuṇīs* and *śrāmaṇerikās* in Korea as well as a large number of others in training. Because it is considered essential to safeguard the standards of discipline within the *Sangha*, five years of rigorous training are required before permission to receive *bhikṣuṇī* vows is granted. One has to work conscientiously for the privilege of obtaining this higher ordination. A master may even refuse permission year after year until he or she feels that a disciple is fully prepared and worthy. Some nuns prefer to remain *śrāmaṇerikās* all their lives.

For some time now ordination has been nationalized, so that rather than receiving ordination on an individual basis, the disciples of various masters from all over Korea gather together in one place once each year. The site of the ceremony changes every few years. Candidates receive uniform training in discipline, deportment, and *Vinaya*, in addition to receiving the vows of higher ordination. This system has greatly improved the standards of discipline among the *Sangha* in Korea.

As elsewhere in the Buddhist world, the upholding of *Vinaya* by the ordained community is considered essential. The practice of Japanese Buddhism, however, differs somewhat from the original monastic tradition in this respect. It seems that gradually the Mahāyāna practices began to take precedence over the *Prāṭimokśa* practices. In Japan it was thought that if one held the Mahāyāna (*bodhisattva*) vows, one need not adhere so strictly to the rules of *Vinaya*. As a result, during the thirty-six years of Japanese occupation in Korea (1909-1945), those sects of Buddhism which allowed the monks to marry flourished, while the monastic school suffered a decline. Lacking political and economic support, the monks and nuns had to struggle under adverse conditions to keep their monasteries going. Nevertheless, the monastic tradition was preserved and both the *bhikṣu* and *bhikṣuṇī* lineages survived.

In the *Vinaya*, it is prescribed that a *bhikṣuṇī* must be ordained by a full complement of *bhikṣus* and a full complement of *bhikṣuṇīs*. This procedure of dual ordination is clearly outlined in the *Bhikṣuṇī Karman* (*Bhikṣuṇī Procedures*), a text which explains the methods for receiving ordination, making confession, and so forth. Due to the difficulties in assembling ten qualified fully ordained *bhikṣus* and ten qualified fully ordained *bhikṣuṇīs* under the above-mentioned circumstances, however, the tradition of giving the dual ordination was discontinued for some time in Korea.

In 1981, the Chogye order, the leading monastic order in Korea, decided to reinstate the dual ordination procedure, and the *Vinaya* master Venerable Il Ta Sunim revised the ancient text for the dual ordination ceremony, interpreting the ancient language into a modern style which was more meaningful and understandable to the monks and nuns of today. All of this was unknown to me when I arrived in Korea. I had made preparations to take *bhikṣuṇī* ordination in Taiwan, and decided to stop in Korea to visit some nunneries on the way. It just so happened that the first dual ordination ceremony to be held in Korea in about one hundred years was to be given a few days after I arrived. I traveled to Song Kwang Sa, where the master Kusan Sunim gave me my Korean name, He Gon. With his kind help, I registered for the ordination, along with a number of novice monks from that monastery who intended to become *bhikṣus*. We boarded a bus and went to a monastery in Pusan, called Beomeo Sa, where the ordination ceremony was to take place.

There were 180 monks and 120 nuns assembled at Beomeo Sa to receive the *Vinaya* training rules. Included were one English *bhikṣuṇī* and several Korean *bhikṣuṇīs* who were re-taking their vows to be ordained according to the dual ordination procedure. They wanted to receive the training rules from both *bhikṣus* and *bhikṣuṇīs*. There were also more than 400 monks and nuns receiving *śrāmaṇera* and *śrāmaṇerikā* precepts. This was the first year that novice ordinations were also nationalized. Discipline was extremely strict, and I heard that the training for novices was even more severe than that for the higher ordination candidates.

During the five-day ordination procedure, we were given instruction in all the various actions: how to walk, how to sit, how to prostrate, and so forth. Most of the other nuns, having trained for so many years knew everything perfectly already. Most difficult to learn was the system of eating. The service of each meal is extremely formal and prescribed. One must learn how to lay out the four large bowls, the chopsticks and the spoon; how to receive the food; how to wash the bowls. Each action must be well-timed and precise and must be done with mindful precision. Once the food has been served, a chant is done and the food is eaten very quickly. After eating, the napkin is folded, the bowls are arranged together and tied with a cloth just so and after another chant everyone sits until all are ready. For the duration of the ordination, no one was permitted to eat in the evening.

During the days of preparation, we also received the oral transmission and teachings on the *Bhikṣuṇī Prāṭimokśa Sūtra*, given by a well-known *bhikṣuṇī Vinaya* master. Finally, the day of the actual ordination arrived. In the morning we were called into the courtyard of the nunnery, all in strict, single-file order—for kneeling, bowing, recitation, and circumambulation. We then received the training rules from ten highly respected elder *bhikṣuṇīs*. Just as we concluded the morning ceremony and received the rules, a gentle rain fell, which was considered an auspicious omen.

After lunch, we proceeded to the main temple where the *bhikṣus* had been staying and underwent a second ordination ceremony, administered by ten renowned *bhikṣu* masters. This procedure was similar to the first, with bowing, kneeling, chanting, and receiving the rules. Just as we went outside to be photographed and to receive the certificate which verified our ordination in a valid ceremony, again a gentle rain began to fall. Once more people remarked that this was a very auspicious sign, equivalent to divine approval that the dual ordination procedure had been re-established in Korea after such a long time. I felt so fortunate to have had the experience of participating in such an ordination, and I treasure the kindness shown to me by my Korean sisters.

THERAVĀDA NUNS OF NEPAL
by Anagārikā Dhammawati

Even though Nepal is the birthplace of Lord Buddha, the history of Theravāda Buddhism in modern Nepal has not been a long one. The revival of Theravāda Buddhism began there only sixty years ago when a few Burmese monks visited Nepal from Kushinagar and some Nepalese people came forward to be ordained. About that time five Nepalese women were ordained as nuns. Thus the ordination of monks and nuns began at almost the same time. Since then, Burma, Sri Lanka, and more recently Thailand, have been helping in the training of the Nepalese *Sangha*. Since it was not possible for a woman to get an education during the Rana autocracy (1846-1950), most Nepalese nuns remained uneducated. They were also generally quite old when they took ordination. Ours is the first generation of nuns who became ordained at an early age.

Since there were no facilities for the study of Buddhism in Nepal when I became ordained, I decided to go to Burma. I was fourteen years old at the time (1948). I could not get permission from my parents, so I had to run away from home. During the Rana period, it was not possible for a woman to go abroad to study. Since I had no passport, I had to walk to Burma where I was arrested for entering the country illegally (1949). Finally I was able to get a passport and to study *Dhamma* there.

After studying in Burma for fourteen years, specializing in *Abhidhamma*, I went back to Nepal with a strong determination to work for the *Dhamma* and for the advancement of women. At first there were not many people interested in listening to the *Dhamma*, so we began by teaching young students. Gradually, the number of people who came to listen increased.

Eventually we acquired a small piece of land and were able to establish a nunnery in Kathmandu called Dharmakirti Vihar. In the twenty-three years since I returned from Burma, there has been considerable progress. At present there are fourteen nuns studying and practicing at this *vihar.* In addition to study and practice, the nuns are also engaged in teaching various other *Dhamma* activities. The *vihar* is supported by laypeople and every *uposatha* day, when Buddha Puja is held at the *vihar,* about nine hundred lay disciples, mostly women, attend the ceremony.

The *vihar* also has a youth group called Dharmakirti Buddhist Study Circle. This study circle has four main objectives: to study the *Buddhadhamma* and teach others; to go to rural areas to propagate the *Dhamma*; to invite and welcome foreign Buddhist scholars; and to publish literature on the *Dhamma*.

To make the teachings available to as many people as possible, we are publishing books and magazines in both Newari and Nepali languages. The *vihar* is also actively involved in the fields of education, social service, culture, health, and sanitation. Some of the young students we first taught have now earned university degrees and are able to work very effectively for the *Dhamma* and the welfare of their communities.

At present there are about sixty Theravāda nuns in Nepal. Most of them live alone or in small groups. About half of them are quite old; the other half are younger and working hard for the *Dhamma*. The nuns are called *anāgārikas* (homeless ones), and are respectfully addressed as *guruma*. They observe ten precepts, but instead of the precept not to handle money, they observe a precept to have loving kindness for all living beings.

There is great need for an organization which will unite and coordinate the activities of all the nuns in Nepal. Thus far, for example, there is no institutionalized system of education for them. We are eager to progress and hope that, together with the nuns of other countries and traditions, supporting one another with loving kindness, we will be able to help the *Dhamma* flourish.

NUNS OF SRI LANKA
by Mr. Abhaya Weerakoon

The order of nuns in Sri Lanka has a long history. After the Indian emperor Ashoka was converted to Buddhism, his son Mahindia and his daughter Sanghamitta entered the *Sangha* and each attained the state of arahantship. In time, the Arahant Mahinda Maha Thera led a mission to Sri Lanka where he established the *Bhikkhu Sangha* in the third century B.C. When Sri Lankan women appealed to Mahinda Maha Thera to admit them too to the order, he explained that a team of *bhikkhunīs* was required to perform such an ordination. At his request Arahant Sanghamitta Theri traveled to Sri Lanka for this purpose with a group of *bhikkhunīs*.

In anticipation of taking full ordination, the Sri Lankan queen Anula, along with 500 other women who wished to enter the order, gave up their lay lives, lay attitudes, lay endeavors, and lay appearances, and observed the ten precepts in preparation for this great step. This was similar to what Queen Mahā Pajāpatī Gotamī had done with her retinue of ladies when they sought entry to the *bhikkhunī* order from the Buddha. Subsequently, Queen Anula and the 500 women were ordained and the *bhikkhunī* lineage was established in Sri lanka.

History shows the disappearance and reintroduction of the orders of *bhikkhus* and *bhikkhunīs* in various countries from time to time. We know for instance that missions had to be sent to Thailand from Sri Lanka when the order of *bhikkhus* was extinct there. Sri Lanka also had to depend on Thailand and Burma for the reintroduction of the order several times in a similar way. Similarly, Bhikkhunī Dewasara is believed to have taken the *bhikkhunī* order to China from Sri Lanka.

In recent times the order of *bhikkhus* was reintroduced to Sri Lanka, once from Thailand by Welivita Saranankara Sangharaja Thero in 1753, and again from the city of Amarapura in Burma by Welitara Gnanawimalatissa Thero in 1803, and from the district of Ramanna in Burma by Ambagahawatte Indasabhavara Gnanasami in 1863. Immediately prior to 1753 there were persons with the outward appearance of monks who observed the ten precepts (*dasasila*). They had renounced lay life and were referred to by some as *bhikkhus* and by others as *ganninnanses*, even though the *bhikkhu* lineage was not existent at the time. These monks played a very important role and were instrumental in preserving the Buddhist tradition in Sri Lanka in the succeeding years.

In 1905, a woman named Sri Sudharmachari returned to Sri Lanka from Burma. Having renounced lay life, she observed ten precepts and was referred to as *anāgārini* (homeless one), or what is known in the present-day language of Sri Lanka as *dasasil mātā*. Thus, in common parlance the word "nun" can have two meanings. It can mean *bhikkhunī*, a fully ordained nun, the lineage of which is now extinct in Sri Lanka; it can also mean a woman who has given up worldly life and lives the life of a *bhikkhunī* but observes only ten precepts. These women are referred to as *dasasil mātās* in Sri Lanka, or *maejis* in Thailand, and are not formally recognized as part of the *Sangha*. The lifestyle of the great women Pajapati Gotami and Queen Anula with their followers, living as nuns in anticipation of *bhikkhunī* ordination, can be viewed as the inspiration for the vocation of *dasasil mātās* of the present day.

The number of *dasasil mātās* in Sri Lanka did not increase for about the first fifty years after the arrival of Sri Sudharmachari. A decision to renounce lay life and join the order of *bhikkhus* was greeted with great respect and celebration, but renunciation on the part of a woman was received with surprise and suspicion. It aroused the curiosity of many to find out what prompted such action, whether such a person needed psychiatric treatment or whether taking ordination was a convenient way to eke out an existence. This attitude was only one reason for the very slow growth of the population of nuns. Other reasons include the following:

1. There was no royal patronage for the new order as there was during the time of Arahant Sanghamitta Therī. Sri Lanka in 1905 was under British colonial rule, and official religious emphasis was Christian.

2. Sri Lankans who had risen to the higher echelons were heavily influenced by colonial ideology and did not support the country's Buddhist heritage.
3. Sri Lankan monks did not canvass for the rights of women to lead lives as nuns.
4. The knowledge of *Dhamma* among the laypeople was minimal. *Dhamma* was taught in *Dhamma* schools which were quite scarce then, and the popular way of receiving teachings was at the feet of a monk or at sermons held at a temple at night, which virtually precluded the participation of women.
5. Society dictated that women were relegated to the tasks of running a home and attending to the needs of their children, husbands, and parents-in-law. Therefore, renunciation or even listening to teachings was not possible for them until they reached old age.

With time, however, as Buddhism gained status in the eyes of society and as *Dhamma* schools increased in number, greater opportunities were provided for the young to learn the *Dhamma*, and a new era dawned. The *Dhamma* schools were in effect a passport to forbidden territory for young girls. They provided new access to religious education and wisdom. The path of renunciation came to be appreciated and the numbers of women giving up worldly life for the religious life began increasing. It seems that women tend to have certain qualities which are stronger in them than in their male counterparts, and one such asset is *saddha*, respect supported by appreciation. This abundance of devotion in women is amply displayed by their enthusiastic participation at religious functions. With the opportunities for living as *dasasil mātās* now available to women, the day is not far away when nuns will outnumber monks. This should open our eyes to the facilities currently available to nuns, as well as those still needed for helping them lead the religious life.

Religious devotion may indeed lead women to wear the robes of nuns, but thereafter they are almost stranded. Lacking an organized support system, they live as individuals in scattered locations. They have lost the world they renounced, yet there is hardly anyone to receive them in their new environment. Bereft of companionship and encouragement, there is a resulting lack of self-confidence. Many changes are needed to help give the nuns strength and confidence. Improved conditions for nuns will no doubt give rise to more congenial, supportive communities.

Throughout Sri Lanka there are *ārāmas* (hermitages), where one or two nuns stay. A nunnery of fifteen or twenty is very rare. Each *ārāma* is supported by the village, so there have been occasions of competition and rivalry between monks and nuns, which is very unfortunate. Friendliness with the *Sangha* is essential.

Efforts are currently being made to improve the difficult situation of nuns in Sri Lanka. In each of the twenty-five districts, monthly get-togethers for nuns have been organized which are designed to improve communications, leadership qualities, deportment, mutual respect, and organizational skills. This program has become very popular and successful.

The December full moon is enthusiastically celebrated each year in commemoration of the arrival of Sanghamitta Therī and the establishment of the order of *bhikkhunīs*. On this day in 1986 almost the entire body of Sri Lankan nuns gathered in the sacred city of Anuradhapura under a new flag and a slogan from the Buddha's words: "Patience is the highest form of asceticism." It is clear that patience is necessary for the tasks that nuns are now undertaking.

The Anuradhapura congregation was very successful in promoting unity among nuns. There have been several requests to make this an annual event. A number of nuns have suggested drawing up plans for the future, a code of conduct for nuns, and several other projects. There is a new awakening among *dasasil mātās*, an increasing feeling of confidence, acceptance of responsibility, a feeling of solidarity, and an expression of dedication, sacrifice, and eagerness.

The time is now ripe, therefore, for further steps which can partly be accomplished through improved education. The knowledge of *Dhamma* most nuns have was received at the *Dhamma* schools meant mainly for lay children. While monks have educational centers known as *pirivenas*, the nuns have had difficulty in getting religious education. A few *Dhamma* classes for nuns have been organized in some districts, with monks volunteering their teaching services. There is need for setting up suitable libraries and a residential training center for nuns. Another very beneficial potential project is that of setting up an international nuns' center, where nuns from various parts of the world are afforded an opportunity to study Buddhism and undergo training. There is also a great need for a hostel for nuns visiting Colombo and other cities.

To meet the financial needs of *dasasil mātās*, wherever possible I think it is a very good idea to create trusts and investments of funds in banks which would generate interest to provide their essential requirements. There are a few cases of this happening in Sri Lanka already, and I hope that this trend will continue to increase. Our country has received massive amounts of financial assistance for its development from many friendly countries both in East and West. Perhaps these countries can also help the world community of *Sangha*. Even minimal amounts of assistance would be sufficient to look after the needs of our nunneries and to make possible future international gatherings of nun. In the past in Sri Lanka, lay support for *Sangha* has been directed more towards monks than nuns, but we hope to ensure that nuns will not be an ignored sector in the future.

NUNS OF THAILAND
by Dr. Chatsumarn Kabilsingh

The kingdom of Thailand began 700 years ago with the establishment of the Sukhothai Dynasty. It is recorded that at that time lay men and women were able to practice side by side. For example, they would observe the eight precepts on *upostha* day, offering flowers and chanting together. However, there is no mention of nuns.

The *Bhikkhu Sangha* is a long-standing tradition in Thailand, and it is interesting to speculate on why women never requested ordination. By contrast, not long after Buddhism went to Sri Lanka, the women came forward themselves with great enthusiasm to seek full ordination within the Buddhist system. We must seek an explanation of why this never happened in Thailand.

In the early Ayudhya period, about 500 years ago, the Thai army attacked Cambodia and captured its capital. In the process, the Thais absorbed considerable Brahminical influence from the Cambodians. In Brahminical societies, women occupy a much lower place in the social order than men, and this attitude was transmitted to Thailand. Subsequently, Thai women did not enjoy as much social freedom or as many educational opportunities as men. This state of affairs continued for centuries and still prevails today. I believe this is the main reason why Thai women have never stepped forward to assert their rights and request *bhikkhunī* ordination.

There are records of Western Christian missionaries who visited Thailand during the Ayudhya period (thirteenth to eighteenth centuries) in which they mention local nuns called *maeji*. Most of these *maeji* today take eight precepts, though some receive ten. They wear white robes and shave their heads. Even though some may have taken ten precepts, they are not considered *samanerīs*. The history behind this is that about fifty years ago, there were some women who took *bhikkhunī* precepts, but without the participation of a *Bhikkhunī Sangha*. After this incident, a committee of elder *bhikkhus* passed a regulation stating that monks are not allowed to give either *samanerī* or *bhikkhunī* ordination. As a result of this ruling, even though a woman may receive and uphold the ten precepts, she is not called a "*samanerī*." Consequently, in Thailand we have neither *bhikkhunīs* or *samanerīs*.

There are some nuns who wear brown robes. They do not call themselves *maeji*, but rather *dhammajārinī*, "a woman who practices *Dhamma*." Their numbers are very limited—you can almost count them on your fingers.

We speak of the four groups of Buddhist followers—*bhikkhu*, *bhikkhunī*, layman, and laywoman—but the *maeji* who wear white are none of these. They are suspended somewhere in between. If you ask a monk he will tell you that these *maeji* are considered as *upāsikās*, or laywomen. Yet, they are not actually laywomen either. They are poised midway between the *Sangha* and the laity, and a double standard is applied to them. For example, *maejis* cannot vote because they are ordained, yet have to pay full fare when traveling by train because they are not considered ordained. They are also not exempt from the 1000 *baht* travel tax when leaving the country, because they are not ordained. This is the sort of double standard that exists. The *maeji* themselves respond by saying, "Oh, we are seeking *nirvāna*; we don't fight for this kind of thing." The problem is quite irritating, but there is not much interest in changing the situation either among the monks or among the *maeji* themselves.

Research on the *maeji* shows that eighty percent of them come from farming backgrounds and poor families. Second, more than eighty percent of them have only four years of compulsory education. Lacking economic means and educational background, they have low social status. We would expect the *maeji* to be spiritual role models for society, but in fact they are not heeded by society at all and enjoy no prestige whatsoever. We hope to improve their standing.

Most of the *maeji* live in the poorest part of the temples where they stay. Their activities include cooking, cleaning the temple, washing the dishes, and maintaining the temple grounds.

Others are attempting to pursue an education. A few have come to study in India, and a few have obtained Ph.D. degrees. Still, those who are educated are so few in number that they do not as yet have power to effect changes in the religious structure or to improve conditions for *maejis* in general.

An Institute of Thai *Maeji* has been established which is specifically for nuns wearing white robes. Those wearing white robes are under the close supervision of the monks, an association which obviously has some built-in limitations. The brown-robed ten-precept *dhammajārinī* are not included and do not participate in the programs of the institute.

The Department of Religious Affairs of the Thai Government has given the figure of 20,000 *maejis* in Thailand. This figure is disputed by the secretary of the Institute of Thai *Maeji*, who says that only 4,000 have registered with the institute. She speculates that the figure could not be more than 10,000 for the whole of Thailand.

Economic considerations also affect the ordination of the *maeji*. Since they are poor, they cannot afford to invite many monks or nuns to participate in the ordination, but instead usually receive the eight precepts from just one monk. Those who plan to stay in a temple specifically for nuns often receive the precepts from the *maeji* who heads the temple. Whenever a nun wishes to give back her vows, she can go to the preceptor to return them and resume wearing lay clothes.

What are the main objections to establishing a *bhikkhunī* order in Thailand? Why is it that Thai society does not accept *bhikkhunīs*? First, many object that the lineage never existed in Thailand. This is not a logical objection; we never had discotheques before in Thailand either, yet we have welcomed them with open arms. I believe that the *Bhikkhunī Sangha* is something that would be beneficial to society and that there are good reasons for its establishment.

Second, objectors point out that the *bhikkhunīs* in China are Mahāyāna, whereas the Thais are Theravāda, and, like oil and water, the two never mix. To this I respond that the *bhikkhunīs* of China originally received their vows from Sri Lankan nuns, who are our Theravādin sisters, so like milk and water, they *can* mix.

One important factor here is that many people do not understand the differences between Mahāyāna and Theravāda, which lie in their philosophical interpretation of the *Dhamma* teachings. This is where the distinction exists. In terms of *Vinaya*, of ordination lineage, however, they are the same. My studies on *Vinaya* have revealed that there were eighteen schools during King Aśoka's time; the Theravāda branch was subdivided into twelve schools, and the Mahāsānghika branch was subdivided into six. The *Paṭimokkha* vows which the Chinese *bhikkhunīs* follow are those of the Dharmagupta school, which is a sub-sect of Theravāda. So, in fact, the Chinese nuns are following Theravādin *Paṭimokkha* vows. When speaking of ordination lineage, we cannot speak of Theravāda and Mahāyāna. There may be different interpretations of the *Dhamma* between Theravāda and Mahāyāna, but in terms of *Vinaya*, there is no such split. Thus it is illogical to base one's conclusions about the validity of the *bhikkhunī* lineage on such prejudices. As I am still a laywoman, I feel free to speak frankly about these matters.

There are also some misunderstandings regarding the history of the *bhikkhunī* lineage. For example, people often say that the Buddha never wanted a *Bhikkhunī Sangha*, but that women kept pestering him, so he had to allow the *bhikkhunī* ordination. It is true that the Buddha hesitated when his aunt asked for ordination. He hesitated, mind you, three times. And three times Ananda repeated the request.

The Buddha also hesitated in another instance. When he became enlightened, he hesitated to preach. Even though he hesitated to preach, we never question that the *Dhamma* he preached was faulty. Just as we cannot use the fact that the Buddha hesitated to preach as a reason to invalidate the teachings, we cannot use the fact that he hesitated to admit women into the order as a reason to reject the *Bhikkhunī Sangha*. This would be illogical. In my opinion, the Buddha naturally had to admit women into the order, since he accepted that women are as capable as men of spiritual salvation.

A double standard is being applied to justify the exclusion of women from the order. We should reflect carefully on the objections that have been raised at different times in different countries, so that we will be able to refute them with logical reasoning.

People always find objections to raise with regard to *bhikkhunīs*. For example, when a woman requests full ordination, she is required to accept the eight *gurudharmas* from the outset. The very first one of the eight, which people find so objectionable, is that a *bhikkhunī* ordained even for one hundred years must bow down to a *bhikkhu* ordained even for one day. My mother happens to be the only Thai *bhikkhunī*, having been ordained in Taiwan in 1970. On one occasion when she traveled to a rural area and was introduced to the monks as a *bhikkhunī*, the first thing they asked was why she did not bow to them!

To have a sensible view of such issues, one needs to study the texts. We must not take things superficially. We must delve into the social context, read the stories that tell what occasioned the creation of the vows, and understand why each rule was laid down. I believe that we need a new interpretation of some points, especially those regarding the interaction between monks and nuns. We must realize that there are various ways of explaining things. We should not think that the Buddha was so narrow minded! I think that if he were alive today, he would change many of the rules, and my guess is that monks probably would have to observe many more rules in relation to nuns.

In the *Bhikkhu Paṭimokkha* there are many rules for monks regarding *bhikkhunīs*. I always challenge the monks on this and say that they are not observing the 227 rules, because there are no *bhikkhunīs*. To observe the 227 rules they must have a *Bhikkhunī Sangha*!

NUNS OF TIBET

by Śrāmaṇerikā Lobsang Dechen

Buddhism reached Tibet in the seventh century, during the reign of King Songtsen Gampo. The first monasteries for monks were founded in the eighth century, under the rule of King Trisong Deutsen. The nunneries were founded later, beginning in the eleventh century. The first nunnery is said to have been established in a place called Phenpo, to the north of Lhasa, the capital of Tibet.

Among the celebrated female practitioners of Tibet there were a large number of nuns. The isolated settings of the nunneries provided conducive circumstances for religious practice, and the earnestness of the nuns in their spiritual endeavors was greatly appreciated by the lay community. Among the most revered and respected nuns in recent times were Samding Dorje Pagmo, Abbess of the State Nunnery of Tibet located seventy miles from Lhasa, and Jetsun Lochen Rinpoche of Shugsep, who was considered exceptionally realized and lived to be more than 115 years old.

In 1959, when the communists took over the country, there were 618 nunneries with 12,398 nuns. Forty-four of these nunneries were large, housing more than one hundred nuns each. Under the communist regime, Buddhism suffered many setbacks and most monastic institutions were totally destroyed. During the 1960s not a single robed figure could be seen anywhere in Tibet. Under the new Chinese policy of "relaxation," although members of the *Sangha* have reappeared and joined the few monasteries remaining, there are still severe restrictions on teaching and propagating the *Dharma*. Among the twenty-four monastic institutions now being reconstructed, only two are nunneries: Gari Gonpa and Tsang Khung, both in Lhasa. Even these are being promoted chiefly for propaganda purposes and are not functioning independently as nunneries did in the past.

Fortunately, before the communist incursion the Tibetan tradition had spread widely in neighboring Asian countries. More recently, it has taken root in many Western countries as well. There are still too few organized nunneries, however, among the exile communities in India and Nepal. The majority of nuns live widely dispersed in villages and remote areas. For this reason, it is difficult to give an exact account of nuns in the Tibetan tradition. Nevertheless, I have attempted to gather information to serve as a basis and reference for understanding the current conditions of these nuns.

In India, there are approximately 839 nuns following the Tibetan tradition. There are about 250 in Ladakh, 100 in Zanskar, 103 in Lahaul and Spiti, and 106 in Kinnaur. There are 138 in the Dharamsala area, including Tilokpur, 62 in Rewalsar and Pangang in the Kula area, 35 in Darjeeling, and 45 in Mundgod. Many other young women wish to become nuns and to join nunneries, but they are unable to do so because the limited accommodations of the existing nunneries are already filled.

The neighboring country of Nepal is the home of about five hundred nuns practicing in the Tibetan tradition. Thirteen nunneries have been established there, but again due to a shortage of living space many nuns live on their own.

Bhutan is a purely Buddhist country. There are about six hundred nuns living in Bhutan. Of these, only one hundred live in nunneries; the remainder live on their own. Those who are from wealthy families are supported by their parents. The others go from place to place to beg for grains during the harvest season, then resume their practices the rest of the year.

The same is the case with nuns who live in other Himalayan regions—if they have no means of support they are compelled to go from place to place for their basic necessities. Some also stay with their families during the cultivation and harvest seasons to help with work in the fields.

Currently there is only one nunnery of the Tibetan tradition established in a Western country: the Dorje Pamo Nunnery in France with five nuns. There are another 240 Western nuns in this tradition who either live in monastic communities of both monks and nuns, in *Dharma* centers, or on their own. Many move between India and Nepal with no permanent base, while others live in North America, Europe, and Australia. These nuns earnestly hope that plans to build more nunneries can soon be realized.

Traditionally, Tibetan monks have had ample opportunity for education, but opportunities for nuns to receive religious education have remained very limited. The principal emphasis in the nuns' training is the memorization of prayers. Each day a nun memorizes a certain number of lines and recites them before the elder nun who serves as her teacher. To retain previously memorized material, they recite the full text from memory in the evening.

The majority of the nuns know how to read the scriptures, but are unable to write. This indicates that the main concentration of their *Dharma* practice is chanting and meditation. Recently, however, changes of great significance have taken place. Nuns at Geden Choeling Nunnery in Dharamsala have begun to take classes in basic logic and philosophy, and to debate them as well. This is the first time in history that Tibetan nuns have undertaken such training in the traditional monastic curriculum on a formal basis. The nuns are also learning Tibetan literature, grammar, and calligraphy. Likewise, in Nepal, classes in logic, Tibetan grammar, and English are being held both at Keydong Thukche Choeling and at the new nunnery being established at Kopan Monastery. The other nunneries are gradually instituting similar educational programs.

The biggest challenge that faces nuns today is the lack of adequate facilities. There are many nuns from Himalayan border areas and many arriving fresh from Tibet who, after long difficult journeys from these regions, cannot find a place to live in the existing nunneries. Unfortunately, this severe housing shortage discourages young Tibetan women from taking ordination who would otherwise be interested. In nunneries, the main source of income is performing ritual ceremonies requested by the lay community to help accumulate merit and remove obstacles for the sponsor. This subsistence income is inadequate to fund plans to develop the nunneries.

The community of nuns within the Tibetan tradition has a long history and has produced numerous virtuous and realized practitioners. Now, as opportunities for women are increasing, we wish to improve and expand the circumstances of ordained women in the Tibetan order. Even for those fortunate enough to have a place in a nunnery, instruction is still insufficient. Current emphasis must be on expanding educational programs. It is essential that the fundamentals of religious education be taught to all nuns and that general subjects such as languages, history, and mathematics, be introduced as well. Retreat facilities also need to be constructed for those particularly interested in intensive meditation practice.

In 1984, four Tibetan nuns received full ordination as *bhikṣuṇīs* in Hong Kong. We hope that this year again more nuns can receive this higher ordination, and that in time a strong *Bhikṣuṇī Sangha* will evolve. By raising the level of education, by providing better facilities, and by slowly establishing the *bhikṣuṇī* lineage, we will strengthen the order of nuns in the Tibetan tradition so that the female *Sangha* can better serve the general community and the Buddhist faith.

NUNS OF VIETNAM
by Bhikṣuṇī Dr. Karuna Dharma

In Vietnam, Buddhism is practiced in a non-sectarian way. The people feel comfortable practicing the Theravāda and Mahāyāna traditions together. I believe that this openness is one of the strengths of Vietnamese Buddhism. Most of the Buddhism practiced in Vietnam today is Mahāyāna, but Theravāda practice also continues. The Theravāda *bhikkhus* and the Mahāyāna *bhikkhus* and *bhikkhunīs* still assemble and perform ceremonies together from time to time. Even people who belong to one particular temple feel very happy visiting and supporting other temples, whether they are Vietnamese or not. They feel that any temple that practices *Buddhadharma* should be revered and supported. This non-sectarian viewpoint is truly praiseworthy.

Historically speaking, Vietnam has been under the domination of China and European powers, particularly France, for long periods. During periods of foreign rule, it has been difficult for the Buddhists to practice their religion. Until Vietnam overcame French imperialism in the fifties, opportunities for higher education for either men or women were very limited. As in many Asian countries, monks tended to take ordination at a young age, twelve or thirteen, or even younger. Much of their education, therefore, was carried out in the temples where fine schools developed. It was not until the late 1950s that some of the *bhikkhus* were sent abroad to study at well-known universities. By that time, the college system in Vietnam could grant the equivalent of a bachelor's degree, but further higher education was not available. Thus it was that two groups of Buddhist monks, who showed outstanding promise in their academic ability as well as in their knowledge and practice of *Buddhadharma*, were sent abroad.

One of these groups went to Japan where they studied at the very best universities. The Empress herself was the one who granted scholarships to some of the monks and became their personal sponsor. My own teacher was with this group and received the first doctoral degree to be granted in Japan in twenty years. This created a bit of a stir, since he was a foreigner and his field of study was Yogāchāra philosophy, a Mahāyāna system analyzing mind and reality. At this same time, the second group went to India to study. (The governing body of the *Sangha* in Vietnam chose the two countries that they felt had the finest universities for Buddhist studies.)

When the *bhikkhus* returned to Vietnam after completing their degrees, they established a Buddhist university in the city of Saigon. It was named Van Hanh University after a very profound Vietnamese Zen master of the eleventh century. The courses offered were not only in Buddhist and Oriental Studies, but also included liberal arts. At the time of the fall of Vietnam, there were 20,000 students enrolled and although it had been operative for only about fifteen years, it had considerably improved the prospects of education for both men and women. Nuns as well as monks were able to receive a very fine university education there and were encouraged to do so. Both ordained and lay people could get excellent university degrees at the Buddhist university, as well as at the University of Saigon, University of Hui, or the other public universities. Even today, educational opportunities are said to be equal for men and women, and many of Vietnam's lawyers and doctors are women.

The *bhikkhunī* tradition in Vietnam goes back in an unbroken line to the time of the Buddha. Their practice is primarily Mahāyāna. There are many currents and traditions in Vietnam, all of which were transmitted at different periods in history. Buddhism arrived early from India, around the third century A.D., and its first Zen introduction also came from India, in the sixth century. Later on, around 700 A.D., Zen was also transmitted from China. It developed simultaneously with the Pure Land form of Buddhism, which emphasizes Amitabha Buddha. These two traditions actually merged into a syncretic whole in Vietnam, combining the meditative tradition of Zen with the devotional practices of the Pure Land tradition. My original training was in Zen, but when the Vietnamese refugees came to Los Angeles in 1975, it became necessary for me to be trained in Pure Land as well, in order to benefit the laypeople. In general, the laypeople feel more comfortable with the devotional practices of Pure Land than with formal meditation practice.

The Vietnamese people are very religious and are similar to the Tibetans in that Buddhism is deeply integrated into their lives. Therefore, after Vietnam came under socialistic rule, the government embarked upon the systematic eradication of the Buddhist hierarchy and clergy. One of the first things the government did was to try to return as many monks and nuns as possible to lay life. Sometimes this was accomplished by force, but more often by removing the economic support of the laity. Financial constraints compelled many of the monks and nuns, particularly the younger ones, to leave the *Sangha*. Quite a few of the young monks were inducted into the military, and young nuns were required to return to their homes and villages.

Before the fall of Vietnam, there was a vast number of monks and nuns. The percentage of nuns was higher than that of monks, since all young men were pressed into military service. These nuns had great influence in Vietnam. Although they tended to be less visible than monks and to have lesser positions, some of them were highly respected as meditators and teachers. There are many accounts of their great spiritual achievements. These days the active monks and nuns are primarily those older ones whom the government failed to force into other lifestyles.

Buddhism is so integrally linked with the cultural identity of the Vietnamese people and their sense of national pride that the present government has worked very systematically at destroying all Buddhist influence. When elder monks speak out against repression and injustices of the current regime, they are dealt with as harshly as under the old colonial regime. When the *bhikkhus* and *bhikkhunīs* spoke out during the period of American involvement, they were denounced as communists. Today, the very same *bhikkhus* and *bhikkhunīs* are being held as C.I.A. informants or operatives. Such charges are simply being used as a pretext for preventing laypeople from associating with and supporting them. As a result, the lives of the monks and nuns have become very difficult. They are commonly sent to the villages, where they live under a form of house arrest. While the government tries to avoid blatantly harmful measures toward the *Sangha*, they make it a policy to withhold medical attention and proper nutrition when they are ill.

Despite these repressive measures, Buddhism has not been eliminated in Vietnam. Although many of the temples and pagodas have been taken over by the government (which appropriates them on the pretext of turning them into medical centers and then uses them for other purposes), there are still a few temples that are actively functioning.

Approximately eighty percent of the population of Vietnam is Buddhist. This proportion is not accurately reflected among the Vietnamese emigrants, because the first immigration had large numbers of Christians. In spite of this, large numbers of Buddhists have managed to go abroad. I worked in the camps when the Vietnamese refugees first began coming to the United States. About three months before the fall of Vietnam, the Supreme Patriarch cabled my master and asked him to take young monks for proper training. Unfortunately, the red tape was so complicated that these young monks were not able to leave before the government collapsed. After that, the Supreme Patriarch requested that monks and nuns not leave Vietnam, because they would be needed by the people. Consequently, there is a lack of properly trained *bhikkhus* and *bhikkhunīs* in the refugee communities in various countries today.

Some monks and nuns who were in imminent danger of being placed under house arrest were practically forced into fishing boats by their disciples and managed to escape to Southeast Asian countries such as Thailand and Malaysia, and then emigrated to France, Germany, and the United States. Many of them had actually kept their suitcases packed and ready, waiting for the moment of their arrest. It was very touching when we first received communications from some of the Vietnamese monks whom I had met earlier, and learned that they had arrived safely in the United States. I wept when I read their letters, realizing the tremendous suffering they had undergone.

Today, in the exile communities the majority of the *Sangha* members are *bhikkhus*, the reverse of what the situation had been in Vietnam. A Vietnamese Buddhist monastery has been established in California under the direction of an excellent young *bhikkhu* in his mid-forties who is training both men and women. Due to limited resources, it will be some time before we have the separate facilities for monks and nuns required by tradition. While a few other monasteries are being developed in the United States for the religious training of young Vietnamese, at present most of this training is being carried out in temples in the various overseas Vietnamese communities.

It is difficult to determine exactly how many Vietnamese *bhikkhus* and *bhikkhunīs* there are now in the United States and other countries abroad. In the main temple in Los Angeles, which was the first of the Vietnamese temples to be established in the States, there are currently ten young monks residing with their master. At the nearby A-Di-Da Temple, there are three or four nuns. Vietnamese temples around the United States have multiplied tremendously; there must be about one hundred temples at this time.

The greatest difficulty we face is that there are still not enough *bhikkhus* and *bhikkhunīs* to take care of the spiritual needs of the people. It is a problem similar to the one the Tibetans face. At times we have been so busy with the problem of the survival of the community that the elder monks have not had enough time to transmit properly all the traditional practices to the young monks and nuns. Monks and nuns alike are encouraged to receive a good education and obtain at least a bachelor's degree, in addition to their Buddhist education. This Buddhist education goes on all the time at the temples. Two or three classes on various aspects of *Buddhadharma* are given throughout the year.

Through working in the Vietnamese community, I have come to understand some of the very real problems faced by these temples. There is a tremendous generation gap between the older generation who will always be Vietnamese and the younger children who are not truly Vietnamese. There is a whole generation of children growing up who do not speak Vietnamese, yet some of the temples are still conducting all their classes in Vietnamese. The temples do not seem to be adapting quickly enough to the Western lifestyle, and there is a danger of the young people becoming completely integrated into mainstream Western society and christian culture. These problems are extremely difficult for the monks and nuns.

As I see it, one of the main obstacles for the Vietnamese *bhikkhunīs* is that Vietnamese Buddhism is quite paternalistic—the result of old Chinese customs. There is considerable Confucian influence in the Vietnamese Buddhist tradition, not in the doctrine, but in the structure. There is a rather rigid hierarchy, on the paternalistic model, which places women at the bottom. In terms of the roles they play in the community, in theory *bhikkhus* and *bhikkhunīs* are equal, but in actual practice such is not always the case. I speak quite frankly to the abbots about the adaptations that need to be made in this regard, about eliminating these Confucian elements and upholding Buddhist egalitarianism. As long as the Vietnamese remain in the West, I feel that inevitably there will be changes in the structure of the Vietnamese Buddhism.

A second obstacle is that the Vietnamese *bhikkhunīs* themselves tend to be too shy and retiring. They need to learn to put themselves forward more. A very interesting process of change is occurring as a result of the meeting of cultures, but the Vietnamese nuns are still not as confident and outspoken as their American counterparts. As the *bhikkhunīs* become better educated and accustomed to American society, however, it is my hope that they will play a greater role in this cultural dialogue.

5 *Education for Buddhist Women*

In the Buddha's time, women were able to listen to discourses directly and to request instruction from whatever qualified teachers they chanced to meet. Nuns were expected to invite a learned *bhikṣu* to give instruction at their nunneries twice a month and to continue their studies of the teachings independently in the interim. Whether or not their opportunities to listen to discourses were completely equal to those of men is something we cannot know, but it is certain that many learned nuns of that day are cited in the chronicles.

In Buddhist countries in general, a man interested in spiritual training enters a monastery and has immediate access to in-depth literary, liturgical, and contemplative training. This training, often gained at a young age, in turn qualifies him to serve as an instructor to future generations. In many countries, the Buddhist education that evolved for women was somehow less formal and systematic than that available to men. Obviously, where a lack of opportunities for higher academic training existed for women, fewer qualified teachers emerged. In the absence of highly qualified women teachers, women had less access to religious education, a cycle which was self-perpetuating. Once education systems begin to devolve, the downhill trend perpetuates and the loss is difficult to recover even within generations. Conversely, once an organized educational system gets set in motion which regularly produces qualified teachers capable of continuing the momentum, the system will regenerate automatically. Given concerted efforts, great strides forward can be accomplished. Where educational systems for women have degenerated, female students will naturally have to rely on male teachers until they themselves gain expertise.

Universal education is a relatively recent development. In the past, girls were usually educated in the home in those areas which were felt to be of practical concern for them, namely, cooking, sewing, childrearing, and related domestic arts, as well as agriculture, foraging, and skills related to livelihood. By and large, training in letters had not been seen as particularly necessary for women until modern times. For the most part, religious lore has been transmitted orally in the home and in the local religious setting.

Where formal religious education has been primarily the prerogative of men, fewer women have gained thorough comprehension of the teachings and been able to fulfill their spiritual potential to the fullest extent to serve as guides for others. The only possible opportunity for women to gain spiritual training has been on a one-to-one basis in private tutorials. Particularly where the teacher is a monk and the student is a woman, the situation is circumscribed and awkward, in that the parties are subject to societal strictures and gossip. Hence, in some traditional Buddhist societies, opportunities for women to gain in-depth instruction and spiritual guidance are decidedly limited. Consequently, women *Dharma* teachers are not being produced in large numbers. In these societies, the situation of religious learning for women has reached a low ebb and stagnated. Something dramatic is required to call attention to the situation and set improvements in motion.

In many Buddhist countries, a girl with strong spiritual aspirations will decide to enter a nunnery at quite a young age. Being strongly attracted to the spiritual life, she may consciously reject secular education, even where it is available, in favor of a religious discipline. In such a discipline, memorization may be emphasized, obviating the necessity for literary training. A lack of writing systems in the Buddha's time did not prevent people from attaining *arhatship* and high states of realization, so we can see that it is not necessary to be literate to become enlightened. The existence of illiterate monks, nuns, and lay practitioners need not be viewed as shameful; nevertheless, in a world of widespread literacy, the prestige of such practitioners is low and their usefulness in spreading the teachings is minimal.

On the other hand, for centuries Buddhist institutions have played a major role in education, which explains the high degree of literacy in countries such as Thailand. In many Buddhist countries, written literature has principally been religious in character and the chief vehicles of literary transmission and oral commentary have been the monks. There are cultural factors that may explain why the education of nuns has not kept pace; investigation of these factors will help us determine how to best restore the balance.

Nuns deprived of basic literary skills will out of necessity opt for contemplative and devotional practices rather than scholarly pursuits. As long as nuns lack the tools, facilities, and the incentive for intellectual development, however, there is no justification for asserting that nuns lack the interest or ability to develop themselves academically. On the contrary, throughout Buddhist history, particularly in China, we find examples of highly learned nuns. Nuns in Taiwan today, filling the Buddhist colleges to capacity, may be seen as the trendsetters. The strictest of the colleges there have the longest waiting lists, having to turn away three applicants out of four. The prognosis for unprecedented developments in women's Buddhist education are excellent, with nuns taking a position of leadership among women. The magic ingredients in this somewhat spectacular development have been adequate facilities, inspirational role models, and encouragement from teachers. Similar opportunities for women's Buddhist education and similar results are found among the nuns of Korea today.

A strikingly different picture presents itself in Thailand and

Sri Lanka, where opportunities for religious education for women are barely existent. As with Tibetan nuns, organized systems of religious instruction are painfully lacking. What learning occurs is largely a private, individual responsibility handicapped by a dearth of facilities and qualified female instructors. Unless structured systems of religious education are implemented soon, Buddhist women in these countries will remain disadvantaged for several generations hence. Though they may well progress spiritually despite learning handicaps, they will not be able to take their rightful places in the religious hierarchy as teachers, administrators, role models, and perpetuators of the *Dharma*. Lacking a solid educational foundation themselves, they will have no footing from which to make a lasting contribution in the spread of Buddhist culture just at the very time when women's participation could have such a far-reaching and profound impact.

The situation of these disadvantaged nuns is quite distressing. Many are quite content to chant prayers without really understanding their meaning. They may never have received any hint that they are capable of scholarship or meditation. There are often cultural and social innuendos, implanted in young minds, that women are mentally inferior or are temperamentally unsuited for higher studies. Preconceptions have grown up that women are less qualified for spiritual mastery and should rest content with basic devotional exercises. Many women in traditional cultural cultures are convinced that they do not have what it takes to develop themselves intellectually and that their greatest hope lies in supporting monks and making prayers to become a male in the next life. Even where secular education is accessible for women, nuns are somehow getting left behind. Some nuns in these countries now realize that they could improve their minds if they had a chance, but the conditions for such improvement elude their grasp. The public tends to make offerings more generously to the monks than to the nuns who, being economically handicapped, spend much of their time fending for food or saying prayers to generate donations. Both their mental and spiritual advancement are therefore severely restricted by mundane realities, though they generally accept their lot uncomplainingly despite hardships and rejoice in their freedom to practice the *Dharma*.

Some nuns, however, are acutely aware of their limitations and bristle under them. These nuns have keen intelligence, intense dedication, and a strong desire to see improvement made. There are also highly qualified women eager to take ordination who are waiting until the time that suitable facilities become available. These, I submit, are the nuns who will engineer the future of women in Buddhism. They love to say prayers, but they feel that they have a right and a duty to know what these prayers mean. They are not ambitious to become scholars and teachers, but they feel an obligation and sincere inclination to study the Buddha's teachings as thoroughly as possible. They are not envisioning themselves as great *yoginīs*, but they know that intensive meditation practice is vital for transforming the mind. After having devoted their lives to the *Dharma*, sacrificing worldly pursuits and material comforts, they become utterly disillusioned when they find the doors to religious advancement closed to them. These women are not blind to the fact that men enjoy all the advantages for educational and spiritual development. They are not jealous or resentful in the face of such inequities, yet they would like to go forward. Many realize that these advantages will not be theirs without great struggle, but they do not even know where to begin to set things right. Still they sense that they could do better and must do better if they really are to be able to serve the *Dharma*. They realize that education is the key to their improvement. They are struggling to find their voices, to find sympathetic support, and are responding to any encouraging word with great enthusiasm. To ignore the needs of these committed nuns would be a pitiful waste of human potential, for each one could become a spiritual leader among women.

At the conference, three well-defined topics were presented each day for discussion by participants. Each day thirty to fifty Tibetan nuns met to discuss the topics in their own language, and each time they discussed nothing but the need for education. When it came time to name the new international association of Buddhist women, they wanted a name that included the word "education"!

It is clear that even without a *bhikṣuṇī* order, there is a need for improvements in the field of education for Buddhist women. As desirable as it may be to have as teachers women who are fully ordained, it is important that women in whatever aspect begin to serve as *Dharma* instructors and role models for other Buddhist women. We cannot wait until the *Bhikṣuṇī Sangha* is instituted in every country before we start to improve facilities for women's learning and practice. A campaign to fashion a *bhikṣuṇī* order among nuns who lack even a rudimentary knowledge of the *Dharma* may be a bit premature. At the same time, it must be recognized that where full ordination exists for women, and thereby equal status, roughly equal educational possibilities also exist. Where full ordination does not exist and nuns are of secondary or inferior status, educational opportunities are fewer and of inferior quality. The relationship between equal status and equal opportunity does not seem to be entirely coincidental.

As women gain an equal footing in various spheres of secular life, many women with excellent spiritual potential will be dissuaded from religious life if blatant inequalities exist. After enjoying equal rights in worldly life, what intelligent young woman would knowingly trade them for a life of subordination in spiritual pursuits? Buddhist institutions must keep pace with social changes or risk appearing antiquated and unfair.

Without improvements in religious education, few intelligent and educated women will be attracted to the spiritual life. Once better opportunities for Buddhist studies are available, more qualified young women will be drawn to the *Dharma* and to the monastic life. The general quality of nuns will therefore improve in relation to the educational opportunities afforded them.

Ultimately, of course, Buddhist education is far more than curriculum and institutions. It is training in the development of enlightened awareness. It is becoming accomplished in the practical application of Buddhist principles and in the awakening of unimpeded wisdom. Nevertheless, the enlightening process presupposes knowledge of these basic principles and methods set forth by the Buddha for gaining enlightened awareness. Not everyone may be capable and willing to take on the hardships of intensive study, but all should have the right of access to the Buddha's teachings if they wish. Buddhist nuns and laywomen should at least have the option to study the teachings in depth, but at the moment their opportunities are very limited in certain countries.

Educationally disadvantaged nuns are meeting many obstacles, both psychological and material, but their aim to study the Buddhist teachings, like any just and worthy goal, cannot be thwarted or postponed much longer. They are receiving strong encouragement from their spiritual masters and are ready to throw off centuries of mental bondage, cultural preconceptions, as well as both real and imagined constraints, in the quest for an understanding of the *Buddhadharma*. All possible cooperation should be extended to support them in this quest.

TRAINING AT GAMPO ABBEY

by Bhikṣuṇī Pema Chodron

The ideas to be presented here are primarily the results of my experiences while working to establish a monastic center in Canada, which is for monks as well as for nuns. Since this work is still in process, my ideas on the training of seekers of the way are also in the process of evolving.

Our basic assumption or view of this educational training program is that all beings naturally have tremendous insight, precise minds, gentle hearts, and open attitudes that can be cultivated and awakened. The basic purpose of education is to further awaken and ripen our inherent qualities. Such potentiality may be given different names, but we aspire to recognize the Buddha nature which is intrinsic in all beings.

Our fundamental concept is to establish a training program in the hope that a person wishing to become ordained as a novice would first undergo at least one, two, or three years of preparatory training. The length of training necessary would depend on the extent of the person's familiarity with Buddhist studies and meditation. By the time that a candidate has received such preparatory training, their ordination as a novice would have more significance and putting on robes would represent something substantial. After novice ordination, there would be a minimum of two years of training required before receiving full ordination as a *bhikṣu* or *bhikṣuṇī*, so this would also represent a significant step. The education process would also continue after that.

At present this educational process is a pilot program which is constantly evolving. None of us has been through it before—we are all going through it together. Therefore, the program that is evolving at Gampo Abbey is very lively and energetic. It has three major parts, which we sometimes refer to as the three wheels of *Dharma*, consisting of study, meditation, and work.

The study curriculum that has been established is a three-year program, which just began in 1987. The first year concentrates on history, *Vinaya*, and *Abhidharma*. The notion is to first give an overview of the subject, and then go into the subject in greater depth. The basic underlying view of our approach is attempting to realize the true meaning or essence of the teachings. This is the aim of our studies, rather than simply acquiring facts and figures. Tremendous emphasis is placed on discussion, on probing, and questioning. We all write papers, take examinations, and are expected to give talks.

For example, in the study of *Vinaya*, we follow a method of teaching and learning that goes through text rule by rule. How intensively one goes into the subject, of course, depends on each person's level of ordination. Our approach includes familiarization with each rule, analyzing and questioning it, coming to an understanding of it, and then considering its relevance for us now, and how we can live by it. As our study has evolved, we have come to question what the Buddha really meant at the time he established each *Vinaya* rule and to try to assess what the motivation was behind each one.

As a result of this method, our *Vinaya* study is extremely lively and healthy. Consequently, the people at Gampo Abbey have an enormous interest in the *Vinaya*; it is not a dry, boring, academic affair, but something that is very interesting for us. Since the *Vinaya* is our code of conduct, it is intensely relevant to us, and we are beginning to get a sense of what was actually intended by each of the rules. Even the ones that do not seem applicable to us at the present time, such as the rule not to carry black wool on one's head, give us insight into the intent behind formulating rules.

It is important to emphasize that in our concept of study and the ongoing curriculum, we also have teacher training. We put a lot of stress on requesting each person to teach the *Dharma*. We have found that this practical experience fosters a person's appreciation of and identification with the teachings and helps to ripen their understanding. for instance, suppose you have heard the teaching on the four Noble Truths so many times that you nod off in class. You think you know it thoroughly because you have heard it so often. Then someone says that they would like you to give a talk on the Four Noble Truths three days from now. Suddenly, you realize that you do not understand the teaching at all: you do not want to just stand up before people and be like a parrot, just saying dry dusty words; you want to speak from your own experience. Suddenly, it is like starting fresh again. This sort of practice teaching experience is therefore a very important part of our study program.

Thus, one can say that while we have a high regard for intellectual development, we also have a high regard for experience. There is an attempt to find the meeting point between the two. This summarizes the study part of our educational program.

The second part of the program, the second wheel of *Dharma*, is meditation. Most students come to the Abbey from different spiritual traditions. Thus, rather than presenting a rigid course of meditation that everyone has to follow, we are trying to provide an environment that gives people space to practice the meditation teachings that they have already been given. We do give instruction in basic *samatha-vipassanā* meditation, but so far we have been encouraging people to continue individual meditation practices they have already been trained in.

Those who are fully ordained, as well as novices and candidates for ordination, are required to do at least one month a year of individual retreat in one of our retreat cabins. We also have one month each year when everybody sits together, doing basic sitting meditation. Sometimes this takes the form of a Japanese-style *sesshin*, sometimes it takes the form of a *vipassanā* retreat, and sometimes it takes the form of what we call a *dathun*. *Dathun*, a tradition established by Trungpa Rinpoche, is essentially a month of basic sitting meditation practice, during which a student engages in at least ten hours of meditation per day.

In addition to sitting meditation, contemplation on the teachings is also highly valued. Such reflection is an integral part of the education process and is greatly encouraged. We provide a quiet section in the library and periods of silence which are conducive to contemplation. Already the environment at the Abbey is very conducive to meditation, contemplation, and study, and in the future we hope to improve conditions even further so that each ordained *Sangha* member will have their own room and so forth.

In keeping with the meditative atmosphere, we also encourage those who are so inclined to take time for walking in the woods, sitting on the cliffs, looking at the sea, and appreciating the natural surroundings. If one has just been in the middle of an intensive study session or intensive meditation retreat, these activities actually have a profound effect.

Once people are ordained, we expect them to participate in a program of training in meditation instruction. They undergo a prescribed course of study and practice which includes a large number of mock interviews for practice in giving meditation instruction. It is quite a disciplined course of training. Eventually we encourage them to actually give meditation instruction to students that are ready for it. In this way they develop their abilities both in meditation instruction and counseling. Development of such skills, of course, depends on individual aptitude, but everyone is encouraged to go through the training.

The third part of the program, after study and meditation, is work. Our attitudes toward work at Gampo Abbey are strongly influenced by the Zen tradition, that is to say, we regard work as practice. We have found that there is a tendency either to feel that work is standing in the way of one's practice or to become totally caught up in one's work. We are trying to find a middle way. We are working very hard, encouraging each person to take part in all the work that needs to be done in the community, while at the same time implementing the concept that work is a mode of practice. The results have been very encouraging and inspiring.

The essential aim of this educational process of study, meditation, and work, however, is to utilize it to bring out the inherent qualities, even brilliance, of each person. The ultimate intention of all these activities—the study, the meditation, the work—is to tame the mind. We have found that it is very important however difficult, to encourage each person—through the teachings of the Buddha, through meditation practice, and through personal insight—to evolve toward certain realizations. We need to cross beyond certain stages where the training program begins to squeeze the individual and bring out specific egocentric habit patterns. Such patterns become accentuated to some extent during intensive training because the ego is somehow starved. There is a natural tendency to feel ruffled and disturbed as if the sharp points of our personality were continually being worn down. It is understandable for the ego to react defensively during this smoothing process.

We feel that an important aspect of the educational program is beginning to understand in our own hearts and minds that we no longer need to cling to our own points of view or to imprison ourselves by having to have everything on our own terms. It is a matter of realizing that we are going through a process; beginning to delight in being awakened is a crucial part of the training program.

When resentment or any kind of fixation or solidification of viewpoint arises, the individual becomes the first one to realize it, rather than blaming others and holding on to resentment or harshness of any kind. Instead, there is a sense of softness and flexibility that begins to occur. We emphasize these qualities in our training. We find humor to be extremely important and continually emphasize the development of loving kindness—gentleness for oneself and sympathy for others. We need to have time for developing these qualities, and to realize that each person's evolution is unique. We need to have something in the monastic schedule that allows for individuals to ripen according to their own style, in tune with their own inclinations and way of understanding *Dharma*.

The monthly schedule that we have developed at the Abbey may be of interest. This schedule is followed except during *yarne* (rainy season retreat), extensive practice sessions, or study sessions. One week each month is devoted to intensive practice and study. Two weeks each month are termed "contemplative weeks'' in which we rise together as usual in the morning for chanting, meditation, and a formal breakfast in the shrine room. For the rest of the day, from about 7:30 a.m. until about 3:00 p.m. when the work period starts, we are free to explore our spiritual growth in the way we see best. For example, some people feel that they never have enough time for studying, others feel a need for more practice or more contemplation, and so forth. This schedule allows time for each person to pursue their particular interest. To assure that this program benefits all of us, we meet on Saturdays during these weeks to discuss our mutual journey. This arrangement has proven extremely helpful. We also meet on the *sojong* (confession) days when we review our vows.

The fourth week of the month (though these are not always consecutive) is devoted to work. During this week the morning and evening services are the same, and there are three hours of meditation practice daily, but the rest of the day is devoted to work. We noticed that people were feeling short of time to paint a room, to do correspondence, to do the bookkeeping, or whatever. So we started allowing time for catching up on work.

The main point is to never lose sight of why one is doing these activities. It is very easy somehow to become businesslike or to get caught up in normal *samsāric* views. Therefore, it is essential to continue re-evaluating what we are doing, to continually discuss the goal of our meditation and study. The idea is never to lose sight of the basic purpose of *Dharma* practice, which is to remove all obstacles to seeing clearly the true nature of reality.

A BHIKṢUṆĪ'S OBSERVATIONS ABOUT THE TIMES
by Bhikṣuṇī Shig Hiu Wan

Prajñā (exalted wisdom) is the eye of the *Buddhadharma*, as well as the path of behavior of *bodhisattvas* and great beings. When practiced by *bodhisattvas*, this *prajñā* leads to the state of ultimate reality (*bhūtatathata*), a state which is without characteristics, and is, therefore, devoid of male/female discrimination. All living beings are essentially equal and independent. Men and women, monks and nuns, are alike in that they equally possess Buddha nature. When just beginning to practice the *Buddhadharma*, beings depend on phenomena as they develop toward becoming *bodhisattvas*, but the *Mahāprajñāpāramītā Sūtra* teaches practitioners to "consider form as being empty," and then to go deeper into the essential meaning of the *Dharma*. Therefore, there is no point in attaching ultimate significance to male/female distinctions.

On the relative level, we *bhikṣuṇīs* owe a great deal to the Buddha's aunt Mahāprajāpatī, the *bhikṣuṇī* who repeatedly requested permission to lead the homeless life and to become a member of the *Sangha*. We should also feel grateful to the honorable Ānanda who, on her behalf, reported Mahāprajāpatī's earnest wish to the World-honored One. To repay the kindness of his aunt for having raised him, the Buddha finally consented to her becoming a *bhikṣuṇī*, on the condition that she observe the eight commands (*gurudharmas*) of paying reverence to monks, and so forth. In addition to these eight commands, *bhikṣuṇīs* keep more precepts than *bhikṣus* do. Once a woman firmly sets her mind on becoming a member of the *Sangha*, she is required to abide by the *bhikṣuṇī* discipline. At the same time, a monk who is qualified to receive respect from nuns, in accordance with the eight commands, should also keep the *Bhikṣu Vinaya* rules required of him.

The first *bhikṣuṇī* Mahāprajāpatī once said, "I have heard that a woman who zealously practices the *Buddhadharma* is sure to attain the four paths of a *śramaṇa* (recluse): (1) the path of increasing endeavor, (2) the uninterrupted path, (3) the path of liberation, and (4) the path of surpassing progress.'' Due to their strong faith and yearning for pure, disciplined conduct and their longing for the splendid, liberating *Buddhadharma*, Prajāpatī (the Buddha's stepmother and aunt) and Yaśodharā (the Buddha's former wife) were able to receive ordination as *bhikṣuṇīs*.

Later there were many Buddhist scriptures taught for Buddhist nuns and laywomen. The Buddha taught the *Sūtra of Sixteen Contemplations* (*Sadasavipasyana Sūtra*) for Lady Vaidehi and the *One Vehicle Lion's Roar Sūtra* for Lady Malyasri. Two other teachings were *Sūtra of the Virtuous Maiden's Questions* and the *Sūtra of the Maid in the Moon* (*Candrottara Darika Vykarana Sūtra*). All of these are teachings of the Mahāyāna Buddhist doctrine. In the *Mahāprajāpatī Sūtra*, there are numerous precepts for nuns to abide by, and there are even many discussions concerning women we may find unthinkable and inauspicious. For example, there is mention of a woman's body as being filthy, ominous, and an unsuitable vessel for the *Dharma*. We must understand, however, that such unfair viewpoints concerning women came about as a result of the very discriminatory caste system in India of that day. Now, with modern civilization, such views have changed a great deal.

In the spread of the *Buddhadharma*, it is the provisional and expedient methods that change, not the *Buddhadharma* itself. The Buddhist teachings remain essentially the same throughout the ages. Yet, to spread the teachings in a particular age, changes of methodology are made in a contemporary light. That is to say, the *Buddhadharma* should be spread in a way that complies with current trends of thought.

In China, Buddhism has always been considered a religion full of boundless compassion and merciful resolve. Therefore, different teachings and various means of practice have been taught to different kinds of practitioners according to their receptivity and capabilities. Thus, Buddhism in China is quite different from that of India. When Buddhism was transmitted to China during the Han dynasty, there were already historical records of Chinese women becoming nuns. There were various *Dharma* methods for women to practice through which they could attain Buddhahood. Some practiced meditation, others mastered the doctrine, some recited *mantras* or chanted the holy names of the Buddhas. In the book *Wu.teng.heui.yuan*, there is a story concerning a woman named Chit-t'ong who, through the study and practice of *Buddhadharma*, became enlightened and subsequently pronounced this verse,

> There being no difference between the self and material things,
> Kaleidoscopic phenomena are all reflected in the same mirror.
> So transparent is the mind, that it has transcended master and mastered;
> Enlightened is the mind that has penetrated true emptiness.

This verse reflects her enlightened insight. Later on, her practice of Ch'an meditation became legendary. She entered into *nirvāna* while seated cross-legged in meditation. Her book, *Analects of the Enlightened Mind*, has been circulating ever since.

Emperor Ming of the Han Dynasty authorized the ordination of a woman from Loyang called Ah-p'an, this being the first historical record of a Buddhist nun in China. In the Eastern Chin dynasty, another nun, Bhiksuni Tao-hsing of Tong Temple in Loyang, became famous for her understanding of the *Lotus Sūtra*, the *Vimalakirti Sūtra*, and many other profound Buddhist scriptures. She was the first nun to expound *sūtras* and to propagate the *Buddhadharma* in the history of Buddhism in China. In the Western Chin dynasty, Bhikṣuṇī Chien-ching established the Chu-lin Temple to the west of Loyang and served as its abbess. She was the first nun to be in charge of a Buddhist temple in China.

Because Chinese nuns were able to zealously practice and cultivate the *Buddhadharma*, expound *sūtras* and propagate the *Dharma*, and to take charge of temples, they were also revered as great masters and ranking clergy, as related in *The Brief Bi-*

ography of the Sangha. The appellation "Orthodox *Bhikṣuṇī Sangha*," given to the Chinese nuns, did not appear until the Southern Sung dynasty. Emperor Wan bestowed the title "Orthodox *Bhikṣuṇī Sangha*" on the nun Pao-hsien, as mentioned in Chapter 27 of the *Book on Buddhism*.

From the above examples, we see that nuns who master the scriptures, practice Ch'an meditation, and keep the precepts well, occupy a position equal to that of monks both in Buddhist circles as well as in ordinary society. Nowadays, the number of nuns in Taiwan is far greater than that of monks. Though monks are still in charge of certain large temples, nuns often serve as their assistants, sparing no effort to foster Buddhist activities. More and more nuns now maintain large temples themselves. Furthermore, the educational level of the *bhikṣuṇīs* in Taiwan is steadily improving, and the number of nuns who receive college educations is increasing year by year. Some nuns have obtained Ph.D. degrees abroad in Japan and the United States, returning to Taiwan afterwards to lecture in colleges and universities.

It is necessary and urgent for *bhikṣuṇīs* to receive both Buddhist and practical education. Those nuns who have received higher education need to receive further education to enrich their understanding of *Buddhadharma*. Those nuns who were ordained at an early age and have already pursued Buddhist studies and practiced *Buddhadharma* diligently also need further education to enrich their practical worldly knowledge. In recent years, many such nuns have gone on to graduate from colleges and universities. Thus, in Taiwan, there is a prevailing trend for nuns to pursue both the profound Buddhist studies and practical worldly knowledge.

The modern world is a world rich in all kinds of useful, advanced knowledge, and the present trend is the effect of this explosion of knowledge. I believe that the good effects of this trend outweigh the bad ones. A nun should focus on the study of *Buddhadharma* and not get carried away with the trifling details of worldly knowledge. In general, Chinese nuns are deeply convinced that they should prepare themselves with the practice of the *Dharma* as well as with worldly erudition in order to expound and promote the Buddhist teachings in the modern world. With this intention, they continue learning and practicing. They also clearly realize that they must take a share of responsibility equal to monks in fostering the *Buddhadharma*. Thus, they work as hard as monks in the development of Buddhism.

Due to their heartfelt respect for the *Buddhadharma*, more and more Western women have also become Buddhist nuns. In recent years, there have been a dozen Western nuns from England, France, the United States, and West Germany, who have studied and practiced at my Lotus Buddhist Ashram. According to my observation, it seems far more difficult for Western nuns to learn Buddhist teachings and to practice meditation than it is for Asian nuns. Owing to different living habits, Western Buddhist nuns need special training and considerable psychological adjustment to adapt themselves to life in an Asian monastic environment. To do so, it is valuable for them to learn all the necessary formalities of a Buddhist nun's way of life. Therefore, it is my opinion that to avoid giving up their vows or living an unhappy and uneasy life, Western women who wish to become Buddhist nuns should first learn to understand Asian thought and customs, which are completely different from their own. A year or two of training at a Buddhist school or temple in Asia will facilitate their adjustment to the Buddhist monastic lifestyle.

Worldwide, female adherents of Buddhism outnumber male, and since women suffer more trials and tribulations than men, it is appropriate that nuns become trained to help guide those Buddhist women who are in difficulty. In this way, nuns can play a very significant role, both in Buddhist communities and in secular society.

As a Chinese *bhikṣuṇī*, I sincerely hope that all Buddhist nuns and laywomen constantly enrich themselves inwardly to the best of their abilities. With refinement, virtue, and unflinching courage, Buddhist women, both ordained and lay alike, should contribute to society by exemplifying purity and goodness. I hope the Buddhists of Southeast Asia, who esteem Buddhism as we Chinese do, can improve the status of their practicing nuns and help them to obtain full ordination. In this current age, we should restore the *bhikṣuṇī* ordination which was initiated and instituted by Śakyamuni Buddha. By doing so, we will strengthen the Buddhist *Sangha*. It is my fervent wish that all *bhikṣuṇīs* of all countries become deeply aware and industriously cultivate themselves by practicing the *Dharma*. We *bhikṣuṇīs* should cultivate humility and kindness, practice meditation and morality in combination, nurture noble and worthy attitudes, and most importantly, observe the eight commands of reverence. These are the disciplines bequeathed us by the Buddha, the World-honored One.

Simultaneously, we should strive to serve our communities and the general public in the field of Buddhist education, Buddhist culture, charity work, medical treatment and so forth. Already there are some hospitals run by *bhikṣuṇīs* in Taiwan. These hospitals serve the needy, the poor and the sick. We *bhikṣuṇīs* do not always have to depend on donations from philanthropists to do charity work, but should actively devote ourselves to whatever activities significantly benefit humanity.

6 *Nuns in the Community*

In earlier times, the spiritual practices of the ordained community, such as their upholding of the *Vinaya* and their serving as an example of renunciation, were considered their chief contributions to society. For example, if a Tibetan nun today is asked what she and her ordained sisters are doing to benefit society, she is likely to answer, "Praying for the welfare of all beings." A Theravādin nun is likely to cite striving for liberation as her major contribution. While no one can deny that these are noble goals, in today's troubled world the welfare of society seems to depend on much more than prayer and meditation alone. There is clearly scope for greater social involvement on the part of Buddhist monks and nuns.

The recent participation of some Theravādin monks in social service activities has been controversial and has even been frowned upon by the more conservative members of their society. Monks in some countries are expected to remain aloof from involvements with laypeople and social problems. In Thailand during the 1970s, for example, there was a great outcry when some monks began working among the Cambodian refugees in camps along the border. There is, however, a growing number of people who criticize practitioners who attend solely to their own spiritual practice while neglecting the needs of others around them. Many feel that Buddhist monks and nuns should devote more time and energy to serving the needs of humanity directly. At the same time as the incident related above, the efforts of some monks in Bangkok to set up drug rehabilitation programs began to elicit popular appreciation and support. Clearly, ideas concerning the role of *Sangha* members in society can change with time and in accordance with social conditions.

His Holiness the Dalai Lama often exhorts his followers to look to the example of Christian monks and nuns, and to begin taking a more active part in social service work. He has said that the age of *Sangha* members merely sitting and praying all day is past. The sufferings of humanity are too acute to be ignored. Monks and nuns, free of family responsibilities and having virtually no private life to attend to, have more time and energy to devote to others and are thus ideally suited to social service. Their training in awareness and compassion should make them responsive to the miseries of others and equip them to serve as attentive nurses, skillful counselors, and caring teachers. Buddhists helping society in tangible ways will also benefit it intangibly, by demonstrating the Buddhist teachings of compassion and loving kindness.

In places such as Taiwan and certain Western countries, where *Sangha* members are well educated and trained in various fields, programs to serve the wider community have already begun. Ordained *Sangha* in these countries are working constructively in the fields of health, education, geriatric care, counseling, and other social services. Their efforts have proven highly successful and are greatly applauded by the secular community. Participation in community welfare programs sends a very positive message to society, translating into reality the Buddhist ideal of benefiting others. Buddhist social welfare programs also generate much interest in the *Dharma*. Plans are being laid to expand Buddhist social services wherever possible.

In countries where nuns are not trained and are living in very poor circumstances themselves, it is unrealistic to expect them to provide social service to the community. They must first be provided with decent living conditions and educational opportunities before they can effectively assume their roles in these fields. As Mr. Abhaya Weerakoon expressed during the conference:

> We often hear people asking why the nuns do not go out to do hospital work, social work, and provide services for the laypeople and the very unfortunate ones. I think people who ask these questions do not fully understand or appreciate the difficult conditions under which the nuns themselves are living. I do not think the nuns can be expected to provide these services for others until they are equipped to look after themselves and to do their own essential work. First they need to receive proper education and training, and develop to a level at which they are able to look after the spiritual needs of the people who support them. Only then can they begin thinking of other services. These other services are definitely important, but we should be patient and see that nuns are properly qualified to provide these services in order to inspire the respect and appreciation of the people.

Providing support and education for nuns to take up social action programs is a wise investment of energy and resources which will pay great dividends to the society at large.

The development of one's own mind and service to the human community are very compatible and closely linked. Benefiting others is itself a form of *Dharma* practice. *Sangha* members who apply their professional skills to help others may inspire others to do likewise. At the same time, social service may be a solution to the problem of livelihood for monastic communities, because it will directly or indirectly generate financial support from the laity.

There are many possibilities for Buddhist monastics who wish to embody compassionate activity such as fostering peace projects, working with battered women and substance abusers, teaching in the prisons, consoling the ill and dying, and providing retreats for parents and working people. They may engage in conservation work, in developing crafts projects for the handicapped, or in blending Buddhist psychological methods with Western psychotherapy.

Since the needs of living beings are endless, there is barely any limit to the ways in which these needs may be served. The key is in balancing one's time carefully to maintain the formal practice necessary for developing spiritually to be of greater service. As one's own mental defilements are purified and egotism loosens its grip, one becomes freer to attend to the miseries of humanity and other suffering creatures.

Now, with improved world communications, areas of great poverty and urgent need are more visible and more accessible. Consequently, opportunities for selfless service are greater than ever before. Nuns training in mindfulness and loving kindness are in an ideal position to devote themselves wholeheartedly to relieving suffering in a very immediate and meaningful way. In the field of social service activities, a new chapter in Buddhist history is just beginning.

BUDDHIST SOCIAL SERVICE IN AUSTRALIA
by Śrāmaṇerikā Thubten Lhundrup

Although I have only been ordained as a nun for a short while, I have lived and worked among monks and nuns for some time, even while serving in the Air Force. I will also be returning to work in such an environment. I am speaking from my own experience, all of which has come about while living in a Western country.

Everyone seems to agree that living in a monastic community or nunnery has numerous benefits. The support of Dharma friends, the material support, the activities of the laypeople, and the laying of a foundation or spiritual background to learn from are all incredible advantages. It is not always possible to be in a nunnery, however, or even to start out in a nunnery, particularly in the West. Sometimes this is because there is no nunnery, and sometimes it is because the nunnery is not self-supporting and we do not have the money to be able to stay there. Sometimes we find ourselves taking a position in society because we are asked to by our teacher, either to teach or for some other reason.

For whatever reasons, we in the West often find ourselves living in society and not necessarily in a Dharma Center. Sometimes we are fortunate enough to stay in the supportive environment of such a center, but not always. Western nuns can relate to the situations and difficulties that all *Sangha* face, such as problems encountered while wearing robes, problems of supporting oneself, of facing hostility from the community, facing loneliness and other trying circumstances.

When His holiness the Dalai Lama was giving us teachings on the *Sun Rays of Thought Transformation*, he referred to transforming adverse circumstances into the path. This type of text gives me great strength to face such circumstances. It teaches how activities actually become our *Dharma* practice. We need to remember that the reason we are practicing the *Buddhadharma* is to relieve the suffering of ourselves and other sentient beings. Living in society we certainly have many opportunities for doing this. The same applies to practitioners of other religions as well.

Buddhist nuns can learn a lot from Christian nuns, particularly in the field of medical care, health education, and general education. We can do practical things; we are not just meditators. Some Buddhist practitioners think that they can do nothing but meditate, that the only valid way of practice is to pray and to meditate. Certainly these are very valuable things, but there are also other things that we can do.

Many problems we face in the West are different from those faced in the East. Our main problems in the West are loneliness, unhappy feelings, and particularly fears. If we can help relive some of these sufferings, either by counseling or by other work, than it would be very valuable.

The center I work with in Australia is not outwardly a *Dharma* center, but it is quite unique. It was founded by an Australian monk named Thubten Pende (Ken Hawter) who was asked to begin a center by Ven. Thubten Zopa Rinpoche. Being a practicing physiotherapist, Thubten Pende established a clinic called Karuna Center in Brisbane. Since then (two years ago), the services of the clinic have expanded and I have been employed there as a massage therapist and receptionist. Other services offered by the clinic include acupuncture, podiatry, and relaxation classes. We also have a part-time counselor.

One of our special areas of interest at the clinic is working with the dying, as well as with cancer patients. In the process of our work, we have found that a lot of the patients coming in for treatment of physical conditions also had emotional problems, many of which were related to unresolved grief. As a result, we have taken a great deal of interest in this area.

We are also engaged in teaching to various groups in the community. For example, we teach to a group called TALAG which is The Association for Loss and Grief. We also teach at a Cancer Foundation, to nurses, and to young mothers who have difficulty coping with their babies. Normally, these are relaxation classes, which are free or run on a donation basis for those who cannot afford to go to other relaxation centers.

Another aspect of our work at the clinic is visiting lonely or sick people. We visit nursing homes and also private homes. We provide volunteer services at places such as the St. Vincent de Paul Hostel for men, which serves as a home for the destitute. Many of the people are alcoholics or drug addicts. There are surely many, many other possible areas of community service, but these are just a few examples of the areas in which Karuna Center is involved.

One area that we are particularly interested in is hospice work. I am not sure whether hospices exist in Asian countries, but basically a hospice is a place where you go when it seems likely that you are about to die. The majority of patients in hospices are cancer or leukemia patients. Apart from actual illnesses they also have other problems. In the West, death is a cause of great fear, something very negative, which we do not like to talk or even think about. When a death occurs in a family, it can be absolutely devastating for those who are not prepared or willing to accept what has happened. This does not seem to be as great a problem in the East, where death seems to be more accepted.

Members from Karuna Center visit a hospice in Brisbane called Mt. Olivet Hospice once a week. Basically, we just visit patients; it is nothing exotic, nothing you have to be highly trained for. It is just visiting and sitting with people. Sometimes people want to talk about their situation and sometimes they do not. Sometimes they just want to sit and have their hand held, to be read to, or to be taken for a walk in a wheelchair. Sometimes just that is enough. They may not feel comfortable talking about their situation, but if they do, then they do have the opportunity.

Staff members at the hospice are aware that people from Karuna Centre are Buddhist, although we do not wear robes to visit. This is partly because the robes may set up a sort of barrier in a hospice-type environment. I have noticed that even the Catholic priests and nuns who visit the hospice occasionally encounter hostility from the patients because of their religion, perhaps because the dying patient feels anger towards

"God." Death is such an emotional time that sometimes people do not want to be reminded of religion. We rarely talk about religion when we visit, unless the patient brings up the subject. We just try to remain open, caring, and compassionate.

Thubten Pende teaches relaxation at the hospice, while I must visit the patients and do general volunteer work. Teaching relaxation to the patients can be very useful, especially as the time of death comes closer. In the classes, the patients who cannot walk are brought to the room in a wheelchair. If someone is too sick even for this, then we go and visit their bedside, talking and taking them through the relaxation process, even as the time of death approaches. This can be incredibly beneficial for the person.

These are all examples of the sorts of community services that are possible for Buddhists, but I am sure that there are many other things that could be done. We just need to think of more. I remember when I first started looking for things I could do, for avenues where I could help people. The more you look, the more you find. People's needs just seem to keep expanding. The more volunteers you find, the more you need. I am sure that there are many more areas that we could be serving; we just have to start somewhere. The laypeople contribute enormously to the volunteer numbers, but most of them have families to care for and so their time is usually limited. The reason for being a nun is to devote one's whole life to the *Dharma*, hence nuns actually have much more time to dedicate themselves totally to others.

One does not have to practice in a way that is obvious *Dharma* practice, such as giving teachings or leading meditations. Helping others may not be such an overt form of practice, but it can be tremendously beneficial, nevertheless. Sometimes while doing volunteer work, one may become a bit tired or disillusioned, but if one is practicing purely and has pure motivation, with a positive approach, then that will definitely affect people in a very positive way.

CHINESE NUNS IN SOCIAL WORK

by Bhikṣuṇī Shih Yung Kai

At the turn of the century, women in the West slowly awakened to the fact that there was more to life than being subordinate to their male counterparts. They wanted to be liberated and to be equal to their male partners in terms of their moral, social, and domestic status. They were seeking something that had already been attained by the Buddhist women in India over 2,500 years ago.

Women during the Buddha's time were living in a much more unfortunate situation than the women of the twentieth century. They were regarded as very lowly and mere child-bearers. They had little authority at home and did not play any part in public activities at all. A large number of these women followed the courageous example of Mahāprajāpatī and embraced the homeless life advocated by the Buddha. They decided to break out of their accustomed roles and to achieve freedom not only from the moral, social, and domestic restraints, but also in the realm of spiritual endeavor.

These liberated women played a very important part in their communities. They served as examples to women who remained in the household life, as reminders that they too could become liberated and lead an independent life. They were sources of light and hope for bereaved mothers and childless widows. They gave a sense of purpose to the wives of kings and rich men who led empty and idle lives of luxury. They helped relieve poor men's wives from problems and drudgery. They saved young girls from the humiliation of being handed over to the suitor who bid the highest. They liberated thoughtful women from the ban imposed upon their intellectual development by convention and tradition. If we read through the Buddhist texts, we find many examples of *bhikṣuṇīs* of great ability and spiritual accomplishment.

As a Buddhist nun ordained within the Chinese tradition, I would like to give an account of my experience of living at Fo Kuang Shan and the work that the nuns of this monastery are doing for the community.

With a population of more than three hundred monks and nuns, Fo Kuang Shan is the largest monastery in Taiwan today. It is the only forest monastery in Taiwan that welcomes people from all traditions and walks of life to study, teach, and serve the *Dharma*. Of the more than thee hundred residents, over seventy-five percent are nuns. Therefore, most of the responsibility is taken by nuns.

Fo Kuang Shan was established in 1967 by Venerable Hsing Yun who came to Taiwan from mainland China in 1949. He became a novice when he was twelve years old. When he first set foot on the soil of Taiwan, he was only twenty-three. As a refugee escaping from the communists, he was homeless and penniless, without anyone or any place to turn to. Inspired by Venerable Tai Hsu, a famous Chinese Buddhist monk at the beginning of the century, through faith and dedicated work, Master Hsing Yun managed to succeed in his new environment. He has been very active in the revival and reformation of Chinese Buddhism in Taiwan. He promotes "humanistic Buddhism," that is, integrating Buddhism into daily life.

The operation of Fo Kuang Shan is centered around four main objectives. These are: (1) spreading *Dharma* through cultural activities, (2) training *Dharma* teachers through education; (3) benefiting society through social and medical programs, and (4) purifying people's minds through pilgrimage.

The popularization of *Dharma* is essential for the survival of Buddhism. Buddhism spread to many different countries and has continued for centuries because people made efforts to teach it. There are many different ways in which one can spread the *Dharma*, but the most important and far-reaching method is by means of cultural activities. The cultural activities of Fo Kuang Shan include publishing books on Buddhism and circulating cassette tapes of *Dharma* talks and Buddhist chanting.

We publish a bi-weekly newsletter, "Awaken the World," which has a circulation of over 25,000 copies, as well as a monthly magazine, "Universal Door," which has a circulation of over 13,000 copies. Both of these publications have worldwide distribution. Venerable Yi Kung, a graduate of Tokyo University with a master's degree in Indian Philosophy is the director of these publications. Previously she was the principal of our private high school and currently she is the abbess of a Buddhist nunnery. She also teaches in universities and is the Dean of Academic Affairs of our Buddhist college. The editors of our newsletter and Buddhist magazine are also nuns.

About ten years ago, we set up a special editorial committee. We are planning to re-edit the entire Chinese Tripitaka by adding new punctuation and footnotes, since the existing Chinese Tripitaka was written in classical Chinese with no punctuation at all. These additions to the earlier edition will facilitate easier understanding of the Tripitaka. So far we have completed the four *āgamas* (collections of scripture). We are also compiling a Chinese Buddhist dictionary in twelve volumes, which will be completed very soon. The director of the editorial committee is Venerable Tzu Yee, a graduate of the Buddhist University in Japan with a master's degree in Buddhist history. Presently she is the abbess of Fo Shan Ssu, one of our branch temples, and is also the president of Fo Shan Buddhist College.

The second objective of Fo Kuang Shan is to train teachers of the *Dharma* through education. The educational activities of Fo Kuang Shan are many, the first aspect being Buddhist education. We have established five Buddhist educational institutions in Taiwan. Both members of the *Sangha* and lay Buddhists come from all over the world to study at these institutes. Their school fees, food, and lodging are provided free of charge by Fo Kuang Shan. The directors of three of these Buddhist colleges are nuns.

The second aspect is the education of disciples. We organize a variety of seminars geared toward people of different interests and aptitudes, such as lay devotees, administrators and *Sangha* members.

The third aspect is education for college and university students. We organize summer and winter camps and lectures on Buddhist topics and have recently set up a center to make Buddhism more accessible to these students.

The fourth aspect is social education. We send people to prisons and factories to teach, and organize large public *Dharma* talks every year in large cities in Taiwan and abroad. Three to four thousand people usually turn out for these talks. We have also produced special TV and radio programs on Buddhism. Recently, we have started to give evening classes on Buddhism to city dwellers.

The fifth aspect is spiritual training. We organize short-term retreats for members of the *Sangha* and for laypeople. During these retreats, which usually last for seven days, the participants lead a strict religious life. We conduct ceremonies for taking refuge and observing precepts. Such a ceremony for *bhikṣus* and *bhikṣuṇīs* generally lasts for thirty-two days, while the ceremony for lay and *bodhisattva* precepts lasts from five to seven days. The ceremony for the eight precepts lasts for one day and one night. Various *Dharma* functions, chanting, and ceremonies are held either regularly, on special occasions, or during festivities.

The sixth aspect is children's education. We organize summer camps, Sunday schools, and vocational classes especially for children, as well as operating nursery schools and kindergartens.

The seventh aspect is secular education. We established a private high school ten years ago, which currently has about a thousand students. Two of the previous principals were nuns. In fact, most of the activities mentioned above are organized by our nuns, who not only do the administrative work but are also involved in the actual teaching.

The third objective of Fo Kuang Shan is to benefit society through social and medical programs. We have set up a home for the elderly, retirement homes, an orphanage, and a public cemetery. The home for the elderly is run by two nuns who have completely devoted their lives to the old and sick. The director of the orphanage is Venerable Tzu Jung, who has a

B.A. in social work. At the moment, she is also the abbess of Pu Men Temple, our branch in Taipei, and has been appointed by the government as a probation officer for delinquent children. In 1985, she was given the National Humanitarian Award for her contribution to social work.

We also have a clinic which gives free medical care and medication (both Western and Chinese) to the general public. Several mobile medical units are affiliated with this clinic, and go to remote areas and villages where medical help is not readily accessible. During the winter and at times of natural disaster, we set up emergency relief programs to help the poor and needy.

The fourth objective of Fo Kuang Shan is to purify people's minds through pilgrimage. All branches of the monastery organize pilgrimages to bring devotees from various parts of Taiwan and overseas to visit Fo Kuang Shan. To date, we have almost twenty branches around Taiwan and overseas, and almost all of them are run by nuns. We have seven shrines of different sizes at Fo Kuang Shan, as well as a Pure Land cave, a Buddhist cultural museum, a devotees' education center, a pilgrims' hall, and many other facilities. These facilities provide for the needs of pilgrims and other visitors who thereby have a chance to come into contact with Buddhism and learn something about it. Often a visit to Fo Kuang Shan helps people clear up misconceptions they may have about Buddhism and helps them change their outlook on life and religion.

The whole monastery and all of its activities are flourishing under the wise leadership of Venerable Hsing Yun. Without him, none of this would have been possible. He is assisted and supported by many people, both *Sangha* and lay members. Among the *Sangha* are many nuns, and besides the examples of illustrious contemporary nuns such as Venerables Tzu Chang, Tzu Hui, Chung Yen, and Hiu Wan, there are many touching and inspiring stories about other nuns in the Chinese tradition. Such examples give assurance that nuns have very strong potential for contributing to society and are very capable to help make this a much better world for our fellow beings. May we all join hands and work together for the sake of Buddhism and for the happiness of all!

8 *Living by the Vinaya in the Present Day*

The issue of moral responsibility may not ring many bells or draw large crowds in this age of tremendous social fluidity and libertine behavior, but it deserves a few moments of reflection in view of the pervasive discontent and dis-ease of contemporary society. What is rampant consumerism if not desire? What is conspicuous consumption if not pride? What is communal tension if not anger? We need to be honest about these emotions and the actions they engender if we are to get at the root of personal and social problems and attempt to remedy them.

The Buddhist teachings explain that human happiness derives from well-intentioned, thoughtful, wholesome behavior, whereas problems naturally arise from ill-intentioned, thoughtless, unwholesome behavior. In the Buddhist view, *karma*, meaning "action," denotes a process of ceaseless, universal interaction. Living beings create actions, some better, some worse, and experience the results of their actions, until they sooner or later gain liberation from the cycle of existence. The process of cause and effect is totally impersonal in the sense that there is no creator god figure who controls, rewards, or punishes. At the same time, it is intensely personal in the sense that individuals are totally responsible for their own choices, attitudes, and conduct from moment to moment. The three trainings in morality, concentration, and wisdom are the key to making us more aware of the quality of our choices.

Basic morality for Buddhists consists of refraining from the ten non-virtuous actions: killing, taking what is not given, sexual misconduct, untruthfulness, harsh speech, divisive speech, idle gossip, malice, covetousness, and wrong views. Beyond this, there is the positive moral conduct entailed in formally receiving and maintaining precepts as a lifelong commitment. There are five precepts that are to be observed by Buddhist laypeople,[1] ten precepts to be observed by ordained novices, and hundreds of precepts to be observed by fully ordained nuns and monks.

The *Vinaya*, the section of the Buddhist canon which deals with monastic discipline, is called "the life-blood of the teachings." The *Vinaya* texts are specifically concerned with the outward behavior of those who enter monastic life, enumerating and explaining the precepts or training rules which regulate the conduct of the *Sangha*, the fully ordained nuns and monks.[2] The other two sections of the canon, the *Sūtra* section and the *Abhidharma* section, deal with *Dharma*, denoting here the universally applicable teachings on mental cultivation.

Regulating outward behavior in accordance with *Vinaya* discipline is considered essential for fostering inner development. At the same time, outward behavior is said to naturally reflect the extent of a person's inner cultivation. Thus, inner discipline and outer discipline go hand in hand. If it were possible to achieve enlightenment by indulging in whatever actions we like, we would all be enlightened already and the Buddha need not have bothered to teach.

The *Prāṭimokśa*, perhaps the oldest of all Buddhist texts, enumerates the precepts to be observed by the nuns and monks, and is recited in assembly twice each month. There is a *Bhikṣuṇī Prāṭimokśa Sūtra* for fully ordained nuns and a *Bhikṣu Prāṭimokśa Sūtra* for monks. These *sūtras* open with verses proclaiming the preciousness of moral discipline and proceed to enumerate the *Prāṭimokśa* precepts, arranged into categories according to their gravity. A transgression of any of the precepts of the first category (*pārājikas*, or "downfalls") entails immediate expulsion from the order; transgression of a precept of a lesser category can be confessed and purified by various procedures.

Elsewhere in the *Vinaya*, stories are related to describe the circumstances under which each precept is said to have been formulated, with the Buddha himself cast as the principal adjudicator. There is an explanation of the terms used and of the extenuating circumstances under which a prohibited action is allowable. For example, a nun or monk is not normally allowed to request certain special foods, such as milk or cheese, but is permitted to do so when ill. By investigating the precedents, the test cases that led up to the original formulation of each precept, we get an idea of the intent behind each one, as well as useful insight into the social values of the Buddha's time. By studying the allowances made for extenuating circumstances, we gain an understanding of the parameters of allowable departure from the stated norms.

The monastic discipline detailed in the *Vinaya* is undertaken voluntarily by nuns and monks with the understanding that wholesome, morally responsible actions undertaken with positive motivation lead to pleasant results. This system of ethics is the essential foundation for the spiritual practice of the *Sangha*. It is the very core of a life of renunciation.

Because *Sangha* members are cast as role models in Buddhist society, they not only need to maintain the *Vinaya* discipline for their own spiritual development, but also need to be aware of their behavior as it appears to the public eye. While one purpose of the *Vinaya* is to help nuns and monks refrain from unwholesome deeds, another is to protect the *Sangha* from the criticism of others. Thus they must carefully judge what is the appropriate action in any given situation. Although the main point is the intention of the mind in doing the action, since *Sangha* members represent the *Sangha*, they need to be aware of the effect their actions have on others so as not to incite blame.

The ramifications of attempting to live by an ancient moral code in the present age is a topic worthy of thoughtful consideration. Present-day dialogue, especially in Western countries, is concerned with the ways modern nuns and monks can honestly yet comfortably live by this ancient code of discipline. Cutting oneself off from society completely does not seem to be a realistic alternative, although a protected environment is highly advisable during the first years of ordained life. Unless they are fortunate enough to live in a monastic community, practitioners trying to maintain precepts are constantly confronted by tremendous challenges. It is certainly not an easy matter to maintain monastic discipline in society today.

Whether changing the monastic code is allowable or desirable is another issue that is being hotly debated. Some argue that the *Vinaya* strictures are antiquated, obsolete, and stand in need of revision. Others counter that changing the code would be tantamount to rewriting the scriptures. Although the Buddha himself changed and amended the precepts, it is debatable whether others are at liberty to do so. Such changes would meet with stiff opposition because the *Vinaya* texts belong to the oldest strata of the Buddhist canon and are held sacred by all Buddhist adherents. Many people also question whether such changes are desirable, in that the changes themselves would soon become outdated in this rapidly changing world and thus would require continual revision. The *Vinaya* has served as the foundation and has helped maintain the vitality of what is presumably the oldest continuous monastic community the world has ever known. We must seriously consider the possible repercussions of altering a moral system that has so admirably withstood the test of time.

Correct interpretation of the *Vinaya* is not an easy task. It requires a deep overall understanding of the *Dharma* and a detailed study of the complete *Vinaya* code in all its complexity. Before starting to interpret the rules, we have to know clearly what they are and must be thoroughly familiar with well-disciplined monastic life from an experiential standpoint. To judge what constitutes proper conduct places an enormous responsibility on each individual. To develop mature judgment of situations, it is essential to receive proper guidance from a qualified *Vinaya* master over a long period of time. For this reason, nuns and monks are required to train intensively with a teacher for five to ten years to gain a firm grounding in the proper attitudes and behavior of an ordained person.

Obviously, it is not possible to gain an accurate sense of allowable conduct if we are completely on our own after ordination. For this reason, it is important to set up centers where nuns can receive intensive training in monastic discipline and study under *bhikṣuṇī* masters. There need to be *bhikṣuṇī Vinaya* experts who are qualified to interpret difficult points of *Vinaya* and are knowledgeable in matters that particularly relate to nuns.

Originally the *Sangha* was a unified whole with members observing a common body of precepts. The order functioned quite smoothly during the Buddha's lifetime and for about a century thereafter. During the time of King Aśoka, however, divisions arose. Whether these divisions arose primarily as a result of language differences, cultural differences, points of view, matters of monastic discipline, or a combination of these factors, is difficult to determine. Naturally, various reasons for the divisions were advanced by opposing parties in the dispute. In any event, the Mahāsānghika (the majority) split away from the Theravāda about that time.

In the beginning, the majority of the *bhikṣus* were attracted to the Mahāsānghika with its more liberal interpretation of the precepts. Due to its stricter interpretation of the discipline, the Theravāda school had fewer followers at that stage. Yet it would seem that precisely because of its orthodoxy and careful adherence to precepts, this school managed to avoid dissension and averted a split within its community. "Since it was a small community and maintained strict discipline, it was a unified and strong order which survived for a century without a schism."[3] This would indicate that a well-defined and precise interpretation of allowable behavior brings consensus and cohesiveness to monastic organization. Once disagreement is broached in regard to interpretation of the monastic rules, diverse views tend to emerge and dissension often results. Such dissension may threaten the strength, harmony, and unity of the community, giving rise to splinter groups.

Although the Theravāda and Mahāsānghika schools both eventually gave rise to a number of sub-schools,[4] it was ultimately those who maintained a more stringent interpretation of the precepts that maintained their vitality and have survived up to the present day. The Dharmagupta school prevalent in Korea and China, the Mūlasarvāstivāda school of Tibet, and the Theravāda school followed in Burma, Cambodia, Laos, Sri Lanka and Thailand, all belong to the Theravāda, the stricter of the two branches of *Vinaya* that originally developed. That is to say, all the traditions of *Vinaya* that exist in the world today are actually branches of the original, more orthodox Theravāda school. No lineages from the more liberal Mahāsānghika have survived. Thus we may conclude that close adherence to monastic discipline helps account for the strength and endurance of an order in the long run.

Stability is one of the benefits that may result from exemplary discipline; popular support and internal harmony are others. This was observed by Holmes Welch when he studied the large, well-disciplined public monasteries of China and compared them with the smaller, more relaxed local temples: "It is stated in a monastic code of rules: 'The more strictly the rules are applied, the more people there will be living in a monastery. The looser the rules, the fewer people.' This was partly because strictness attracted donation from the laity and partly because it would be impractical to have several hundred persons living together in disorder."[5] The conclusion implicit here is that monasteries following the *Vinaya* regulations closely are better supported, more livable, and more durable.

This evaluation should be kept in mind as we consider what

concessions nuns and monks should make to today's lifestyle. If we wish to create lasting monasteries and a stable *Sangha*, relaxing the rules unnecessarily may prove to be a big mistake. We should strive to create an optimum balance between monastic ideals and everyday realities, fashioning healthy, agreeable communities, without sacrificing orderliness and moral rectitude.

NOTES

1. The precepts undertaken by Buddhist laywomen and laymen are to refrain from killing, stealing, lying, illicit sexual conduct, and intoxicants.

2. Although the term *Sangha* is commonly being used in the West these days to refer to *Dharma* practitioners in general, it actually means an assemblage of four or more fully ordained nuns or monks.

3. Akira Hirakawa, *Monastic Discipline for the Buddhist Nuns*, p. 3.

4. Jeffrey Hopkins, *Meditation on Emptiness*, pp. 713-19.

5. Holmes Welch, *The Practice of Chinese Buddhism*, p. 4.

LIVING BY THE *VINAYA* IN THE WEST

by Bhikṣuṇī Jampa Tsedroen

Although I am not a scholar of *Vinaya*, I have gained some experience through trying to live according to the *Vinaya* over the last few years, living mainly in the West, but also for short times in Asia. It is my view that there is no Buddhist country where *Vinaya* is really practiced any longer in the way it should be. In my opinion, the practice of *Vinaya* in the Theravādin tradition has become a little bit too rigid, while in the Mahāyāna tradition, it has become a little too lax. By saying that in the Theravādin tradition *Vinaya* practice has become too rigid, I mean that the rules sometimes seem to be followed too literally. By saying that in the Mahāyāna tradition it has become too lax, I mean that by giving more importance to Bodhisattva practice than to *Vinaya* practice, it sometimes seems to be forgotten that one can usually practice both at the same time.

I feel that trying to live according to the *Vinaya* in the West can only become something very meaningful and important for us if it is mainly practiced in its original sense and not just according to traditions. The true sense of the *prātimokśa* vows of monks or nuns is to change our unwholesome physical and verbal actions into virtuous actions. One meaning of *prātimokśa* is "individual liberation." To become a monk or nun therefore means to engage in a basic practice that helps to improve one's daily outer behavior to attain one's own liberation from the cycle of existence. It is a primary Buddhist principle to strive for one's own liberation by harming others as little as possible. Therefore, it seems understandable that every action that is ruled by the *Vinaya* is based on doing as little harm as possible and as much benefit as possible for oneself and others.

Although this is the principle upon which the training rules of the *Vinaya* have been given by the Buddha to the monks and nuns, the rules were given under certain circumstances. Therefore, if the rules are kept literally even though circumstances are changing, they can sometimes be harmful rather than beneficial. I think that it is very important to always consider the reasons and meaning of rules and not to practice them only word by word without reflection. On the other hand, one also has to be careful not to fall into the other extreme of thinking that only our motivation is important and not our outer behavior. We have to find the middle way.

Our personal assessments today are not comparable to those of the ordained people who had a chance to live close to the Buddha during his lifetime. Since that time various Buddhist traditions have developed. The Buddhist traditions we find today follow the interpretations of highly respected Indian masters as well as of indigenous masters. These interpretations are interwoven with the respective cultures. This does not mean that Buddhism has not been preserved authentically, but shows that Buddhism is flexible enough to assume various forms without changing its true meaning. Yet, we see that traditions have both advantages and disadvantages. People in different countries follow different traditions and some accept these traditions unquestioningly, but our situation as Westerners is a little different. Not having grown up in a Buddhist country, we are apt to question everything that differs from our own Western, Judaeo-Christian heritage. Most of all, we tend to question things that we have reacted against among those traditions. I think we are facing two main problems: first, the problem of deciding how to put the original meaning of the ancient rules into practice in modern life, which is a problem Asians have, too; and second, the problem of lacking a Western Buddhist culture, which is a problem that Asian countries also had to overcome when they first introduced Indian Buddhism into their own cultures.

Many questions and problems arise when Westerners nowadays try to live by the *Vinaya*. In the first years after becoming a Buddhist, I questioned why the Buddha instituted so many minor rules concerning external behavior, and I discussed this topic with my teacher at length. From Buddhism I learned that the most important thing is to have a good heart and that the mind is more important than external behavior. Therefore, in the beginning I thought that some *Vinaya* rules appeared to be in contradiction to this basic teaching of the Buddha. Yet in the process of discussions, I began to recognize that it is very important to have a foundation of moral discipline as a basis for daily practice and mental development. I learned that these rules were simply a realistic and beneficial foundation for one's own life and for life in a community.

Buddha Śakyamuni did not create rules from the beginning when the *Sangha* was first established. It was the *Sangha* who asked advice when problems arose in their communities as a consequence of unwise behavior on the part of some *Sangha* members. Each rule is to be viewed as a recommendation for a specific problem which required a solution in those times. The *Vinaya* contains many legends describing situations where followers of the Buddha were criticized because they did not behave according to the teachings or because laypeople might draw false conclusions about the meaning of the teachings, thus losing faith. In this way, whenever *Sangha* members jeopardized their own goals or those of other people, rules were set forth one by one by the Buddha to regulate the life of the *Sangha* community.

Everyone recognizes that throughout the world and throughout history the majority of human beings have lacked the maturity to act wisely. Thus there is no way but to have rules to help people act more competently with respect to the needs of themselves and others. Rules or vows are an expression of our good intention to follow a pure mode of conduct in daily life. Rules also do restrict our lifestyle, however, and it is difficult to explain concisely the significance of a rule without explaining the circumstances which led to its creation.

Before the Buddha passed into *nirvāna*, he stressed once more the fact that the rules do not all have to be followed. Our task must be to find out why the Buddha has given each rule and to determine whether it is still applicable to these times, circumstances, and the challenges we have to cope with. For this reason, we need to examine the rules in relation to the teachings as a whole.

In the West these days, we find a certain tendency for monks and nuns to conclude on their own which rules are still applicable and which are not. But of course we cannot handle it in this way. Consider for instance, the case of a *Dharma* center where there are rules regulating daily life, born of many years' experience and found suitable to improve the life in the community. It would not be appropriate for a newcomer to step in and immediately decide independently which of these rules to accept and which to reject without bothering about the other members of the center. If someone were to discuss the meaning and the necessity of the rules from long years of experience, however, and after having studied the basic teachings of Buddhism, including a study of the situations which led to the rules, then the person would surely be cooperative and contribute to the improvement of the regulations.

The situation of the *Sangha* is similar in some respects. When speaking of the *Vinaya*, we are not dealing with rules for just one household, but with the rules for the whole *Sangha* community. After all, when we come together we can speak of one *Sangha* of monks and one *Sangha* of nuns, even if they are scattered over the whole world. If we do not want to contribute to the degeneration of the discipline of Buddhist monks and nuns, we can only decide on modifications worldwide. Since there may be situations where the rules Buddha has given may be applicable in the future, one cannot just skip the rules, but surely more work on interpreting them needs to be done. This work can only be done by monks and nuns who have studied the *Vinaya* thoroughly, and are experts in the theory *and* practice of the entire *Tripitaka* as well.

Personally I feel that it is helpful in the modern age to wear robes and to practice as an ordained person, as long as one tries to do so as the Buddha intended. Being ordained is something which should make life very easy, giving time for the practice and spread of the *Dharma*. It should not become a hindrance. In the traditional monasteries of Buddhist countries Asian people show much respect to the *Sangha*, offer many donations, and always behave with great kindness and devotion toward those who are ordained. In the West, the situation is completely reversed. People very often approach us and ask, "Why have you become a nun? It is very strange." "Aren't you dealing with your emotions?" "Are you repressing something?" Such attitudes make things very difficult. Many people cannot understand the purpose of ordination. Some Buddhists even say that we really do not need *Vinaya* here in the West at all.

Many people in Germany and other European countries think that it would be better if all *Dharma* teachers came from the lay community. They think that it would be easier for lay teachers to communicate with the laypeople. I do not completely agree. It is very good to have lay teachers, but it is difficult for laypeople to study Buddhism extensively. Having a family and job in the West makes full-time study impossible. There are some cases of people who have tried to manage it, but it only seems possible if they live alone, following a celibate lifestyle.

A celibate life in the West these days is viewed with mixed feelings. Some people have the impression that celibacy leads to repression and rigidity. But in fact there are many stories of holy beings and highly developed people who utilized for higher goals all the strength they retained by renouncing worldly life. In addition I have learned that many laypeople are more inclined to discuss their personal problems with monks and nuns, provided they are monks and nuns who diligently apply *Dharma* to their own mental development and thus can function as role models. Sometimes there will be a "black sheep," meaning people who do not live up to the expectations and do not even try to, but within the "world *Sangha*" one can certainly find serious practitioners. We should not forget that very often, especially in the West, monks and nuns have only been ordained for a short time and are, therefore, only beginners. The expectation that those wearing robes should already be highly developed spiritually, to be an object of respect, is totally unrealistic.

Besides the respect one should show toward sentient beings in general, the Buddha clearly indicated that those who dedicate their whole lives to the practice and study of *Dharma*, who are ready to give up material comforts, worldly reputation, family, and so on, deserve a special sort of respect. This may be one of the reasons why monks and nuns are designated "fields of merits." Certainly it is a wholesome action within the subtle functioning of the law of cause and effect to support men and women who dedicate their lives to the *Dharma* and take on the required commitments. Ordained people have time to engage more intensively in *Dharma* study and practice. That does not mean that one cannot practice *Dharma* the whole day in worldly life, too. Monks and nuns nowadays also do much other work in addition to their studies and meditations, especially with respect to looking after the needs of the lay community. After many years of training, ordained people become like professionals in *Dharma* practice; thus they can benefit the lay community greatly, not in a material way, like the laypeople can benefit monks and nuns, but in a spiritual way. Nowadays, especially in the West, some are of the opinion that ordained people cannot correctly advise laypeople since they do not have the same worldly experience. I disagree. Monks and nuns still live in the world, and therefore they hear and see the problems that laypeople face day to day. By acting as advisers to lay people, they hear about similar problems and experiences from many different points of view. Being not personally involved, maintaining a certain inner distance, and being close to the *Dharma* day to day, ordained people can help the laypeople to look at their problems from the *Dharma* point of view.

To act as advisers, monks and nuns first have to find the right outer circumstances for preparatory training. In this regard, nuns especially lack many basic conditions. For example, shortly after I decided to follow the Buddhist path, like many other women, I asked where one could find female teachers and meditation masters. It was quite difficult for me to accept the fact that there were no *bhikṣuṇīs* in the Tibetan tradition who function as role models for women. It seemed like a real setback to find myself in a position of inequality, lacking equal rights and opportunities, being a novice Buddhist nun amidst a community composed largely of fully ordained monks.

It is true that the question of becoming ordained is totally unrelated to and should not be confused with that of striving for equal rights in a worldly sense. The decision should be motivated solely by an aspiration to be freed from cyclic existence. In the West, however, women have successfully fought for equal rights and sometimes react quite irritably if these basic rights are not respected. Many young women and also young men in the West find it a big obstacle to discover discrimination against women in the Buddhist world. It runs counter to their expectations and makes Buddhism seem "old-fashioned" along the lines of other world religions which are governed patriarchically and undemocratically, though ultimately this is a false conclusion.

After many years of struggle, discussions, and contemplations, I finally became convinced that the Buddha did not discriminate between men and women, nor between high and low castes, different races, and so on, but that the Buddha really intended to give women equal responsibility and opportunity to practice the *Dharma*. Though social realities may sometimes be at variance with this ideal in the present world, united, and in harmony with men, we must demonstrate that the revolutionary truth the Buddha taught is still seriously being practiced.

These days there is a great opportunity for the growth and development of the *Bhikṣuṇī Sangha*. Except for China, Vietnam, and Korea, where the *bhikṣuṇī* lineage is already well established, we will be building something new. This will give us the opportunity to investigate the *Vinaya*, to do research in our respective traditions, and to determine what the practice of *Vinaya* should be. This is a very important opportunity. It is clear that the practice of *Vinaya* needs to be adapted to present-day conditions.

For example, there is the question of touching money, which is prohibited in the *Vinaya* regulations. In all countries these days, the restrictions against handling money is a problem. It is nearly impossible to avoid transgressing this rule. My teacher explained, however, that as long as we are not handling money for our own purposes, but for the purpose of spreading the *Dharma*, building temples and *Dharma* centers, it is permissible. Many people think that we should change the rules, but I do not agree. The issue is one of interpreting the rules, not of changing the *Vinaya*.

When I returned to Germany after receiving *bhikṣuṇī* ordination in Taiwan, I felt a responsibility to try to observe the rules strictly, but problems arose. For instance, I was no longer allowed to touch a man, as such contact transgresses one of the chief rules of a *bhikṣuṇī*. All traditions agree that a *bhikṣuṇī* should not touch a man, because one comes very close to committing one of the *pārājikas* (root downfalls). To do so with attachment means that a major precept is broken and one becomes expelled from the *Sangha*. I realized that it is better not to put oneself in a potentially difficult situation and that it is best not to touch a man at all. Now, this point of view is easily understood by Buddhists once it is explained, but when new people who are interested in the *Dharma* first walk into a *Dharma* center, things are different. As you know, in Germany, we always shake hands, so when a man first arrives and extends his hand, to leave him standing there without responding is considered very impolite. Then the situation cannot be left as it is, but needs to be explained. So I have to say that I am not allowed to touch a man, and immediately a barrier is created. A wall has gone up which is impassible. New people already feel a bit uncomfortable and afraid, coming into a temple for the first time. They do not know what these strange Buddhists are doing, but they are interested, and immediately I have set up this wall. It makes for an awkward situation.

When his Holiness the Dalai Lama came to Germany I had

the opportunity to ask his advice on this matter. He said that for the time being, I should be patient. If people give their hand to me, then I should respond. Otherwise I should leave the situation as it is and should not make any effort to extend my hand first. Then slowly, meeting people over and over again, one should try to explain the matter to them. Gradually people in Western countries will become accustomed to the fact that Buddhist nuns do not shake hands. Some Western nuns may think that we do not need to pay attention to these kinds of rules in the West, but I do not think we can ignore them, since this would be a step toward the degeneration of *Vinaya* practice. The reasons why Buddha Śakyamuni set up these rules are still present.

In the West, problems sometimes arise when we wear our robes in public. Several times monks have been attacked by punks, skinheads—members of certain social movements we have in the West—or by drunkards. This poses a very difficult problem, because the people who attack them collect a great deal of negative *karma*. Wearing robes is not such a problem for nuns, but a man wearing a skirt in the West is always looked upon as being very strange. His Holiness seems to have given permission for some Western monks to wear lay clothes when they go outside their centers or monasteries. Of course, in Asian countries, this would mean that one had left the order. Even though to wear robes is not a major rule, not wearing robes is one of the three circumstances which lead to degeneration. Nevertheless, vows are not dependent upon clothes and as long as a *pārājika* has not been committed, one still possesses the vow.

Here again, as in the Buddha's lifetime, special permission was given in a particular case. Still, one has to decide how to handle special situations in a way that corresponds with the teachings. Unforeseen results may arise that contrast markedly with the intended meaning of a prescription, prohibition, or permission, which are the three types of *Vinaya* instructions. These days we find many monks and nuns in the West who even from the very first day of their ordination wear blue jeans, sunglasses and quite long hair, even longer than a customary short hair cut. They do not look ordained at all. I trust that they are keeping their vows, but it is difficult for me to see any difference between such ordained people and laypeople, and it is understandable if people do not treat them like monks and nuns. In the future, it may be possible to find a style of robes which is both in accordance with the *Vinaya* and also acceptable to people in the West. Such changes may be warranted, but to let things develop as they are poses a real danger. People may begin to feel that the *Vinaya* rules are no longer significant. It shows that *Vinaya* practice in the West is still in the very beginning stage and needs much improvement. Otherwise, what has lasted for centuries in Asia could be destroyed in the West in a few decades. I am worried about this and feel that we must be very careful.

It is not a question of our being ashamed to go outside in robes. If we feel uncomfortable when people criticize us in the streets, that is our problem. This surely happened also in Buddha's lifetime and it can be overcome. But when wearing red robes in Europe, we are often called "Bhagwan" (Rajneesh), and Theravāda monks are identified with the Hare Krishnas. Therefore, it is a question of whether continuing to wear robes despite such associations is helpful in spreading the *Dharma*. Nevertheless, we should remind ourselves that the first monks and nuns in Christianity and other religions surely faced similar problems, yet today their orders are socially recognized.

It is very worthwhile to come together to discuss the *Vinaya* rules and their adaptation. There are many complex points to consider which cannot be reasoned out by people individually. It would be beneficial to have national and international committees working to come to an understanding on these points. We are not dealing merely with correct interpretation of rules, but with the introduction of Buddhism into new non-Buddhist countries as well. To take an example, it is very difficult to recite the confession *sūtra* in a foreign language, so first I translated the *Prāṭimokśa Sūtra* from English into German, thinking it would be best to recite it in my own language.

Now, it seems that for international *Sangha* gatherings, it is best to recite the *sūtra* in English. This is a great opportunity. Whenever we come together from all different countries, we can recite the *Prāṭimokśa Sūtra* in a common language. It is difficult enough to learn it by heart in one language. Therefore, for the time being, all of us should use one and the same reliable translation. This is the kind of project that requires the efforts of an international committee.

It would be very good to have an opportunity to hold workshops on the *Vinaya* commentaries to revise the practice of *Vinaya*. It is important to receive and comprehend the teachings of Buddha genuinely and also in a way which is meaningful for people today in new environments. I think that monasteries in the West are going to play an increasingly important role, especially with respect to communicating Buddhism fully and authentically. We may never have such great numbers of monks and nuns as in Asia, but we should feel responsible to contribute at a high standard to their work. Constant endeavor to emulate right behavior on the path in accordance with the teachings will diminish the prejudices against monasticism that exist in some minds. We will then meet people who give wholehearted understanding and support to the aspirations of monks and nuns.

Living by the *Vinaya* in the present day in the West is something that has begun but is still developing. One difficulty we face is that the various Buddhist traditions are grounded in different cultures. Another problem is that we lack monasteries. There are a few monasteries for monks already, but few specifically for nuns. I feel that we need to set up nunneries led by experienced *bhikṣuṇīs* who are learned not only in *Vinaya*, but in the teachings as a whole. Being a Western nun in the Tibetan tradition means that one must take responsibility to undergo thorough training and in addition must help to establish nunneries. Certainly, in building up a new nun's *Sangha* we will face many difficulties, but it is also a great opportunity. By starting anew, we can try to find a middle way in the practice of *Vinaya* without having to change existing traditions. In other words, we can build up modern nunneries based on old traditions. Surely this is something worthy of support.

8 *The Bhikṣuṇī Issue*

During his lifetime, the Buddha gave the right of full ordination to women and personally established the *Bhikṣuṇī Sangha*. The order has continued to exist until the present day in some countries but no longer exists in others. Where the order does exist, nuns serve a useful function in the religious life of the society; where the order does not exist, women are at a distinct disadvantage in terms of gaining spiritual nourishment and instruction.

Some observers doubt the importance or wisdom of receiving full ordination as a *bhikṣuṇī* these days. They maintain that upholding the five precepts of a layperson or the ten precepts of a novice is sufficient, even ambitious, considering the mores of modern-day society. Be that as it may, the fact remains that full ordination is available for those men who wish to receive it, so it stands to reason that it should be available for women as well. Certainly not everyone is interested in undertaking more than three hundred precepts for life, but it can be argued that those who seriously wish to do so should have the option.

What are the merits of full ordination? Why would someone wish to become a *bhikṣuṇī*? What is to be gained from taking such a drastic step?

The value of upholding moral discipline in general, as a basis for the development of concentration and wisdom, has already been discussed. The benefits of abiding by precepts as a method for increasing individual awareness in daily activity and for fostering communal harmony have also been mentioned. Full ordination intensifies *Dharma* practice further, increasing the practitioners's mindfulness from moment to moment by regulating even more aspects of everyday conduct. The more precepts one holds, the less chance there is of committing negative actions and creating future suffering. Maintaining full ordination provides a matrix for bringing practically every action into concord with the Buddha's enlightening teachings. One's identity becomes thoroughly intertwined with the *Dharma*, allowing hardly an instant's lapse. While this total immersion method represents an immense responsibility, it is also a tremendous opportunity for advancement on the path.

The life of a *bhikṣuṇī* or *bhikṣu* is said to be the ultimate pure and simple life—"free as a cloud." It is so conducive to *Dharma* practice that many realized beings are recorded to have received ordination even after attaining *arhatship*. Living by precepts restrains a person from engaging in meaningless and unnecessary actions, thus assuring time, quietude, and freedom to practice. Radically changing the outer lifestyle to the monastic mode protects a person from becoming entangled in the shortsighted goals of this life and propels one toward wholesome attitudes. Standing somewhat apart from the complications of worldly involvements one is often better able to develop the strength and objectivity that are necessary to help others with their problems. Dwelling in contentment, rejoicing in the precepts, one experiences inner happiness and freedom.

In addition to the advantages gained in this lifetime, it is said that maintaining pure morality leads to a human rebirth in future lives. It is also said that wherever ordained *Sangha* members abide by the morality of the *Prāṭimokśa*, the Buddha's teachings will continue to exist. This is a significant statement in a world where many Buddhist cultures are being threatened by political problems and are fighting for their very survival. It is equally significant for the spread of *Buddhadharma* to new countries. Since the term *Sangha* actually denotes an assemblage of four or more fully ordained nuns or monks, we can see that *bhikṣuṇīs* contribute to the flourishing of the *Dharma* simply by their presence. This is one contribution the *Bhikṣuṇī Sangha* has to offer the world.

People ask why there are objections to the establishment of a *bhikṣuṇī* order in certain countries. Although it is somewhat uncomfortable to reveal, part of the reason may be economic. In some countries there have been no *bhikṣuṇīs* for centuries, so the *bhikṣus* alone have enjoyed all privileges, support, and power. Since both *bhikṣus* and *bhikṣuṇīs* depend upon the laity for their sustenance, to establish a *Bhikṣuṇī Sangha* would mean a division of resources. This could be one reason why there is opposition to its establishment—to give the nuns equal status might erode the *bhikṣus*' basis of support. In many traditional Buddhist countries, it is mostly women who patronize the *bhikṣus*; if they began patronizing the *bhikṣuṇīs*, it could cause a conflict of interests.

Other objections to the establishment of the *Bhikṣuṇī Sangha* can be countered with logical reasoning. The foremost objection relates to the question of the lineage. Opponents claim that there is no *bhikṣuṇī* lineage today. It is clear, however, that *bhikṣuṇī* lineages do exist in several traditions, namely, the Chinese, the Korean, and the Vietnamese. Others claim that these lineages have not been transmitted continuously. This is a difficult claim to refute, since to conclusively prove a millennia-old lineage to be unbroken would require omniscience, but the onus of proving that the lineage has not been transmitted continuously clearly falls upon the challenger. Why should those with faith in the purity of the lineage they hold feel any compulsion to validate it? Thus far, no one has been able to produce evidence of any break in the existing *bhikṣuṇī* lineages.

Detractors claim that the Buddha prophesied a decline in the doctrine if women were admitted into the order. This refers to a hotly debated statement which warns that as a result of the creation of the *bhikṣuṇī* order, the teachings would decline after five hundred years and disappear after one thousand years.[1] Some people maintain that the eight important rules (*gurudharmas*)[2] accepted by the first *bhikṣuṇī*, Mahāprajāpati, achieved their intended effect of nullifying the dire consequences predicted. Others doubt that this prophecy is a genuine statement of the Buddha, in that "...far from disappearing after 500 years, the *Dhamma* is very much alive and kicking even today after 2,500 years."[3] My own opinion is that if the Buddha possessed omniscience and was able to perceive all phenomena of past, present, and future, surely he was aware of women's equal spiritual capabilities and of how long the doctrine would last. The notion that the Buddha was averse to the idea of establishing an order of nuns and was coerced to do so by Ānanda against his better judgment is both unreasonable and demeaning. The *bhikṣuṇīs* constitute a major component in the *Sangha* and Buddhist society is not complete without them.

Some opponents have charged that efforts to revive the *Bhikṣuṇī Sangha* are equivalent to the heinous crime[4] of creating a schism in the *Sangha*. This charge can also be countered with calm, clear logic. First of all, it is clearly those who *oppose* such a revival who are actually responsible for creating dissention. Surely there is no fault in upholding the Buddha's injunctions to create a balanced society composed of *bhikṣuṇīs*, *bhikṣus*, and laypeople. Furthermore, as mentioned previously, it is impossible for a woman, either ordained or lay, to create a schism in the *Bhikṣu Sangha*. It is specified that only a fully ordained monk is capable of creating such a schism. Female proponents of the *bhikṣuṇī* order need not worry that they are creating a heinous crime.

Despite the opposition of conservative elements in some countries, support for the full ordination of Buddhist women is gathering rapidly. The *bhikṣuṇī* issue has become increasingly relevant now that the Buddhist teachings are spreading to the West. In the past, practitioners in Asian Buddhist countries have remained somewhat insular, well aware of the historical background of their own traditions, but less aware of historical developments in other Buddhist countries. Until fairly recently, many did not realize that the Chinese, Korean, and Vietnamese traditions have preserved the *bhikṣuṇī* lineage intact. Thanks to improved global communications, this information is quickly becoming more widespread.

Currently the existence of Buddhist nuns is gaining sympathetic recognition, and opportunities for Buddhist women to receive ordination are increasing. As full ordination becomes more widely available to women in different countries, we will see the emergence of an international *Bhikṣuṇī Sangha*, a unified alliance of *bhikṣuṇīs* from many countries and traditions who combine their efforts to promote the *Dharma* and the monastic way of life. A mutual support system like this will be a spur to intercultural exchanges and a source of encouragement for nuns everywhere. Together they can inspire one another and share ideas for improving conditions for Buddhist women in general. Eventually such an alliance could form itself as an official organization, furnishing information about upcoming *bhikṣuṇī* ordinations and available training centers, as well as providing other useful services. In the meantime, women will have a communications system operating under the aegis of Sakyadhītā which can provide services and information to *bhikṣuṇīs*, novices, and others.

The need for a worldwide alliance of *bhikṣuṇīs* is felt because, although *bhikṣuṇīs* are already recognized in some countries, there are many others in which full ordination for women has yet to gain acceptance. Where there are very few *bhikṣuṇīs*, communications and moral support from sisters in other lands will lend encouragement to those who are still striving for such acceptance. Furthermore, where *bhikṣuṇī* ordination is a recent development, as in Western countries, links with elder *bhikṣuṇīs* from traditionally Buddhist countries are desirable so that aspirants and the recently ordained may learn from these masters. There are advantages to be gained on both sides from opening up lines of communication and achieving a solidarity among the *bhikṣuṇīs* living in different parts of the world. A confederation of *bhikṣuṇīs* from East and West, whether formally established or operating as a loose network of like-minded individuals, will lend strength and a sense of purpose for those leading the monastic life. It will also give impetus to further research in the study of the *Bhikṣuṇī Vinaya* texts, which is widely recognized as an important task.

The views presented at the conference, while varied, are those of people who earnestly wish to find a solution to the ordination issue which will benefit all Buddhist nuns. Since the vast majority of nuns are Asian, all were concerned to elicit the approval and support of Asian Buddhists, particularly the monks. It is essential that the *Bhikṣuṇī Sangha* be established in accord with the *Bhikṣu Sangha*. Those monks who do not agree need to be convinced of the viability and usefulness of a strong and well-organized order of nuns. Therefore, we must understand the points of view of all the various traditions and persuade the monks with cogent reasoning. Efforts to establish full ordination for Buddhist women are not to be treated as a struggle for worldly gains and recognition, but rather as an assertion of women's rightful place in the field of religion. The hope is that nuns will be accorded a place within the Buddhist establishment in each country as a means to the end of benefiting women more extensively. By maintaining a worldwide perspective, we can proceed toward our just and valid objective of improving opportunities for the spiritual development of women within the Buddhist fold.

Some proponents of the *Bhikṣuṇī Sangha* feel that we should dispense with the dual ordination process and initiate ordinations of *bhikṣuṇīs* by *bhikṣuṇīs* alone, circumventing the participation of men altogether. This is not permissible, however, since it is a transgression for a *bhikṣuṇī* to administer full ordination to a woman without the confirmation of the *Bhikṣu Sangha*. Besides being one of the eight important rules for *bhikṣuṇīs*, ordination by both *Sanghas* is stipulated in the text on procedures. An ordination conducted by *bhikṣuṇīs* alone would not be in accord with the *Vinaya* and would not be accepted in any Buddhist tradition.

Other proponents of the *Bhikṣuṇī Sangha* feel that we should press for recognition even of *bhikṣuṇī* ordinations conducted by *bhikṣus* alone, without the participation of *bhikṣuṇīs*. Monks in some countries maintain that this procedure is allowable. Such proponents contend that an ordination ceremony conducted by *bhikṣus* alone is simpler to organize and should be considered just as valid as a dual ordination ceremony. They argue that since the rules of ordination are not included in the *Prāṭimokśa* rules, they are minor rules, and cite the fact that Buddha has allowed minor rules to be altered when circumstances deem it necessary.

Several points can be raised to counter these arguments. First of all, again, all extant renditions of the *Vinaya* prescribe that *bhikṣuṇī* ordination be given by both *Bhikṣuṇī* and *Bhikṣu Sanghas*. As has been reasoned elsewhere, it is advisable to proceed in accordance with the *Vinaya* wherever possible, not only to abide by these ancient texts and traditions, but also to gain acceptance for the *Bhikṣuṇī Sangha* in the more conservative Buddhist countries.

Secondly, dual ordination is recommended from a feminist point of view. Women should participate in the ordination of women. Why should nuns be excluded from ordaining nuns, when their right and duty to do so is fully elaborated in the *Vinaya* texts? It is correct that *bhikṣuṇīs* should take part in the *bhikṣuṇī* ordination ceremony, not only as spectators and assistants, but as principals in active roles on a par with the *bhikṣu* ordination masters. The *Vinaya* texts explain that the precepts are to be conferred by the *Bhikṣuṇī Sangha* and confirmed or reconferred (traditions differ in interpretation on this point) by the *Bhikṣu Sangha* later the same day. Why should women relinquish their right to participate in their own ordinations? On the contrary, we should stand united in requesting that our right to participate, as prescribed in the original *Vinaya* formulations, be upheld.

Due in part to the widespread interest generated by the conference, educated and progressive *bhikṣus* are showing increasingly open-minded attitudes on the subject of *bhikṣuṇī* ordination. Already, certain Theravāda *bhikṣus* have broken with tradition and begun conducting *śrāmaṇerikā* ordinations in India and the United States. With improved transportation and communications, *bhikṣus* are traveling abroad more frequently and are consequently being exposed to feminist sentiments among Western Buddhists. Many of these *bhikṣus* are highly respected in their home countries. As they become aware of these sentiments and relay them to others, there is every reason to suppose that more liberal attitudes towards ordination for women in traditionally Buddhist countries will gradually result. Substantial reforms can also be anticipated as the coming generation of younger *bhikṣus* begin to move into positions of responsibility in the Buddhist hierarchy.

As far as the Thravāda countries are concerned, it has been suggested that in the beginning a *bhikṣuṇī* ordination be held in a neutral place where the *bhikṣus* are supportive. For example, open-minded Sri Lankan monks living in India or the United States could be invited to participate in an ordination ceremony along with Chinese *bhikṣuṇīs*. Then, gradually, people could work to gain acceptance for the lineage among the rank-and-file in Sri Lanka itself. One Sri Lankan delegate warned that "to attempt a mass exodus would be like upsetting a hornet's nest." The best approach seems to be to start with a small nucleus of sympathetic, educated monks abroad and progressively transmit the lineage to the home country.

Buddhist women, numbering in the millions, possess considerable public relations potential. The rate at which improvements can be made for Buddhist women and recognition gained for ordained Buddhist nuns depends to a great extent on the skill with which the better informed and better educated among these millions wield that potential.

A Buddhist society devoid of *bhikṣuṇīs* lacks a crucial component for creating a balanced social order. It stands bereft of caring, qualified counselors for the spiritual guidance of its wives, mothers, single women, and men. To seek the right to receive ordination and to abide by moral precepts in accordance with the Buddha's instructions is certainly virtuous, provided it is done with skill and knowledge. There is nothing to be gained by opposing the establishment of the *Bhikṣuṇī Sangha* and depriving the world of this source of qualified women *Dharma* teachers. The present age of women's heightened awareness is the perfect time for *bhikṣuṇīs* to take their rightful place in the spiritual fiber of society. It is hoped that the points of view presented in these pages will provide stimulus for increased dialogue on this important issue.

NOTES

1. The passage containing this prediction is found in the Cullavagga, translated by T. W. Rhys Davids and Hermann Oldenberg in *Vinaya Texts*, Part III, p. 325.

2. The eight *gurudharmas* as translated and explained in *Monastic Discipline for the Buddhist Nuns* by Akira Hirakawa (Patna, 1982, pp. 47-98) are: (1) When a *bhikṣuṇī*, even though she has been ordained for a hundred years, meets a *bhikṣu* who has newly entered the order, she ought to rise, venerate, and pay obeisance to him; (2) A *bhikṣuṇī* is to study for two years prior to the *upasampadā* ordination and to receive the ordination from both *bhikṣuṇīs* and *bhikṣus*; (3) A *bhikṣuṇī* must not admonish a *bhikṣu* for his offenses, while a *bhikṣu* can admonish a *bhikṣuṇī* for her offenses; (4) A *bhikṣuṇī* must not receive food, lodging, bedding and cushions before a *bhikṣu* does; (5) If a *bhikṣuṇī* transgresses a *gurudharma* or commits a *saṅghāvaśeṣa* offense, she ought to perform the *māṇatva* for one-half month before the order of *bhikṣus* and the order of *bhikṣuṇīs*; (6) On the day of *upoṣadha*, the *bhikṣuṇīs* should seek instruction from the order of *bhikṣus*; (7) A *bhikṣuṇī* should not pass the rainy season in a place where there are no *bhikṣus*; (8) When the rainy season is over, the *bhikṣuṇīs* should observe the ceremony of repentance of offenses before the two orders.

Some suggest that the eight rules purportedly laid down by the Buddha were not as a result of sexist discrimination, but were a precautionary measure to assure the smooth functioning of the male and female monastic communities. To establish orders of male and female celibates in close proximity to one another is a risky venture. Therefore, to guard against untoward consequences and to provide protection for the female order, the Buddha formulated the eight rules regulating the conduct and interaction of the *Bhikṣu* and *Bhikṣuṇī Sanghas.*

Three examples are given to illustrate the point that accepting women would render the order more vulnerable to attack and an untimely demise. The eight important rules were introduced as if to ward off such misfortune: "And just, Ānanda, as a man would in anticipation build an embankment to a great reservoir, beyond which the water should not overpass; just even so, Ānanda, have I in anticipation laid down these Eight Chief Rules for the Bhikkhunīs, their life long not to be overpassed." (*Vinaya Texts*, Part III, p. 326.)

3. Quoted from the article "Bhikkhuni Order" by D. Amarasiri, printed in the *Sunday Observer*, Sri Lanka, on July 8, 1984. A number of leading scholars, including Bhikkhu Khantipalo and Yuchi Kajiyama, regard the rules as being a later accretion. Akira Hirakawa, a leading scholar of *Vinaya* texts, states: "According to the *Bhikkunīkkhandaka*, when the Buddha, in response to Mahāprajāpatī Gotamī's request, allowed women to become *bhikkhunī*, he also set forth the eight gurudharmas. However, their contents indicate that they were actually formulated later." (*Monastic Discipline for the Buddhist Nuns*, p. 37.)

4. The five heinous crimes are patricide, matricide, killing an *arhat*, intentionally drawing blood from a Buddha, and causing a schism in the *Sangha*.

THE ROLE OF WOMEN IN BUDDHISM
by Dr. Chatsumarn Kabilsingh

Buddhism was the first religion in the world to establish a community of ordained women on the premise that women can achieve spiritual liberation on a par with men. In the present day, we tend to underestimate the significance of this achievement, but in India, at the time of the Buddha, society closely followed the law of Manu. Women were under the protection of their fathers when young, their husbands when married, and later, the protection of their sons. Women were regarded as possessions to be handed down under the dominance of men. The birth of sons became a religious and social obligation for women, failing which their husbands were entitled to take new wives. Women were not allowed to perform religious rituals on their own, but were dependent upon men in every sphere.

Within this social context, Buddhism opened up new horizons. Women under Buddhism were able to step out of their accustomed subjugation and began to fulfill their ideal roles, not only as wives and mothers, but also as propagators of the new religion on an equal footing with men. This social and spiritual advancement for women was ahead of its time, and hence drew many objections from men, including the monks. The Buddha was well aware of the controversy that could arise as a result of this liberal attitude toward women.

During the Buddha's lifetime, many women from all walks of life joined the order. Many of them were successful in learning the *Dhamma* and became eloquent teachers, counting ministers and kings among their listeners. Royal support has always been a key factor in the growth of religions, and we see that Buddhist nuns played a major role in inciting the faith of royal families as well as of ordinary people. Certain of the nuns who were outstanding in remembering past lives, in insight, in observing *Vinaya*, and in teaching, received special praise from the Buddha.

The role of ordained women was intended to be equivalent to that of monks. Acquiescing to prevailing social norms, the

Buddha put the nuns under the protection of the monks, as sisters to be protected by their elder brothers. Unfortunately, due to the Brahminical social backgrounds of the monks, history records numerous incidents where the nuns were treated more as subordinates or servants than as spiritual sisters. The nuns were made to do laundry and clean up after the monks to such an extent that they had no time for spiritual practice. When the Buddha was informed of this, he set down rules forbidding monks to take advantage of nuns. On one occasion, a young monk who was too lazy to go for alms took those of a nun 120 years old. After three days of providing him with her share, the elderly nun collapsed of hunger. When the Buddha came to know this, he set down a rule forbidding monks to take almsfood from nuns. As long as the Buddha was alive, he made provisions to protect the well-being of the nuns' community. He was concerned about the fact that nuns received less support from the laity. This is clearly shown in a rule which provided for the equal distribution of robes between the *Bhikkhu* and *Bhikkhunī Sanghas*. Yet, after the Buddha's passing, the order was guided by the community of monks.

Evidence of discrimination against nuns may be seen as early as the first council held three months after the Buddha's *parinibbāna*. The council consisted of five hundred enlightened monks; none of the many learned and enlightened nuns were invited. Among other censures, the Buddha's attendant and cousin Ānanda was blamed by the council for allowing nuns to pay respect to the body of the Buddha. Another criticism was that he mediated to effect the establishment of the order of nuns. Though he did not lodge a protest, Ānanda made it clear to the assembly that he did not consider these actions as faults. Nonetheless, it is apparent that some monks were not happy to have nuns existing by their side. Such a mentality still persists today in some quarters, despite the Buddha's egalitarian teachings.

The Order of Nuns

There are four groups of Buddhists mentioned by the Buddha as being responsible for the development of Buddhism: monks (*bhikkhus*), nuns (*bhikkhunīs*), laymen and laywomen. The community of nuns was established in India during the lifetime of the Buddha under the leadership of Queen Mahāpajāpatī. Inscriptions tell us that the order continued to exist until the invasion of the Turkish Muslims in the eleventh century. Both the *Bhikkhunī* and the *Bhikkhu Sanghas* disappeared in India after that time. In the third century B.C., during the time of King Ashoka, an order of nuns was established in Sri Lanka under royal patronage. A large number of Ceylonese women received *bhikkhunī* ordination from Indian *bhikkhunīs* and the order continued to exist until both *Bhikkhunī* and *Bhikkhu Sanghas* died out with the invasion of a south Indian ruler in 1017 A.D. The order of monks was soon revived, but not that of the nuns.

Prior to this time, in 434 A.D., Sri Lankan *bhikkhunīs* had established an order of nuns in China. Only this Chinese lineage has survived to the present day in China and Korea. When China went though years of suppression during the Cultural Revolution, certain nuns escaped and resettled in Taiwan, where they now constitute the largest stronghold of fully ordained Buddhist nuns. The monks who escaped, being obligated to the nuns for assisting them with their early establishment, are grateful and pay due respect to the community of nuns. This is the chain of events responsible for the success of the *Bhikkhunī Sangha* in Taiwan.

In other Buddhist countries, such as Burma, Thailand, Nepal, Laos, and Cambodia, it seems the *Bhikkhunī Sangha* has never existed. Yet, in every Buddhist country, Buddhist women have expressed their desire to lead the religious life and in each there developed a group of ordained women, even when they had no access to full ordination. In Nepal, they observe ten precepts, wear pink robes with a brown robe folded over the shoulder, and are called *anāgarikās*, similar to nuns of the Burmese tradition. In Cambodia and Thailand they wear white robes and observe ten and eight precepts, respectively. In Sri Lanka, they observe ten precepts, wear ochre robes much like the monks, and are called *dasasil mātās*. All these women have shaven heads, a sign of having left the family life. Among them, Sri Lankan nuns seem to receive the highest respect from society. Recently, the Sri Lankan government issued identity cards to them as a first step of formal recognition. There is also a movement to bring about the revival of the *bhikkhunī* order in Sri Lanka.

In countries where there is no *Bhikkhunī Sangha*, and hence, no lineage of full ordination for women, the nuns do not fit into any of the four groups of Buddhists mentioned earlier. Generally, they are not classified as *Sangha* members, nor are they laywomen in the full sense since they have left their homes to lead committed religious lives. In Thailand, they are not legally accepted as laypeople with voting privileges. At the same time they are not considered propagators of the *Dhamma* and, therefore, do not belong to the *Sangha* community. In short, they constitute an awkward minority. Theravādin Buddhists insist that the *bhikkhunī* lineage is now extinct, and that the *bhikkhunī* ordination can only be authorized if given by both the *bhikkhunī* and *bhikkhu* communities. They do not accept the Chinese *bhikkhunī* lineage, taking them to belong to the Mahāyāna. This objection is groundless, however, since the *Vinaya* school followed by the Chinese *Sangha* is the Dharmagupta, and the Sri Lanka chronicles clearly show that, among the eighteen *Vinaya* schools prevalent during King Ashoka's time (third century B.C.), the Dharmagupta is a subsect of the Theravādin school.

The status of Tibetan nuns is unique. Due to geographical factors, the *bhikkhunī* lineage has never existed, but the nuns have been able to receive ordination as female novices (*samanerī*). When China took over Tibet almost thirty years ago, one positive consequence was that as Tibetans spread out to different parts of the world, they took Buddhism with them. As a result many Westerners have accepted Buddhism, and those women who want to lead more committed lives have slowly begun to seek full ordination in Taiwan, Hong Kong, and Korea. In 1983, for the first time in Buddhist history, an ordination ceremony for nuns was given in the United States. The movements and activities of these Western Buddhist nuns will eventually have a great impact on the revival of the *bhikkhunī* order in the East.

Nuns in Thailand

The term *maeji* is used in Thailand to refer to ordained Buddhist women wearing white and observing five or eight precepts. These women may stay at home, in a small quarter of a temple (*wat*), or in a separate nunnery. No one knows exactly when or how they first appeared in Thai history. The earliest historical evidence to mention their existence is a letter by J. Schouten, written in 1639, which estimates that *maejis* were established some three hundred years earlier:

> Besides these priests, there are a sort of old nuns, lodged in Chapels near the greatest Temples, who assist very devoutly in all their preachings, singings, ceremonies, and other church services, but all voluntarily, being tied to no rules or prescriptions.[1]

During King Narai's reign, according to the *Kingdom of Siam* by Monsieur de la Loubere, a French envoy who visited Thailand in the years 1687-1688 noticed "*nang tchii*," most of them elderly, who wore white and lived in a separate section of the *wat*. Again, during King Phaetraja's reign, Kaempfer, a German physician noted "*nang chi*" who wore white robes and not yellow ones like the monks. They observed precepts and pursued religious practice in the *wat*.[2]

Nicolas Servese, who visited Thailand during the Ayudhya period, reported that women who became *maejis* must be over fifty years old and that they mainly worked for the monks, helped with cooking, and so on. When they received an invitation to say prayers at a funeral ceremony, they would go in rows and would receive many offerings. It would seem that *maejis* during the Ayudhya period received more respect from society than today.

At present there are approximately ten thousand *maejis* in Thailand. Their status is indeterminate, and they are generally required to support themselves financially. Recently a movement has begun to help improve conditions for them. An Institute for Thai Maejis has been founded under the patronage of Her Majesty. An associated foundation is responsible for the budget and for various projects which the institute carries out. Projects include educational promotion, *Dhamma* propagation, social services, and development of both practice and administration. The institute is a center to unite all those ordained Buddhist women wearing white robes and holding eight precepts who study and practice with the approval of the Thai *Bhikkhu Sangha*. There are currently some 518 nunneries in 47 provinces and 4158 *maejis* registered with the institute. Members prefer to stay in their own nunneries separate from the *wats* and wear a standard pattern of robes. This is a break from the past where *maejis* only stayed in the *wats* and often became subservient to the monks. As yet, the institute has not been able to adequately represent the needs of *maejis* since it is under the guidance of the *Bhikkhu Sangha*. Recently, some *maejis* have been helping at refugee camps and others have begun teaching courses on basic Buddhism and crafts in the villages, but a serious handicap is the fact that they themselves are not highly educated and, hence, are unable to take on more responsibility. A few have successfully completed the highest available standard in Pāli and have proceeded for higher education abroad, but their numbers are very small and their influence is yet to be felt in society.

Whereas *bhikkhunīs* in the Theravādin tradition would hold 311 precepts, a *maeji* holds only eight and has no ordination lineage. Their standards of education are very low: only forty percent have completed the required seven years of primary school and only seven percent have completed ten years. Eighty percent of them come from farming backgrounds, and the majority became *maejis* to escape worldly problems. Only twenty percent express an interest in social service work. In most cases, they are dependent upon relatives for their livelihood, and elderly ones often find it necessary to beg for their sustenance, which further degrades the status of *maejis*. The Institute for Thai Maejis is attempting to cope with these problems.

In actuality, *maejis* find no place in the religious structure of the country. The Department of Religious Affairs does not seem to heed their problems since they are classified neither as being "ordained" into the *Sangha* nor as "propagators." At best, they are considered "residents" of the *wats*, though they are not entitled to any privileges. *Maejis* are not accepted in society and are unwelcome in certain temples where abbots consider them petty and troublesome. Sometimes it seems to be a policy to ignore them altogether. The *maejis*, lacking proper education and a broad social outlook, generally do not recognize or concern themselves about the injustices they experience. Their limited interpretation of Buddhism as a private spiritual goal tends to reinforce their isolated position and to mitigate against both their further personal and social development. In the opinion of Pra Udorn-khanapirak, an active senior monk, until they broaden their perspective and take a more responsible role in society, society can hardly be blamed for devaluing them.

Many ordained women, dissatisfied with the status of *maejis*, have attempted to break away from this traditional religious lifestyle. In 1957, five women were ordained with ten precepts, like male novices, and began to wear brown robes. They are known as *sīlacārinī*, and their center is at Wat Chanasonggram in Bangkok. In 1981, they started a separate nunnery at Chorake-bua in Bangkapi district. Another group also wears dark brown robes and trains under the guidance of Bhodiraksa, a self-ordained monk. This group draws a good number of followers who practice lives of restraint. In yet another temple, Ven. Voramai Kabilsingh began as a *maeji*, but wore a light yellow robe. She received full ordination in Taiwan, becoming the only Thai *bhikkhunī*. Her temple, Wat Songdharmakalyani, is situated in Nakhonpathom, south of Bangkok. The temple is well supported by private donors, but does not have many ordained women.

Looking into the future, is it too unrealistic to hope that these ordained Buddhist women could be better cared for? In return they could become educated and channelled to lead more fruitful lives for the benefit of society as a whole. The problems of this Buddhist minority stem from social attitudes in general and the mentality of the *Bhikkhu Sangha* in particular. Some changes may be expected from the younger generation of monks who are better educated and more liberal-minded than their elders.

Some of the leading monks have been suggesting that the *Bhikkhunī Sangha* is something very idealized, applicable to the Buddha's age, but something that does not fit into society any more. Some of these monks suggest that we form some kind of religious group for Buddhist women. But I disagree, saying that the *Bhikkhunī Sangha* is something granted by the Lord Buddha himself. The rights of women to full ordination should note be denied. Some say that a *bhikkhunī* has so many rules to follow that it is impossible to follow them in the present day. I reject this view also. If the monks can still uphold the *Vinaya*, so can the nuns. There are no good excuses for not having a *Bhikkhunī Sangha*.

The Future of the Bhikkhuni Sangha

Until now, Buddhist women have been playing the expected roles of supporter and practitioner; now they aspire to serve as propagators and teachers of the *Dhamma* as they strive toward their spiritual ideals. Such a prospect may cause trepidation in the minds of many monks. Preaching the *Dhamma* and performing all the rituals has been the prerogative of monks for centuries. Walls of religious belief, social sanctions, and traditional taboos have conspired against the participation of women in these activities. It is time to be broadminded, to perceive the genuine religious need and commitment on the part of Buddhist women, and to open the door for capable women to benefit human society.

People often ask me why I am so involved with the nuns' issue, when I am not a nun. The reason is that I see Buddhist nuns as a reflection of the spirituality of Buddhist women. I see the two in harmony—nuns as the spiritual reflection and the laywomen supporting their development. If we neglect the nuns, our society will be unbalanced and unhealthy. This is one of the many reasons that gives me strength to work on the issue of Buddhist nuns and to help them in any way I can to establish an order of fully ordained nuns.

In the last two decades in many countries, we have begun to find Buddhist nuns in yellow robes springing up here and there. It is an auspicious visualization. Buddhist women are now more ready than ever for spiritual growth. And because they are so few in number, we have to help them to maintain their good qualities. We have to help them to strengthen themselves spiritually, financially, and in every possible way. I see these nuns as catalysts for the foundation of Buddhist women's spirituality.

I feel that the nuns during this formative stage are so few in number that the individual voice is not heard. Even if one *bhikkhunī* is doing something in Thailand, another is doing something in West Germany or Sweden, their voices will not be heard if they remain isolated. Once we come together and develop some unity, once we gain strength and power, then we do some bargaining.

To do these things, we need to have self-confidence. And to have self-confidence, we have to have a certain economic, educational, and social background, as well as reputation and spiritual development. The best possible thing we can do now is to give the nuns education. What I envision is a *Bhikkhunī Sangha* of educated, capable women. The life of a *bhikkhunī* is serious and very committed; it is not advisable for just any woman. *Bhikkhunīs* must have a good Buddhist education and be able to give *Dharma* talks or meditation instruction whenever requested. They should also be able to do counseling, because that is what the laypeople expect of them. The laypeople come to the *Sangha* members with all sorts of problems to seek their advice. A nun cannot simply stand by the altar. She has to understand social problems and give the people guidance.

Professor Richard Gard, a leading Buddhist scholar, said that it is important for nuns to be able to address an audience, to speak up in large gatherings, to hold conferences and seminars. This harks back to the problem that is of special interest to Tibetan nuns, namely, education. The need for education is apparent in every country. Unless one is educated, it is impossible address people at eye-level. Therefore, I think that we need to set certain requirements for those who are interested in receiving *bhikkhunī* ordination. At least in Thailand, people in society are very well educated these days. We cannot have a nun who has only completed grade four addressing a gathering, because the laypeople will know much more than the nun. In China, a requirement has been instituted the last few years that those who seek *bhikkhunī* ordination should have at least a high school education. Of course, some may object that there was no such requirement during the Buddha's time, but that was more than two thousand years ago. At that time, anyone could join the order. Now times have changed so much, and we have to keep abreast of society—not to be with them, but to lead them. To lead them spiritually, we have to maintain certain standards.

At this crucial point of forming an international *Bhikkhunī Sangha*, we badly need unity. Whether we are Nepali, Tibetan, Chinese, or whatever, we must leave our differences behind. Right now we need to stand united, so we must seek unity within the differences. We have to leave our I/me/mine behind and work together. The establishment of the *Bhikkhunī Sangha* portends the spiritual growth of Buddhist women in general. Our aim is to benefit in practical, as well as spiritual ways. Therefore, we must help the nuns on their way, so that the whole community can be guided on the right path.

I feel that there is great strength in a coalition between Buddhist laypeople and the ordained *Sangha*. To strengthen the *Sangha* community, we need cooperation and support from the lay community as well. By working together constructively, we can gain strength and inspiration from each other. In this way, I am sure that our aim of an international *Bhikkhunī Sangha* can become a reality.

Let the door be opened so that the four groups of Buddhist may be complete, so that the spirit of equality prevails. Give women the place to which they are entitled. What authority do we have to obstruct the growth of women as a spiritual community, a privilege granted to them by the Buddha himself?

NOTES

1. Quoted by P. Suwanbubbha in her thesis, "A Comparative Study of the Status and Roles of Theravāda Buddhist and Roman Catholic Nuns in the Community in Bangkok," p. 85.

2. Quoted by Prakhong Singhanart-nitirak, M.A. Thesis, "Roles of Maejis in Social Development," Faculty of Social Welfare, Thammasat University, 1973, p. 42.

PROSPECTS FOR AN INTERNATIONAL BHIKṢUṆĪ SANGHA

by Bhikṣuṇī Karma Lekshe Tsomo

The *Sangha* is very important as a basis for the preservation and spread of the *Dharma*. The *Buddhadharma* cannot truly be said to be established in a country until there is a strong ordained community. As a Westerner, I am very interested in seeing that the *Dharma* is established properly in Western countries, and for this a strong *Sangha* is essential.

In Western countries where women are working to gain equal rights in many new fields, it is important that the *Dharma* be established in a way that gives equal rights for women and for men. These rights should include equal opportunities for higher ordination. We can see that women within the Roman Catholic church are engaged in a valiant effort to gain full ordination for women. Buddhists can avoid such a crisis by establishing Buddhism in Western countries with a community of fully ordained *bhikṣuṇīs* as well as a community of fully ordained *bhikṣus* from the very beginning.

Full ordination is equally as important for Asian nuns as for Western nuns. In view of the fact that nuns in certain Buddhist countries currently occupy a peripheral position without the opportunity to receive a fully recognized ordination, we are in a situation of having to make a case for the benefits that would accrue, both to society and to the *Dharma*, from having fully ordained nuns. We need to proceed extremely carefully in working to attain our goal of instituting the *Bhikṣuṇī Sangha* in these countries. To demand recognition or to protest for *bhikṣuṇī* ordination before the established *Bhikṣu Sanghas* are convinced of its validity and value is futile and will damage our cause by stimulating hostile reactions. We need to study the *Vinaya* and clearly understand the facts of the matter, taking into consideration the views of conservative elements within each tradition. Proceeding properly along these lines, we will gain credibility for the *bhikṣuṇī* lineage and acceptance from the established *bhikṣu* orders.

The *Bhikṣuṇī Sangha*, the community of fully ordained nuns, was instituted in India by the Buddha in the sixth century B.C. and seems to have continued in that country until at least the tenth century A.D. The lineage was transmitted from India to Sri Lanka in the third century B.C. and survived there until the eleventh century A.D. From Sri Lanka, *bhikṣuṇīs* traveled to China in the fifth century A.D., where they established a *bhikṣuṇī* order that has existed until the present day. From China, the lineage was transmitted to Korea and Vietnam. Today *Bhikṣuṇī Sanghas* exist in the Chinese, Korean, and Vietnamese traditions, but not in the Japanese, Tibetan, or Theravādin traditions. The validity of the existing *bhikṣuṇī* lineages is questioned by many *bhikṣus* of the Theravādin tradition, who in fact question the validity of the *bhikṣu* lineages of these Mahāyāna countries as well.

Gaining an Understanding of the Bhikṣuṇī Issue

It is helpful first to clarify the different levels of ordination available to Buddhist *Sangha* members. A *śrāmaṇerikā* is a novice nun and a *śrāmaṇera* is a novice monk. Both *śrāmaṇerikās* and *śrāmaṇeras* receive the ten precepts of a novice.[1] Before receiving the full ordination of a *bhikṣuṇī*, a *śrāmaṇerikā* is required to receive an interim ordination as a probationary nun, called *śikṣamāṇā*, and to maintain these precepts for two years. The exact nature and number of the *śikṣamāṇā* precepts differ among the various *Vinaya* schools,[2] but the *śikṣamāṇā* ordination basically represents a training period in preparation for full ordination. It is not required for monks.

We should understand the history and reasoning behind this *śikṣamāṇā* ordination. At the time of the Buddha, some young nuns left the household life to enter monastic life and immediately took *bhikṣuṇī* precepts. It happened that some of them were pregnant before they took *bhikṣuṇī* precepts. Although their conduct was pure after they entered the nun's life, they became noticeably pregnant after taking vows. This led to misunderstandings by the lay community, as it certainly was not appropriate for a celibate *bhikṣuṇī* to be pregnant. Therefore, the Buddha prescribed an ample two-year waiting period for nuns to avoid such misunderstandings. Instituting the *śikṣamāṇā* ordination was not a discriminatory move but simply a matter of practicality.

Although novice monks and nuns take the same number of precepts, there is a difference in the numbers of precepts taken by *bhikṣus* and *bhikṣuṇīs*[3] and also a difference in the procedure for full ordination. For *bhikṣuṇīs*, there is a requirement of dual ordination. While the history behind this requirement is unclear, the *Vinaya* texts indicate that, after having maintained the *śikṣamānā* precepts for two years, a candidate for *bhikṣuṇī* ordination should receive ordination from *bhikṣuṇīs* first and have the ordination confirmed in a ceremony with *bhikṣus* later on the same day. This procedure requires ordination by a full complement of ten *bhikṣuṇīs*[4] and again by a full complement of ten *bhikṣus*. The method for conducting the ordination is clearly set forth in the *Bhikṣuṇī Karman*, the text which explains the "actions"—meaning the procedures governing confession, ordination, and so forth. Once this procedure has been carried out under the supervision of twenty qualified *bhikṣus* and *bhikṣuṇīs*,[5] the ordination has been properly received and a person is considered a member of the *Sangha* community.

Under ideal circumstances,[6] an ordination of *bhikṣus* should be conferred by a full complement of ten *bhikṣus*. There is a provision that five *bhikṣu* masters may give *bhikṣu* ordination in a remote area, and some say even four in an extreme instance, but never less than four. A *bhikṣus* ordination conducted by three *bhikṣu* masters would be considered questionable in any Buddhist country. We should be clear about the correct procedure: where conditions allow, a proper *bhikṣu* ordination requires an assemblage of ten *bhikṣu* ordination masters. A full complement of ten *bhikṣu* and ten *bhikṣuṇī* ordination masters is required to properly administer the *bhikṣuṇī* ordination. The minimum number for a *bhikṣuṇī* ordination in an outlying area would be five *bhikṣus* and five *bhikṣuṇīs*.[7]

In some countries where there are no *bhikṣuṇīs*, there are also no *śrāmaṇerikās*. For example, in Sri Lanka, Thailand and Burma, women may receive eight or ten precepts and live as nuns, but they are not called *śrāmaṇerikās*. In these countries it is felt that *bhikṣuṇīs* are required in order to give *śrāmaṇerikā* ordination; since there are no *bhikṣuṇīs* to administer the *śrāmaṇerikā* ordination, it is not given. The necessity of having a female preceptor indicates that women are meant to train under women teachers. In the *Vinaya* texts, it is *bhikṣuṇī* masters who serve as instructors for women and who confer the *śrāmaṇerikā*, *śikṣamāṇā* and *bhikṣuṇī* ordinations. In the Mahāyāna countries of China, Korea, and Tibet, however, it is felt that a master may legitimately give the *śrāmaṇerikā* ordination, since the ten precepts received by *śrāmaṇerikās* and *śrāmaṇeras* are the same.

Although modes of practice and interpretation of doctrine may differ between the Theravāda and Mahāyāna traditions, the *Vinaya* texts they follow vary only slightly. Originally the Buddha laid down rules of training as necessitated by cases of misbehavior by individual monks and nuns. These cases became precedents for determing proper and improper conduct for the *Sangha*. After the Buddha passed away, eighteen schools arose as a result of varying interpretations of doctrine and discipline. The variances on points of discipline, however, are relatively minor. In any case, the Mūlasarvāstivāda school followed by the Tibetans and the Dharmagupta school followed by the Chinese, Koreans, and Vietnamese are both generally considered to be offshoots of the original Theravāda, which is the school still followed in Burma, Sri Lanka, and Thailand today. In terms of *Vinaya*, these schools are very closely related.

Since the introduction of Buddhism in Tibet in the eighth century, there was never a sufficient number of qualified *bhikṣuṇī* masters to conduct an ordination, so there has never been an officially recognized *Bhikṣuṇī Sangha* in Tibet. There are references to *bhikṣuṇīs* in Tibetan historical documents, but their nationality and the circumstances under which they were ordained are unclear. Whether these ordinations were given by *bhikṣus* alone or whether they may have included Chinese *bhikṣuṇī* ordination masters is a matter of speculation, but it is known that the validity of such ordinations was disputed and that an officially recognized *bhikṣuṇī* lineage was never established in Tibet.

Although there is no evidence that the *bhikṣuṇī* lineage was ever transmitted to Tibet from India, the relevant texts of the Mūlasarvāstivādin school of *Vinaya* for *bhikṣuṇīs* were translated from Sanskrit into Tibetan language and are included in the Tibetan canon (*Kangyur*). As mentioned previously, in the Tibetan tradition it is considered valid for a *bhikṣu* to give *śrāmaṇerikā* ordination. There have been large numbers of *śrāmaṇerikās* living in nunneries throughout Tibet until recent times. Tibetan masters do not feel that it is proper for *bhikṣus* alone to give *bhikṣuṇī* ordination, however, since the *Vinaya* explicitly states that the ordination is to be conducted by both *Sanghas*.

When I was ordained as a *śrāmaṇerikā* in France in 1977, I was unaware that no full ordination existed for women in the Tibetan tradition. One of my teachers was Ven. Khechok Palmo, an English *bhikṣuṇī* who founded the community of nuns in Dalhousie which later shifted to Tilokpur. She had been ordained as a *bhikṣuṇī* in Hong Kong with the permission of her teacher, H. H. Gyalwa Karmapa, so I had assumed that the *bhikṣuṇī* precepts were available to nuns in the Tibetan tradition. Only later did I discover that this was not the case.

In 1980, I started to take an active interest in the subject and began collecting research materials on the topics of *bhikṣuṇī* lineage and ordination. In the United States I searched for such library materials as the *Vinaya* translations of the Pāli Text Society, and then traveled to Korea and Taiwan to gather further information. In the process, I found that masters of the different traditions, namely, the Korean, the Chinese, the Tibetan, and the Theravādin, have slightly different views on the subject.

To understand the *bhikṣuṇī* issue properly, we need to know not only how many precepts each tradition has and how the precepts are enumerated, but also how they are to be interpreted. Furthermore, we need to investigate the procedures for ordination as well as the very concept and nature of precepts. By thoroughly understanding the views within each of the various traditions on *Vinaya* issues, we will learn how we can most effectively work for the institution of the Bhikṣuṇī *Sangha* in each of the Buddhist countries where the order has either died out or has never existed.

Gaining Acceptance for the Bhikṣuṇī Lineage

There has been a reluctance among some *bhikṣus* to recognize as valid the *bhikṣuṇī* ordinations currently available in the lineages existent in Korea, Hong Kong, Taiwan, and Vietnam. Some people, especially Westerners, feel that if such reluctance continues, women should act independently to form their own order of fully ordained nuns. I personally feel that this would be a tremendous mistake. The traditions of the Buddhadharma are more than 2,500 years old. The *Vinaya* is an integral part of the *Tripitaka*, of the *Dharma* in which we take refuge. We cannot simply dispense with the *Vinaya* to suit our own convenience. It is certainly no easy task to work to gain recognition for the *bhikṣuṇīs* lineage, to study the *Vinaya*, and to do the necessary research, but in my opinion this is the only way to proceed if we wish to gain acceptance of the lineage from all sides.

In the Chinese tradition, there is no problem of recognition. There is a huge *Bhikṣuṇī Sangha* in Taiwan and in Hong Kong. Even on the mainland of China, there are still large numbers of fully ordained nuns, as well as in all the overseas Chinese communities such as Singapore, the Philippines, Indonesia, the United States, and all the other Western countries that have a sizeable Chinese population. In Korea and Vietnam, there are also *bhikṣuṇī* lineages that have existed for hundreds and hundreds of years. There is no question of gaining acceptance for these lineages, since they are already fully accepted within their own traditions.

In those areas where the Tibetan form of Buddhism is practiced, although there has been no *bhikṣuṇī* lineage in the past, there is an understanding that a strong female *Sangha* is an asset to the *Dharma*. Only in Mongolia has there never been an order of nuns. His Holiness the Dalai Lama has expressed his feeling that it would be very beneficial to have fully ordained nuns working for the *Dharma*. He has given permission for a number of nuns to travel to Taiwan and Hong Kong to receive *bhikṣuṇī* ordination. He has stated, however, that he as an individual does not have the authority to speak on behalf of a council of Tibetan *bhikṣus*. His permission for nuns to receive the ordination does not constitute official recognition of the *bhikṣuṇī* lineage, but he seems to be confident that in time *bhikṣuṇīs* will naturally gain wide social acceptance.

From the Tibetan point of view, it would be convenient if there were an existent *bhikṣuṇī* lineage of the Mūlasarvāstivādin school, since then the *Bhikṣu and Bhikṣuṇī Sanghas*, ordained in the same school of *Vinaya*, would be able to perform the ceremonies for ordination, confession, and rainy season retreat together. If its unbroken continuity could be documented and, in addition, the procedures of *śikṣamāṇā* ordination and dual *bhikṣuṇī* ordination were observed, such a lineage would readily gain the approval of *Vinaya* masters. Even in the absence of a *bhikṣuṇī* lineage of the Mūlasarvāstivādin school, however, a valid lineage of another school is likely to gain acceptance among Tibetans. The ultimate intention of the Mahāyāna system ascribed to by Tibetans is to benefit beings. Since the *Bhikṣuṇī Sangha* will bring benefit to society, its institution is not expected to meet stiff opposition; in fact, it will be heartily applauded by many.

The question of gaining acceptance in the Theravādin countries is considerably more difficult. *Bhikṣus* in these countries feel that for an ordination to be considered valid, *bhikṣuṇīs* must be ordained by a full complement of *bhikṣus* and *bhikṣuṇīs*, but the Theravādin *bhikṣuṇī* order died out around the eleventh century and many Theravādins do not recognize the *bhik-*

ṣuṇī lineages that exist in the Mahāyāna countries. Nevertheless, a very good case can be made for the introduction of the *bhikṣuṇī* lineage from China, since that lineage was originally transmitted to China from Sri Lanka, a Theravādin country, in the first place.

It is important to keep in mind the fact that the Buddha did not teach or advocate different schools of *Vinaya*. The eighteen schools, with their varying enumerations of the precepts, evolved long after his *parinirvāna*. The Buddha intended for monks and nuns to follow disciplined behavior and to train in mindfulness in every action; each rule was formulated as the result of some incident of inappropriate conduct. In setting forth such regulations, he meant to guide the conduct of the celibate communities positively to assure harmony within the order as well as between ordained practitioners and the laity. It was surely not the Buddha's intention to divide the *Sangha* along sectarian lines.

When we compare the *Vinaya* texts of the various schools, we see that the numbers and categorization of the precepts differ somewhat, but that the essential points and spirit of the precepts are identical. Different schools with their variant interpretations of both doctrine and discipline grew up in the early centuries of Buddhist development, however, and the *Vinaya* lineages that are extant today follow one or another of the scriptural traditions embodied in surviving texts.

It is incumbent upon an ordained person to recite and to uphold those precepts which she or he has received in the process of a valid ordination ceremony. Therefore, for example, a *bhikṣu* ordained in the Theravādin tradition receives and keeps the 227 precepts enumerated in the Pāli *Bhikṣu Prāṭimokśa Sūtra* and not the 253 precepts of the Mūlasarvāstivādin tradition which are received and maintained by a Tibetan *bhikṣu*. A Chinese or Korean *bhikṣuṇī* recites and uphold the 348 precepts which she receives in an ordination of the Dharmagupta tradition rather than the 311 precepts included in the *Bhikṣuṇī Prāṭimokśa Sūtra* of the Pāli canon. Thus, maintaining the purity of these *Vinaya* lineages should not be construed as sectarianism, but simply as a matter of upholding and transmitting those precepts which one has received. The alternatives, either of mixing the schools and therefore having to study, recite, and keep the precepts of all the schools, or of ignoring the precepts altogether, are impractical and incorrect.

It is actually ideal that the *bhikṣuṇīs* ordained in China, Hong Kong, Taiwan, Korea, and Vietnam all belong to the same lineage and follow the same school of *Vinaya*—the Dharmagupta. This can be a great unifying force. Once nuns have received full ordination either in Taiwan, Hong Kong, or Korea, we will all follow the Dharmagupta *Vinaya* texts and will be able to do confession, ordination, and other ceremonies together, regardless of nationality or the tradition of meditation practice each may follow. Since the Dharmagupta is historically considered a branch of the early Theravāda school, it is hoped that the Theravādin countries will eventually institute kindred *bhikṣuṇī* orders.

Recently a complete *Sangha* of ten *bhikṣuṇīs* (including myself) from Canada, Taiwan, the United States, and West Germany, gathered in Bodhgaya on the full moon to perform the bimonthly confession of faults and the reading of the *Bhikṣuṇī Prāṭimokśa Sūtra*. Since the *bhikṣuṇī* order is thought to have died out in India in roughly the tenth century, this ceremony would constitute the first *uposatha* ceremony of a full *Bhikṣuṇī Sangha* held in that country in about a thousand years. The senior-most *bhikṣuṇī* read the *Prāṭimokśa Sūtra* of the Dharmagupta school, which we all followed in English. Since *bhikṣuṇīs* from different countries and traditions are united in their practice of the same *Vinaya* precepts, they will be able to perform all *Vinaya* procedures together and there will never be any of the difficulties arising from belonging to different schools. The *Bhikṣuṇī Sanghas* in the various countries will essentially belong to the same order, which will foster an international unity among Buddhist nuns.

Meanwhile, until related *Vinaya* issues have been thoroughly investigated and the *bhikṣuṇī* lineage has been firmly established where it does not as yet exist, it is important for us to exert effort in the study of the texts, train conscientiously in the precepts, and maintain impeccable standards of discipline. At the moment, until an international *Bhikṣuṇī Sangha* becomes a reality, we stand a bit outside the fold of the organized Buddhist hierarchy, and need to be mindful of both our speech and behavior to present our case in the most favorable light.

Receiving Ordination

When considering full ordination, one should understand that in the Chinese and Korean traditions it is a lifetime commitment for *bhikṣuṇīs* and *bhikṣus* alike, involving strict vegetarianism. It is regarded as very unfortunate to give back the precepts, much less to break them. So people should be very clear in their motivation and determination to keep the precepts for life, or not even think about going to Taiwan, Hong Kong, or Korea for ordination. If some nuns should fail to take the commitments seriously, it will reflect badly on the *bhikṣuṇī* order as a whole.

The discipline for *Sangha* members in these countries is extremely strict. The proper mode of walking, way of talking, and other forms of behavior are very carefully observed. We need to set up institutes in the West for training in discipline and preparing people to receive *bhikṣuṇī* ordination. Since we do not have such institutes yet, candidates should plan to go to Taiwan, Hong Kong, or Korea for some months before the ordination ceremony to become accustomed to the environment and to get preparatory training. If this is not possible, they should plan to stay on for some time afterwards to receive further training. In this way, the ordination will not only be more meaningful for the individual, but it will also help to gain credibility for foreign nuns who come to take higher ordination. If the nuns who come from various countries are well-disciplined, others will be welcomed in the future.

More important than having large numbers of *bhikṣuṇīs* is having good *bhikṣuṇīs*. Those considering *bhikṣuṇī* ordination should be aware that one becomes an example of a fully ordained being and a representative of the *Sangha*. This means putting certain constraints on one's accustomed behavior. Full ordination is a great responsibility for each individual reflecting on the whole *Sangha* community. It is of very questionable value to take ordination and just carry on as one did before. The excellent training afforded by an extensive ordination ceremony will help set high standards of discipline for *bhikṣuṇīs* everywhere.

In Hong Kong, it is possible to receive ordination in a five-day ceremony which is held every year. In truth, the precepts are transmitted, but the training is so brief that I do not recommend this ordination to people. I recommend either the full month of training given in Taiwan each year or the extensive ordination ceremony which is given in Hong Kong every three years. This is the ordination that a group of four Tibetan nuns received at Po Lin Temple in Hong Kong in 1984. They participated in a forty-five day *bhikṣuṇī* ordination and they are the first nuns that we know of in Tibetan history to do so. Another group of four nuns, from India, Bhutan, and Sikkim, received the precepts in a similar extensive ordination ceremony at Po Lin Temple in 1987. An extensive ordination is scheduled to be held at Hsi Lai Temple in Los Angeles in November, 1988. This will be the first time that a dual ordination ceremony is held in the United States.

As the *Bhikṣuṇī Sangha* grows, *Vinaya* studies become increasingly important. It is not sufficient just to receive the precepts. We have to know what the precepts mean and all the nuances—the spirit of the precepts as well as the letter. Everyone who has taken ordination or is considering doing so should be encouraged to begin studying those *Vinaya* texts which are already available in English. The *bhikṣus* will always be checking the depth of our understanding about the ordination we have taken, so it is important for us to have a thorough knowledge of the *Bhikṣuṇī Vinaya*. We need to begin investigating the *Vinaya* texts and commentaries in all languages. These texts are very instructive, carefully defining and explaining the various precepts, telling how they were established and showing how they are meant to be kept. There is also a great need for us to begin translating *Vinaya* texts into English from Pāli, Tibetan, and Chinese. We should begin this significant task straightaway.

It is my sincere hope that those who are truly dedicated and truly qualified will gradually go to receive the ordination, train diligently, uphold the precepts carefully, and that united we can develop an exemplary international *Bhikṣuṇī Sangha*.

Making a Case for the Full Ordination of Women

Any tradition would face difficulties surviving intact throughout a span of 2,500 years. In a male-dominated society, an institution comprised solely of women would necessarily experience particular difficulties. The requirement of dual ordination (that is, by both *Bhikṣuṇī* and *Bhikṣu Sanghas*) has made the possibility of full ordination for nuns at least twice as difficult as full ordination for monks. Women, as second-ranking members of the monastic community, often lacked the economic self-sufficiency and social mobility required to undertake the long and often arduous journey to the site of the ordination, particularly if it were in another country. The *bhikṣuṇī* order was thus in a precarious position, and has survived against great odds. Even the existence of the *bhikṣu* order has been threatened any number of times in history. The stipulation of dual ordination for *bhikṣuṇīs* has diminished the chances of survival of the *bhikṣuṇī* order, and thus the continuation of the *bhikṣuṇī* lineage, still further.

There are different views on what constitutes a valid *bhikṣuṇī* ordination. In the Chinese and Korean traditions, ordinations conducted by *bhikṣus* alone are usually considered valid, since *bhikṣus* are considered the ultimate authorities responsible for confirmation of *bhikṣuṇī* ordinations. The *Bhikṣuṇī Prātimokśa Sūtra* makes it clear that it is a transgression for a *bhikṣuṇī* to conduct the *bhikṣuṇī* ordination alone, without prior permission and subsequent confirmation by the *Bhikṣu Sangha*. There is no specific mention of the reverse—ordination by *bhikṣus* alone—being invalid or constituting a transgression. The major difference in the viewpoints of the various traditions regarding full ordination for women is that the ordination of *bhikṣuṇīs* by *bhikṣus* only is currently considered valid by masters of both the Korean and Chinese traditions, while neither the Tibetan nor Theravādin monastic establishments consider such an ordination fully legitimate.

It can be historically documented that the *bhikṣuṇī* order was originally established by a *bhikṣu* alone, in that Queen Mahāprajāpatī and her retinue of five hundred noblewomen were ordained by the Buddha himself. This constitutes a precedent for a valid *bhikṣuṇī* ordination conducted without the presence of ordaining *bhikṣuṇī* masters. This precedent was cited in the fourth century by the master Gunavarman of Kashmir who was an eminent teacher during the early days of the transmission of the *Dharma* to China. He said, "At places where the conditions are complete, one must do things according to prescriptions.... It is an offense if *bhikṣuṇīs* do not receive their full ordination from both a preceptor and preceptress at a place where the *Bhikṣuṇī Sangha* exists." However, "If the two orders of the *Sangha* are not found in one country at the same time, female applicants might receive their full ordination from the order of *bhikṣus* alone and it would be considered legitimate."

There is evidence for this viewpoint to be found in *Cullavagga X* of the Pāli canon: "Then the Lord on this occasion, having given reasoned talk, addressed the monks saying, 'I allow, monks, nuns to be ordained by monks.' " Later in the same section we find: " 'I allow you, monks, to ordain through a messenger who is an experienced, competent nun.' " From these quotations, it would appear that under certain circumstances, ordination of *bhikṣuṇīs* by *bhikṣus* alone was sanctioned.

Strictly speaking, the ideal procedure according to the traditional texts is for *bhikṣuṇīs* to be ordained by both *bhikṣuṇīs* and *bhikṣus*. Since many social factors mitigate against the availability of an assemblage of ten *bhikṣuṇīs*, however, the traditional procedure is not always possible or practical. The actual fact is that worldwide some 15,000 or more *bhikṣuṇīs* today have received ordination solely from *bhikṣus*. Unfortunately, some opponents of full ordination for women have taken the variance in ordination procedures as an opportunity to deny the rightful position of nuns in the religious hierarchy.

Naturally, it is important for the *Sangha* to follow the procedures set down in the *Karman* and related *Vinaya* texts to the best of their abilities. It is also true, however, that the Buddha intended his guidelines to accord with time and conditions. After two and a half millennia of historical, social, and cultural development, it is clear that certain procedures and advice detailed in the *Vinaya* texts must be adapted so as to be practicable in the variant climates and conditions of the diverse lands to which the Buddhist teachings have spread. With today's complex social organization and the more involved lifestyle of modern times, it would be difficult to observe to the letter all the minutely detailed instructions of the *Vinaya* relating to the rainy season retreat, the drawing of boundaries, confession, and so on. It is doubtful if any *Sangha* community today could be considered absolutely flawless in their practice of the technicalities when compared with the original prescriptions set forth so many years ago.

A case in point is the bimonthly practice of confessing faults and reading the *Prāṭimokśa Sūtra*. In some temples and traditions, this prescribed practice has lapsed altogether. In others, a variation of the ceremony has gradually evolved; many prayers are recited during the confession service which are not mentioned in the Karman, while certain prescribed and significant recitations are lacking, notably the reading of the *Prāṭimokśa Sūtra* which is precisely the primary reason for the gathering. Sometimes a shortened version of the *Prāṭimokśa Sūtra* is read. Although some scholars defend such an abbreviated reading, in the texts abbreviation is only sanctioned under ten extenuating circumstances, such as fire, theft, insanity, and so forth.

The other primary reason for gathering at the confession ceremony is to confess one's transgressions of the precepts publicly before the assembled community. When precepts have been transgressed, they should be confessed verbally in the assembly and purified by the appropriate procedure prescribed for that particular category of transgression. If a *pārājika* (root downfall) has been committed, for example, the offender is to be immediately expelled from the *Sangha*. For lesser transgressions, other procedures are prescribed. Strangely, no one interviewed in any of several different traditions had ever witnessed such a confession in the assembly. Can it then be assumed that no member of the community has ever committed a fault?

While each tradition may do its best to observe the instructions of the *Vinaya*, lapses and irregularities do occur in actual practice. If flaws in the observance of procedures are not cited to discount, much less invalidate, the *bhikṣu* lineage, neither should variations in procedure serve as a grounds to invalidate the *bhikṣuṇī* lineage. Not only would this be illogical, but in the modern age in which we live, it would be seen as an example of sexual discrimination.

Points of View

The views of *Vinaya* masters of the Chinese and Korean traditions regarding the concept of transmission deserve to be taken into consideration. Masters of these traditions accept the concept of mind-to-mind transmission from master to disciple, particularly in the Zen (Chinese *Ch'an*, Korean *Soen*) school, but deny that such a concept is applicable in the case of *prāṭimokśa* ordinations. Their interpretation of the idea of transmission is similar to the type of mind-to-mind transmission that may occur during *tantric* empowerment. The difference is that a Zen master normally passes a lineage to only one disciple. There may be more than one Zen lineage extant at any given time, but the practice of a master transmitting the lineage to a large number of disciples, as may be the case in conferring *prāṭimokśa* ordinations, is unknown.

Several of the Chinese masters I interviewed stated that of the doctrinal schools of Buddhism in China, all but two have survived in an unbroken lineage until today. They noted that the transmissions of the Yogāchārya school and the *Tantra* school were broken in China, but that the lost lineages of *tantra* were recovered from Tibet and Mongolia. Normally, as with the Zen school, such transmissions tended to be from the head of a particular school to a single designated successor. By contrast, *prāṭimokśa* ordination may be given to many disciples. Still, authorization to conduct ordinations in the *Vinaya* school was conferred on a limited number of disciples, each of whom was thenceforth designated as a master of *Vinaya*.

The most highly respected masters of *Vinaya* in traditional male-dominated societies tended to be *bhikṣus*. Consequently, their authority was considered supreme and final, and they were deemed most highly qualified to conduct and verify *bhikṣuṇī* ordinations. An ordination conferred by *bhikṣu* masters alone would therefore be accepted as authentic, testified by an official ordination certificate issued by a government-recognized *Sangha* organization and presented to each newly ordained participant.

Several of the Chinese masters thought that the notion of lineage transmission has no place in the context of *prāṭimokśa* ordination. They supposed that the Tibetans have applied the concept of lineage to *prāṭimokśa* ordination as a result of their concern for lineage in the context of *tantric* transmissions. These masters denied that the vows are received from a human being, but rather, maintained that *prāṭimokśa* vows are received from the Buddha himself, just as *bodhisattva* vows are received from a visualized host of Buddhas and *bodhisattvas*. When discussing purity of ordination, they considered the moral purity of the ordaining masters to be of utmost importance; they were not concerned with a linear passing of vows from one human being to another.

Dialogue

The following exchange, between a Tibetan Buddhist scholar and myself, is given to illustrate the traditional Tibetan view regarding lineage transmission:

Q: If you assert that, to be valid, the *bhikṣuṇī* lineage must have been transmitted from *bhikṣuṇī* to *bhikṣuṇī* from the time of Buddha Sakyamuni until the present day, what is the process of that transmission? Do the vows pass from the mind of the master to the mind of the disciples?

A: Nothing is transmitted.

Q: But according to the *Abhidharmakośa*, vows are form, is that correct?

A: Yes, vows are form.

Q: But they are invisible?

A: Yes, they are invisible form.

Q: So the invisible form of the vows passes from master to disciple?

A: Nothing passes from the mind of the master to the mind of the disciple.

Q: Then how do you conceive that the lineage must necessarily have passed from *bhikṣuṇī* to *bhikṣuṇī* from the time of Buddha Śakyamuni to the present day?

A: The vows must be given to a *bhikṣuṇī* by a *bhikṣuṇī*, who in turn has received her vows from a *bhikṣuṇī*, who in turn had received her vows from a *bhikṣuṇī*, all the way back to the time of Buddha Śakyamuni. The *Vinaya* says that *bhikṣuṇī*s must be ordained by a full complement of *bhikṣus* as well as by a full complement of *bhikṣuṇī*s for the ordination to be considered valid.

Q: So if a *bhikṣuṇī* is ordained by a full complement of both *bhikṣus* and *bhikṣuṇī*s, as I was in Korea, then that ordination is considered valid, isn't it?

A: No, not only that, but the *bhikṣuṇī*s who ordained you must also have been ordained by both *bhikṣus* and *bhikṣuṇī*s, and so on, all the way back to the time of the Buddha.

Q: The procedure for the ordination of *bhikṣuṇī*s is very clearly described in the *Bhikṣuṇī Karman*. *Bhikṣuṇī*s are to be ordained by a full complement of *bhikṣuṇī*s in the morning and by a full complement of *bhikṣus* in the afternoon. In this manner, they are recognized as *bhikṣuṇī*s and admitted to the *Sangha*. There is no discussion of the necessity of a candidate for *bhikṣuṇī* ordination to check into the type of ordination received by her ordaining masters. Is it not absurd to assert that a new *bhikṣuṇī* should have to assume responsibility for verifying the correct ordination proceedings of 2,500 years of ordained beings?

A: The correct procedures must be followed.

Q: Of course, the correct procedures must be followed. But in modern times, even the precepts themselves are not maintained strictly in many cases. For example, *bhikṣus* are not allowed to touch money or to take untimely food, and yet these days is it not difficult to find *bhikṣus* who keep these precepts strictly?

A: these are only minor precepts.

Q: Certainly, these precepts belong to a secondary category. Nevertheless, if they are transgressed, they must be confessed before the assembly of *bhikṣus* and purified according to the proper procedures. If they are not, then a *bhikṣu* cannot be said to have maintained perfect morality. To transmit precepts purely, it is important that the ordaining masters should have maintained impeccable discipline by observing the precepts strictly. Otherwise, it could call into question the validity of the ordination conferred on their disciples. According to the masters of the Chinese, Korean, and Thai traditions, it is the purity of morality maintained by the ordination masters which is the main question in determining the purity of a lineage, not a mere matter of transmitting precepts from master to disciple. It would be impossible for us to verify the perfect safeguarding of precepts and the thorough observance of every detail of *Sangha* procedures by *bhikṣus* throughout millennia of Buddhist history. Moreover, to require this would threaten the very institution of the Buddhist *Sangha*. The important thing is for *Sangha* members to be aware of all aspects of proper behavior to bring their own conduct in line with the Buddha's guidelines, and more importantly, in line with the spirit of those guidelines.

Conclusions

If an irregularity in ordination procedure is used as a basis to deny the validity of an entire lineage of *bhikṣuṇīs*—be it Chinese, Korean, or Vietnamese—then one would be forced to apply the same verdict to the order of *bhikṣus* as well. There is no way, however, in which denying the validity of the *bhikṣu* or the *bhikṣuṇī* lineage would serve the *Dharma* or the interests of sentient beings.

Furthermore, the fact that a *bhikṣuṇī* at some point in the history of the lineage may not have been ordained by both *Sanghas* is something that cannot be changed, nor is it of particular relevance to a *bhikṣuṇī* today, if she herself has received precepts according to the proper procedure and is sincerely striving to maintain those precepts as the basis of her practice.

Five recommendations are put forth at this point:

1) Qualified nuns should be encouraged to approach the appropriate *Sangha* associations where ordination is presently available and request to receive full ordination vows and in-depth training in discipline to strengthen the *Bhikṣuṇī Sangha*.

2) These nuns should earnestly request *Sangha* administrators in each place to conduct the *bhikṣuṇī* ordination in a dual ceremony every year, rather than only occasionally as is currently the case, thereby making dual ordination available to more women.

3) The *śikṣamāṇā* ordination (as a probationary nun) should be reinstituted to bring procedures into line with the injunctions set out in the *Bhikṣuṇī Karman*, so that the *Bhikṣuṇī Sangha* may gain full acceptance among the Theravādin *Sangha* communities.

4) All manner of support, financial and otherwise, should be extended to the monastic community to facilitate these objectives.

5) The authenticity of over 15,000 *de facto bhikṣuṇīs* should be acknowledged, regardless of the type of ordination these *Sangha* members received.

The Benefits of the Bhikṣuṇī Sangha

Though the dangers of not holding a traceable lineage must be conceded, within the Buddhist traditions it is the wider issue of benefit to living beings that is foremost. A strong and virtuous *Sangha* is essential for the sound establishment of the Buddha's teachings throughout the world, and the *Sangha* can be substantially strengthened and enriched by a fuller participation of its ordained women. The establishment of a *Bhikṣuṇī Sangha* and the restitution of the *śikṣamānā* ordination in the Tibetan and Theravāda traditions would make the seven levels of *prāṭimokśa* ordination complete. It is upon this firm and egalitarian basis of moral discipline that each of the Buddhist traditions can flourish, and upon which a valid synthesis may eventually evolve.

Until now, each of the various Buddhist traditions has been adamant in asserting the purity of its own lineage, while simultaneously putting forth arguments to challenge the validity of other traditions. For each community to rise above this and take constructive steps toward recognizing the *bhikṣuṇī* lineage would be progressive, humanitarian, and a magnanimous gesture contributing toward unity within the Buddhist family. At this critical point in history, a unity between the multiplicity of Buddhist traditions would be a practical demonstration of religious harmony and a powerful force toward world peace.

Implementation of equitable access to full ordination in all countries would be a valuable statement in recognizing the vital role of dedicated female practitioners within the Buddhist community. It would encourage their greater participation and thereby begin to tap the valuable contribution that women can make to the world religious community. Now, as the *Buddhadharma* is being freshly transmitted to Western cultures, it is important that equal opportunities for full ordination be instituted from the start. If correct ordination procedures are established such that the *Bhikṣuṇī Sangha* in Western countries is recognized by all traditions from the start, we shall not have to later wage the lengthy struggles for the full ordination of women in which other religious traditions are now engaged.

In that full ordination for women is a topic of immense concern globally, the establishment of a viable and universally recognized *Bhikṣuṇī Sangha* is of great significance. With full ordination available to qualified women, the rich Buddhist traditions could genuinely claim to be taking sincere, positive measures toward eradicating sexual discrimination both within its ranks and in society at large. In combination with equal opportunities for religious education, the spiritual development of female practitioners everywhere could be advanced qualitatively as well as quantitatively.

Pure motivation and sustained action by all members of the *Sangha* can ensure that the *bhikṣuṇī* order founded so long ago by Buddha Sakyamuni will be restored and eventually thrive in the modern world. This can only serve to bring benefit to the spiritual aspirations of all living beings.

NOTES

1. The ten precepts of a novice nun or monk are (1) to refrain from taking life; (2) to refrain from taking what is not given; (3) to refrain from sexual contact; (4) to refrain from falsehood: (5) to refrain from taking intoxicants; (6) to refrain from dancing, singing, and entertainments; (7) to refrain from beautifying oneself with ornaments or cosmetics; (8) to refrain from using high or luxurious seats and beds; (9) to refrain from handling silver and gold; and (10) to refrain from taking untimely food.

2. In the Theravāda and Dharmagupta schools of *Vinaya*, the precepts of a *śikṣamāṇā* are the first five, plus the tenth, of the precepts of a novice nun or monk given in Footnote 1 above. In *Monastic Discipline for the Buddhist Nuns* (pp. 53-55), Hirakawa mentions the six *śikṣamāṇā* precepts of the Sarvāstivāda school as being the first four of the novice precepts, plus the last two *bhikṣuṇī pārājikas*. In addition, he notes that there are six *śikṣamāṇā* precepts in the Mahīśāsaka school, six root and six secondary precepts in the Mūlasar-

vāstivādin school, and eighteen precepts in the Mahāsānghika school.

3. According to Waldschmidt's *Bruchstücke des Bhikṣuṇī-Prāṭimokśa der Sarvāstivādins* (pp. 2-3), *bhikṣuṇīs* and *bhikṣus* of the various *Vinaya* schools hold the following numbers of precepts:

Vinaya school	*Bhikṣuṇī precepts*	*Bhikṣu precepts*
Pāli (Theravāda)	311	227
Dharmagupta	348	250
Mahāsānghika	290	218
Mahīśāsaka	380	251
Sarvāstivada (Chinese)	355	257
Sarvāstivada (Sanskrit)	-	263
Mūlasarvāstivāda (Chinese)	354	245
Mūlasarvāstivāda (Tibetan)	371	262

4. According to the Tibetan texts of the Mūlasarvāstivādin school, twelve *bhikṣuṇīs* are required.

5. According to the Tibetan texts, a total of twenty-two.

6. This refers to a "central land," interpreted as an area where the four categories of disciples exist, usually meaning *bhikṣus*, *bhikṣuṇīs*, *upāsakās* and *upāsikās*.

7. In the Tibetan tradition, five *bhikṣus* and six *bhikṣuṇīs* would be required.

ESTABLISHMENT OF THE ORDER OF BUDDHIST NUNS AND ITS DEVELOPMENT IN SRI LANKA

by Kusuma Devendra

Institution of Bhikkhunī Sangha by the Buddha

The Buddha made a striking social evaluation in his first sermon at Benares when he described the prevalent trends in Indian society. We may make a brief evaluation of the position of women at that time accordingly. In a society given to sensual indulgence, the plight of the woman in India was to be given away in marriage early in life. As a result she had no opportunity to gain much knowledge or education. She was certainly no match for the highly accomplished male, educated in the Vedas and so much older than herself.

The other trend in Indian society was austere asceticism, involving self-mortification, which the priestly classes practiced. The *jhānic* states and supernormal powers that they acquired with much time and effort were very transitory, however, having been gained by a conscious suppression of sensual desires, so the very sight or sound of a woman was often enough to destroy their spiritual powers. Thus, the priestly ascetics despised women and looked upon them as if they were the very destroyers of their perfected souls. The Buddha criticized both these trends in society and advocated the middle path. For the pursuance of this, the *Vinaya*-disciplines ordained *Sangha* was the ideal circumstance.

It is a truism that even a Buddha needs a mother to take a human rebirth. To generate perfect human beings you need perfect mothers. The higher the values of women, the higher will be the values of that society, for they instill these values in their young charges. While fully cognizant of this, the Buddha never attempted to disrupt the organized social order or change the social mores of the time. He exhorted those who wanted to join his order not to forsake lightly their previous teachers or their religious beliefs. He was even reluctant to preach to the people his radical *Dhamma* and consented to do so only after the invitation of Maha Brahma.

Against this background, it is reasonable to think that the Buddha would never have acceded to a request to enhance the religious status of women unless he was fully convinced that it would not have drastic social repercussions. This undoubtedly accounts for the early reluctance of the Buddha to institute a *bhikkhunī* order, which would completely change the existing social milieu. Woman was the bedrock of society and hence this was an extremely sensitive matter that had to be approached with great circumspection.

There is no other teacher who appreciated the value of womanhood more than the Buddha. He placed motherhood at the highest possible level. He visited Tusita heaven to preach to his mother, Matru Devarājā (Mahamāyā) and he also showed much respect to his foster mother. When Mahāpajāpatī Gotamī Bhikkhunī and her retinue of five hundred *bhikkhunīs* took leave of the Buddha for their final passing away, the Buddha addressed her in very endearing terms and asked her to display her various supernormal powers. Finally, he even followed behind them up to the gate of the monastery as a sign of his gratitude. This is the only instance recorded where the Buddha is seen treading in this manner behind another person. We also cannot forget the very touching incident when Yaśodarā refused to come out and meet the Buddha when he first visited Kapilavastu after attaining Buddhahood, but the Buddha in his magnanimity visited her in her apartment.

The Buddha realized the extent of oppression of women wielded by the Brahmanic society of India in the sixth century B.C. In an attempt to raise their status he made many references to women in most respectful terms in his many discourses; for example, "mother and father are Brahma himself," "one must pay respect to one's mother and father," "the friend in the home is the mother," "women also can hold intellectual roles," "a wife is an absolute friend," and so on.

The force of the Buddha's exhortations with regard to women's abiding intellectual capacity, deep sense of compassion, and ability to cooperate with men, ushered in a favorable environment for the institution of the *bhikkhunī* order. Consequently, there arose a large number of both ordained and lay male disciples who were free from conceit and envy at the achievements of women. On the contrary, they were full of joy and encouragement. When the Buddha declared, "A human rebirth is extremely rare and difficult to obtain," he was emphatic that the human state is gained with great difficulty, without reference to a particular sex. Transcendental benign peace is to be won by both men and women. The institution of both *Bhikkhu* and *Bhikkhunī Sanghas* bears this out.

Moreover, there is no doubt that the Buddha emphasized the need for a four-fold Buddhist society (*catuparisā*), composed of *bhikkhus*, *bhikkhunīs*, *upāsakās*, and *upāsikās*, for the stability of the doctrine (*sāsana*).[1] This has been proven throughout history by the fact that religious and cultural attainments reached their acme in both India and Sri Lanka only when the four-fold society was flourishing. The peril of the present religious system, in spite of the superlative advance of society, can, in fact, be largely attributed to the breakdown of the four-tier system.

The *bhikṣuṇīs* were able to emulate and parallel all the achievements of the great *bhikṣus* and were thus offered equal status as members of the *Sangha*. But since the basis of seniority is a very salient feature of the order, the *bhikkhus* were given priority, being senior by nearly five years. This was merely a matter of precedence and in no way indicates superiority. Certain structures had to be built into the religious system, not only to stabilize the system but to ensure its social consistency, particularly to assure its integration into a society where men had asserted themselves for aeons and where even the women had come to accept this as a working principle. Thus, placing the *bhikkhus* higher in precedence in the order was indeed a very logical and cohesive rule. But *bhikkhus* are requested, in their *Vinaya* rules, to offer protection by rendering services to the female order. In addition, the appointment of *bhikkhunī* advisers having special talent for such services is a required *Vinaya* law for all *bhikkhus*. Even now the question is asked of monks' assemblies for *uposatha*, "Reverend sirs, have you advised *bhikkhunīs*?," to which the answer is given, "Since there are no bhikkunis, reverend sir, we have not advised *bhikkhunīs*."

The Buddha made some concessions to ensure the smooth working of both orders in the future by giving full responsibility to the *Mahā Sangha* to amend any of the existing minor *Vinaya* rules in the interest of the *sāsana*. The Buddha refused to appoint a leader to the *Sangha*. "The *Dhamma* will be your guide and teacher," were some of his last words.

In Theravāda countries such as Burma, Thailand, and Sri Lanka, there are various views of a statement made by the Buddha immediately after the establishment of the *bhikkhunī* order. The Buddha's utterance is as follows:

> If Ānanda, women had not obtained the going forth from home to homelessness in the *dhamma* and discipline proclaimed by the Truth-finder, the Brahma-faring, Ānanda, would have lasted long, true *dhamma* would have endured for a thousand years. But since Ānanda, women have gone forth...in the *dhamma* and discipline proclaimed by the Truth-finder, now, Ananda, the Brahma-faring will not last long, true *dhamma* will endure only for five hundred years.[2]

The Samantapāsādikā, commentary to the *Vinaya* by Buddhaghosa, explains this statement of the Buddha in great detail. The relevant portion can be translated thus:

> A vast reservoir of water, if not bounded all around for protection, will have no water remaining. The embankment must be made first in order that the water will remain. Likewise, to provide for the non-transgression of non-arisen wrongful practices, the Lord has proclaimed the *garudhammas*. If these were not proclaimed, the going forth of females in *pabbajja* would have caused the Brahma-faring to last only five hundred years. Therefore these (*garudhammas*) were proclaimed beforehand. Now that they

> are proclaimed, the Brahma-faring will last another five hundred years. The Brahma-faring will now last a thousand years as was first declared. In this thousand years will appear *arahants* possessed of the four supreme analytical knowledges (*catu-paṭisambhidā*). Thereafter in the next thousand years there will appear *arahants* of 'dry *vipassanā*' (*sukkhavipassaka*). In the next thousand years will arise the non-returners and then there will be the once-returners and then there will be the stream-enterers. In this way the Brahma-faring consisting of the fruits of the dispensation (*paṭivedha dhammo*) will prevail for five thousand years.[3]

In this statement of Buddhaghosa commenting upon the Buddha's utterance, there is no reference to the lifespan of the *sāsana* being reduced to five hundred years due to the ordination of females. On the contrary, it is indicated that the fruits (*magga-phala*) of the *sāsana* will last for five thousand years.

There are many references in the canon which show clearly that the observance of rules of discipline is the essential factor ensuring the longevity of the *sāsana*. The Buddha, with his knowledge of the three worlds (*lokavidū*), would never have instituted the *bhikkhunī* order if it would have ultimately led to the decline of the tenets of Buddhism. The fact that so many disciplinary rules were proclaimed for *bhikkhus* and *bhikkhunīs* indicates his intention to assure that the order should last. This is borne out even in his final discourse where the four-fold society is referred to, including mention of *bhikkhunīs*.

Nuns in Sri Lanka

Doing research on the establishment of the order of Buddhist nuns and its development in Sri Lanka for some years has given me the opportunity to visit about two hundred nunneries and to meet hundreds of Buddhist nuns in all parts of Sri Lanka. During these visits I gathered data and information about the livelihood of the nuns and received a rude shock when I suddenly became aware that the nuns of Sri Lanka are in a marginal position: they do not belong to the *Sangha*, and they do not belong with the lay people. They are neither one nor the other.

It is perhaps one century since the ten-precept *dasasil mātā* nuns movement came to Sri Lanka, but the amount of support given to its development during this time has been negligible. When the nuns take robes, they receive ten precepts. The same ten precepts, however, can be observed by a lay person; they are not given the *pabbajja dasasila*, which are the precepts of a samanerī. So they are not receiving a recognized monastic ordination. They are not *bhikkhunīs*, they are not *sikkamānās*, they are not even *samanerīs*. In fact, they do not belong to the order at all. They are the equivalent of lay people who have renounced their household and taken to monastic living, and they are not recognized as belonging to the *Sangha*.

When you visit a temple in Sri Lanka, you will find that ninety percent of the devotees are women. These women support the *bhikkhus* because they believe that the *Sangha* is the field of merit (*puññakkhettam*), and that through supporting the *Sangha* one reaps the highest benefits and merit. Even if one of our nuns should become a stream-winner (*sotāpanna*), a once-returner (*sakadāgamī*), or even an *arahant*, she still would not be included in the field of merit because she does not belong to the *Sangha*. This is why the nuns are in a marginal position; the problem is no simple matter, but is very deeply rooted and traditionally bound.

The nuns have entered the order through their own wisdom, their intention to observe the precepts, and their intention to tread the path advocated by the Buddha. The nuns believe that due to having practiced this kind of renunciation in past lives, they were motivated to join the order with such enthusiasm, despite great difficulties. Sri Lankan women are fond of long hair, so to cut their hair and take up robes represents great renunciation.

They do so despite repeated protests from their families. The nuns of Sri Lanka have such low social status that no family would willingly allow a young girl to enter the movement.

There are only a few educational opportunities in the nuns' communities, so no rich, powerful, qualified, English-educated woman would normally join the order. Most nuns do not have money to travel, so even when classes are being held in some of the *pirivenas* (traditional Buddhist schools), they have no means of attending them. Neither do they have the basic education to follow these classes. At the moment the order remains stagnant in every respect.

Some of these nuns do not handle money. They have no organizational relationship with each other and they get no support from their homes, from the *bhikkhus*, or from the lay people. They are isolated, and, in such a situation, each has to develop independently with a pioneering effort. They have to depend on their own strength of character to build up a small group of supporters, and then try to live up to the expectations of those supporters.

With all these forces working against them, they are subject to great psychological stress. Their marginal position, along with the lack of support from the monks and the society in general, has given them a certain amount of resistance to organization. Each one has been working independently and has gained some degree of status in her particular environment as an individual, so she is not willing to submit to any external authority. Such a situation has made the organizing of nuns very difficult. It appears that the only solution is to restore the *bhikkhunī* order.

We find a parallel in the sixth century B.C. in India. At that time women were not given any chance at all, so the Buddha instituted a *bhikkhunī* order and the *bhikkhunīs* followed 311 rules. (According to the Theravādin tradition, the *bhikkhus* follow 227 rules.) This was to enable the order to continue into posterity. It was the last wish of the buddha that all four categories of disciples—*bhikkhus*, *bhikkhunīs*, *upāsakās* and *upāsikās*—should continue to exist and that a balance amongst them should prevail, so that the *Dhamma* would be preserved in the future.

The *Vinaya* rules guide the conduct of the monks and nuns

and provide for a certain balance within the *Sangha*. Since the Buddha has enunciated all the possible rules for errant persons, it is not allowable to increase or reduce the number of vows. Up till now, these *Vinaya* rules have had a certain balancing influence to protect the individual *bhikkhunī*, to protect the *bhikkhus*, and to effect their working together in a positive atmosphere. The rules assure a rapport between them which gives strength of character to both the *bhikkhus* and *bhikkhunīs*. The two *Sanghas* together—the *Bhikkhu Sangha* and the *Bhikkhunī Sangha*—can provide the necessary direction to the laypeople.

As a mother of six, I know what a privilege it is for mothers to bring up the forthcoming generation of young people. It is mostly the women who teach the children what is right and what is wrong, what they should and should not do. A mother is concerned with this responsibility. It is not the father who looks after the children. He takes his bag and goes off to work in the morning, while we stay with the children to direct and guide them moment to moment.

To fulfill this responsibility properly, women must be educated. As far as *Dhamma* education is concerned, they would be able to get closer to *bhikkhunīs* than to the *bhikkhus*. Therefore, women would gain much support in their endeavors if there were well-educated, well-established *bhikkhunīs* from whom they could receive guidance. If the *bhikkhunīs* are well established, they can impart their understanding to the women of the country, and the women in turn can impart that discipline to their children from an early age. Their moral conduct, their virtue, is essential for the welfare of entire future generations.

I contend that there is a great need for uplifting the nuns of Sri Lanka. I must pay tribute to the Commissioners of Buddhist Affairs, because recently there has been a sort of renaissance. The *dasasil mātās* have taken *vipassanā* meditation courses and their inner discipline is quite thorough. If the nuns now also follow the *Vinaya* rules carefully, they will get the support of the *bhikkhus* as well as the masses. Their dignity will be raised, and they will be better able to contribute much more to society.

Proper organizational strength, state support, and the benign influence and direction of *bhikkhus* are dire necessities for establishing a *bhikkhunī* order. Fortunately, there are some venerable elders of the *bhikkhu* order who have hearts filled with excellent qualities as of old. These noble sires of the order must now rise to the occasion, having fully understood the contribution of the female recluse, to win back the *bhikkhunī* order. They who have the strength of character and conviction to break down the barriers that prevent women from taking their rightful place within the ordained community, must give proper advice to the state. Has not the Buddha given full responsibility to the order to change any of the minor rules in the interest of the *sāsana*?

It is indeed a heartening fact that the present Minister of State for Cultural Affairs in Sri Lanka has fully understood, in all its complexity, the value and crucial necessity for the resurrection of the *bhikkhunī* order in Sri Lanka and is supporting this cause in every possible way. And we may hope that this epoch-making gathering in the sacred precincts of Bodhgaya will spearhead a renaissance movement toward establishing *Bhikkhunī Sangha* in the four corners of the world.

NOTES

1. The *sāsana* consists of the teachings (*pariyatti*), their application in practice (*patipatti*), and the fruits of sainthood (*pativedha*).

2. I. B. Horner, *The Book of the Discipline*, Vol. 5, Pali Text Society, p. 356.

3. *Samantapāsādikā* (in Pali), p. 1291.

AN INTERVIEW WITH HIS HOLINESS THE DALAI LAMA

On February 14, 1987, the fourth day of the International Conference on Buddhist Nuns, His Holiness the Dalai Lama met in Bodhgaya with fifteen prominent nuns from Burma, Cambodia, Canada, Hong Kong, Japan, Nepal, Sri Lanka, Taiwan, Thailand, Tibet, the United States, and West Germany, in a private audience. He gave advice and answered questions on the *bhikṣuṇī* issue, among others. The following is a transcript of the exchange that took place on that occasion.

Q: During the conference we have been discussing various issues related to Buddhist nuns. Today we talked about the *bhikṣuṇī* issue. Some of the participants have questions about where we stand and where we should go from here in discussing this issue with the *bhikṣus* to create an international *Bhikṣuṇī Sangha*. The people from different countries are very interested in this question. We at the conference all agree that we have to go slowly and carefully to gain the acceptance of the *Bhikṣu Sangha* in the various countries. From the Tibetan point of view, where should we go next?

HHDL: As we have discussed, it is a bit difficult to become a *bhikṣuṇī* in accordance with the Mūlasarvāstivādin tradition. However, there are many different schools of *Vinaya*—actually eighteen different schools in all. So, although there is a specific procedure of ordination in the Mūlasarvāstivādin tradition, there are also other ordination procedures in existence.

One important point is this: I think that it is very important to approach this issue together simultaneously in all those countries where the practice of *Vinaya* is very strong. Unfortunately, Cambodia and Laos are now in difficult circumstances, so I think that it is especially important to undertake the task (of investigating the *bhikṣuṇī* issue) initially in these three countries—Sri Lanka, Thailand, and Burma.

Q: Would you give your permission for Tibetan nuns to go to Hong Kong to take the *bhikṣuṇī* vows?

HHDL: Yes. There are some *bhikṣuṇī* who have gone already.

Q: Will they be officially recognized as *bhikṣuṇīs*?

HHDL: First of all, religious practice depends upon individual initiative. It is a personal matter. Whether [the *bhikṣuṇī* ordination is recognized] officially or not, in any case, there is some kind of acceptance in the community, and this acceptance by the community is most important.

For example, in Tibet, although the majority of people are Buddhists, there are also non-Buddhist religions, such as Bön. At present, Bön practice is similar to Buddhist practice, but originally the practice was something quite different. Still, the original Bön religion received acceptance. People recognized, or simply accepted it. Similarly, there were Muslims and some Christians. It was no problem.

The *bhikṣuṇī* lineage was previously not available in Tibet, but now, gradually, the *bhikṣuṇī* tradition is being transmitted from other Buddhist countries. As time goes on, these *bhikṣuṇīs* will be accepted. This is no problem. The important point is that, in conjunction with accepting the *bhikṣuṇī* ordination, we have to institute the practices of the rainy season retreat, confession, and so forth. If the *bhikṣuṇī* lineage that we adopt is, for example, of the Chinese tradition, and the texts related to these matters in the *bhikṣuṇī* tradition are in Chinese, since we cannot be expected to adopt the language as well, the first important step is that we need to translate these texts into Tibetan.

First we need to make a translation of the *Bhikṣuṇī Prāṭimokśa Sūtra*, then of the *Bhikṣuṇī Karman* (*Procedures for Bhikṣuṇīs*), then of the texts related to the procedures for commencing and completing the rainy season retreat. When these texts have been translated, [the *Vinaya* practices of that tradition] will become very clear.

Then comes the question of the lineage. Once we identify

the source of the lineage, the *Vinaya* school to which it belongs, and the various procedures of the school according to which they are practicing, there will be no difficulties. We cannot say that it is not compatible with the Mūlasarvāstivāda. We are not saying that.

The only problem we will have to consider is that of the robes. There are different robes in the different traditions, with different colors and sizes of patches. Whatever descriptions of the robes are very explicit, whatever aspects are clearly indicated in the *Vinaya*, should be adopted. Where there is no clear source in the texts, it is allowable if it is compatible with what is allowed in the *Vinaya*.

These sorts of decisions cannot be made by just a few persons. When considering the rules of the *Vinaya Sūtras*, the authority does not rest in any one person's hand. Supreme authority lies only with the *Sangha*. Before, in Tibet, when some important action needed to be initiated immediately, Atisa used to ask, "Is it prohibited in the *Tripitaka* or not?" In addition to that, at Vikramaśila Monastery it would also be asked whether it was prohibited in any of the *bodhisattva sūtras*. Therefore, issues should be settled in accordance with what is determined by the deliberations of a *Sangha* council, that is, the *Sangha* community.

For example, when Tibetan schools were first established in the early sixties in India, quite a number of students were ordained as novice monks and nuns in these schools. As students in the schools, sometimes they were required to take part in social activities such as [Tibetan] dance and theater, or other such performances. So it had to be decided whether these activities were contrary to the *Vinaya* or not. It was a matter that could not be decided by just myself nor just by my two tutors here in Dharamsala. So I sent the matter to Baxa [in Assam, eastern India], since the majority of *Tripitaka* masters who had escaped from the communists were congregated there. Then the *Sangha* community there deliberated and determined what was allowable and what was not. On the basis of their recommendations, the matter was decided. This is the proper way.

Q: We made a decision today to set up some committees of Sakyadhītā (the International Buddhist Women's Association) to conduct research into the *Vinaya* and the proper procedures for *bhikṣuṇī* ordination. We plan to write these facts up into research papers and after one year have another conference to which we would invite the monks of the different traditions to come to hear the findings of this research, and get their approval. Do you think that this is a good way to proceed?

HHDL: Yes, that would be good. My impression from our brief discussions is that the situation is more delicate in Sri Lanka and Thailand. At the moment, I feel that there is more work to be done in these countries. As far as the Tibetans are concerned, first of all, we are refugees, and secondly, though I hope this does not sound presumptuous, the *bodhisattva* ideal renders us more flexible. So there is no problem [from our side].

Q: Many of the Tibetan nuns would like to take the *bhikṣuṇī* ordination, but for all of them to go to Hong Kong is very expensive. Do you think that it might be possible in a couple of years to give a *bhikṣuṇī* ordination, here in Bodhgaya for example, with ten Tibetan *bhikṣus* and ten Chinese *bhikṣuṇīs* together?

HHDL: This has yet to be discussed. The problem is that the Tibetan *bhikṣus* have been ordained according to a different tradition, the Mūlasarvāstivādin tradition. The matter needs to be researched and discussed further, and submitted for decision to the *Sangha* community. Or, gradually, we can institute or introduce the *Bhikṣuṇī* lineage when we have a sufficient number of *bhikṣuṇīs* within the Tibetan community who have the lineage, having been ordained, say, in the Chinese tradition.

Q: But then we would still belong to a different *Vinaya* school. Would that be all right?

HHDL: That is fine. That is no problem. For example, [previously, in Tibet, the Tibetan *bhikṣus* belonged to the

Mūlasarvāstivādin school while the great master] Atiśa belonged to the Mahāsāṅghika tradition, yet he could attend the ceremonies for confession and rainy season retreat. It was only ordinations that he did not give, but he was able to participate in the other *Vinaya* procedures.

During the visit of the Chinese scholar Hsuan Tsang, and later I Ching, to Kashmir, both the *bodhisattva* and *śravaka* traditions prevailed, and within these, Buddhist monks belonged to many different *Vinaya* traditions as well. These seem to have existed harmoniously side by side within the community. As far as the confession ceremony is concerned, the chronicles of Atiśa's life give the impression that he participated in the ceremonies of the Mūlasarvāstivādin school, even though he belonged to a different *Vinaya* school. The point is that he and perhaps just a few disciples belonged to a different school. If there were enough of them they could hold their own separate confession ceremonies.

Since we Tibetan *bhikṣus* follow the Mūlasarvāstivādin school, when we have enough *bhikṣuṇīs* of the Dharmagupta school to form a community, i.e., a *Sangha* of more than five *bhikṣuṇīs*, then the question arises as to whether they should hold these ceremonies together, or separately according to the different traditions of their schools. This is another matter that requires further research, but I do not think it will be a problem.

Q: When you say that when we have enough *bhikṣuṇīs* ordained within the Tibetan tradition there could be a *bhikṣuṇī* ordination, do you mean that the *bhikṣuṇīs* could give ordination [without *bhikṣus*]?

HHDL: You must perform the ordination in accordance with the procedures of your particular tradition. For example, you who have been ordained in Hong Kong and Taiwan would follow the procedures of the Dharmagupta tradition. In the Mūlasarvāstivādin tradition, both a *Sangha* of ten *bhikṣus* and a *Sangha* of ten *bhikṣuṇīs* plus two more, a *bhikṣuṇī* preceptor and a *bhikṣuṇī* instructor, a total of twenty-two, are required if it is a central land. When introducing an ordination, things must be done in accordance with the tradition of *bhikṣuṇī* ordination which is being adopted.

In the paper which you gave me, there is one quotation from a Pāli text which says that where conditions are complete, the ordination should be performed in a dual ceremony, but if conditions are not complete, *bhikṣuṇī* ordination may be given by *bhikṣus* alone. If this quotation can be traced in the Pāli source of the Theravādin tradition, you should get the opinion of the Thai *bhikṣus* concerning it.

Q: The Theravādin monks in Sri Lanka do not agree.

HHDL: If it is explicitly stated in the Pāli canon, they should accept it.

Q: But they are not flexible like Your Holiness.

HHDL: If the statement is clear in the Pāli they should agree.

Q: The extensive ceremony is only given once every three years in Hong Kong, but it is given every year in Taiwan. How would you feel about the Tibetan nuns going to Taiwan for *bhikṣuṇī* ordination?

HHDL: That is no problem.

Q: It might be possible to gather the required number of Theravādin monks in the United States to hold a *bhikṣuṇī* ordination. If respected monks there were in favor of such an ordination, hopefully the monks in Sri Lanka would accept it because they belong to the same tradition.

HHDL: Perhaps there are some *bhikṣus* who, as individuals, are broad-minded.

Q: Many Tibetan nuns are wondering, if ordination is given in Hong Kong and Taiwan by *bhikṣus* alone and not in a dual ceremony, why Your Holiness, being a manifestation of Avalokiteśvara, cannot perform the ordination along with some Tibetan *bhikṣus*, and start a *bhikṣuṇī* ordination in the Tibetan tradition this way on your own.

HHDL: The practice of *Vinaya* has to be undertaken as

Buddha himself has prescribed. It is said that there is only one doctrine and there is only one master. So we must proceed in accordance with what the *Vinaya Sūtras* have said. We cannot transgress that.

Now, for example, in the *bodhisattva* vehicle, the *bodhisattva* vows may be taken from an image, a statue, or a vizualized [preceptor], without [an actual living] *guru*. With regard to *tantric* vows, of course, it is possible for a person with high realizations to have direct contact with different *mandalas*. In that case, there is no need to trace the lineage back to the time of the Buddha.

Vinaya, however, is different. Many people have asked me this question before, but I have always replied in this same way. We must proceed according to the *Vinaya* traditions. We Tibetans follow the Mūlasarvāstivādin school and base all our practices on the authentic treatises of this school. These treatises comprise thirteen volumes in all in the Tibetan canon (*Kangyur*). Since these texts, translated from the Sanskrit, are so extensive, for practical purposes we primarily use the *Prāṭimokśa Sūtra* and Gunaprabha's root text on *Vinaya*. The *bhikṣuṇī* ordination procedure according to the Mūlasarvāstivādin tradition is very clearly set forth in these texts.

Q: Even though we belong to different traditions and wear different robes, it would still be a great thing to have an international *Bhikṣuṇī Sangha*, because it would eliminate some of the discrimination that currently exists between the different Buddhist traditions. Differences in robes and practice are not so significant, and we would be united as a *Bhikṣuṇī Sangha*. This would promote Buddhist unity.

HHDL: [There are some differences. For example,] in the Mūlasarvāstivādin school it is clearly explained that sleeves are not to be worn by those who are ordained. Yet in Mongolia, the *bhikṣus* wear sleeves. When Buddhism was transmitted to Mongolia from Tibet the mode of dress was adapted to the different climate and conditions. However, it is difficult to understand why sleeves are worn in Thailand and Sri Lanka where the climate is so hot.

Q: Females are required to wear sleeves, but not males. It is due to the culture. In their societies, it is not acceptable to show the female body.

Q: You have mentioned the possibility of investigating the school of *Vinaya* followed by the Vietnamese *bhikṣuṇīs*.

HHDL: A friend of mine, a German monk, mentioned to me in France that there is a Sarvāstivādin *bhikṣuṇī* lineage existing in the Vietnamese Buddhist tradition. We are currently investigating this matter.[1]

How many precepts do the nuns in Sri Lanka hold?

Q: Ten.

HHDL: And in Thailand?

Q: Eight. They are actually *upāsikās* (laywomen with precepts).

HHDL: And in Nepal?

Q: Ten.

HHDL: So they are *śrāmaṇerikās*, as in Sri Lanka.

Q: Even though they have ten precepts, they are not accepted by the *Bhikṣu Sangha* as being *śrāmaṇerikās*. They are not allowed to go to confession or to participate in the other *Sangha* ceremonies, but they keep ten precepts.

HHDL: So, in reality, they are *śrāmaṇerikās*.

Q: The *bhikṣus* say that *śrāmaṇerikās* can take precepts only from *bhikṣuṇīs* and there are no *bhikṣuṇīs*. That is why they are not called *śrāmaṇerikās*.

HHDL: And in Cambodia?

Q: Ten precepts.

Q: Education is the key to the development of the nuns. We have a few ideas about a Buddhist Women's Institute which we would like to present to you. Eventually, we would like to see such institutes in many different countries, but we thought of starting first in India.

HHDL: As far as the Tibetan nuns are concerned, it would be good if we could first initiate this kind of study program within the already existing nunneries.

Q: But then it would not be really international because it would all be in Tibetan language, and it also would not be recognized as a higher degree in the school system.

HHDL: It would be good to have such an institute, but sometimes if the idea is too grandiose, it does not materialize. Whereas, where there is something already existing, it needs only to be further developed. That is the point.

Q: Do you think that it would be good for Tibetan nuns to attend the Institute of Buddhist Dialectics?

HHDL: Very good, but the nuns at Geden Choeling Nunnery in Dharamsala have already begun a program for the study of dialectics.

Q: Would Your Holiness accept an invitation to attend if the International Conference on Buddhist Nuns were held in Sri Lanka?

HHDL: In the present political climate, Tibetans are not allowed to visit Sri Lanka.[2]

Q: This conference has been very successful because Your Holiness graced the gathering. If the next conference were held in Bangkok, would you be able to attend?

HHDL: Yes, but my presence is not so important. In the Theravādin countries, where there are some obstacles and opposition, more work needs to be done, in quiet ways, until the people get used to the idea of having *bhikṣuṇīs*. Wherever the next conference is held, [the *bhikṣuṇī* issue] will receive the most publicity within that country, and the people will become more familiar with the topic. Articles need to be written on the subject to create publicity and plant seeds that will grow into seedlings.

NOTES

1. Subsequent investigation has shown that there is currently no Sarvāstivādin lineage extant in the Vietnamese tradition.

2. This is due to pressures from the People's Republic of China.

9 *Livelihood for Sangha*

Now we come to a delicate topic which is nevertheless of critical importance for Buddhist nuns. How do they support themselves? How do mendicants manage in the twentieth-century work-a-day world? Where do they get their food? Who pays their health insurance? How do they face the stark realities of survival in a profession without a salary?

When organizing the speakers for the various panel discussions at the conference, it was very difficult to find anyone willing to speak on the topic of livelihood for *Sangha*. Several Asian nuns declined, explaining that livelihood is not an issue for them since they live in temples that provide all their daily needs. Several Western nuns declined on the grounds that they have had a terrible time making ends meet ever since taking ordination and have so far found no solution to the problem. In the end, we managed to solicit some speakers for the panel and to set off some lively discussions, but seemed to merely scratch the surface of this crucial issue.

In general, we can say that people in traditionally Buddhist countries are accustomed to supporting the *Sangha* while new Buddhists in Western countries are not so accustomed. To delineate nuns' experience vis-a-vis livelihood entirely along East/West lines would be to oversimplify. There are Western nuns whose parents, friends, or temples support them, and there are nuns in certain Asian countries who are literally reduced to begging. Still, ordained *Sangha* members in Buddhist countries are generally provided for, while this is not ordinarily the case in other countries.

It is said that no nun or monk who is practicing sincerely will lack the necessities of daily life. This is reflected in a popular passage from the *sūtras*: "One who takes care of by the *Dhamma*, will be taken care of by the *Dhamma*. One who takes care of morality will be taken care of by morality."

In most Buddhist countries, in fact, simply wearing the robes is seen as worthy of support. In many instances, however, the wearing of robes by male practitioners is seen as worthier of support than the wearing of robes by female practitioners. Part of the reason for this relates to their level of ordinations. It is traditionally believed that donating to those who are fully ordained is more meritorious than donating to novices. This belief influences the degree of a donor's generosity, and where the monks are most fully ordained and the nuns are not, the result is naturally that the monks are better supported than the nuns. Donations may be made in cash or in kind, with the amount normally left to the discretion of the donor. These offerings may be given to individuals, or to the monastery as a whole, to be used for communal supplies or to be distributed among the residents.

This raises the question of lifestyle and the level of support to be given *Sangha* members. What constitutes a satisfactory standard of living for nuns and monks? How do we assure their health and well-being, and still help them abide by the *Vinaya* regulations? To what extent should their lifestyle accord with the standards of other members of their society? Will competent women today who are used to a comfortable lifestyle and could be drawing handsome salaries in the job market be satisfied to enter a profession that provides only the bare necessities? These are questions that concern nuns and potential nuns in all countries and in all traditions.

It is clear that people drawn from various backgrounds have

different answers to these questions, different expectations, and different tolerance levels. For example, when contemplating ordination, a single change of clothes, a simple diet, and a bare sleeping mat seem very attractive. What to do a few years later when your health gives out and you find that you can no longer manage under such spartan conditions? A person raised in simple circumstances may find monastic conditions very similar to what they are used to, while a woman from a wealthy urban family may find the adjustments a real ordeal, even insufferable. For each, a life of renunciation has a vastly different meaning, both in terms of physical realities and in terms of psychological transformation. A person faced with great challenges on the material level may find that stripping away accustomed comforts and security accelerate inner development to a remarkable degree. These challenges may also push her beyond the limits of her endurance.

There is no simple formula for predicting how a woman entering the ordained life will react to the changing conditions that her decision entails. The ideal, of course, is to maintain equanimity whether faced by abundance or poverty, feast or famine, seeing them as equally impermanent. For most, however, it takes time to achieve such laudable equanimity.

Buddhist mendicants are not supposed to amass wealth, but neither are they required to live lives of abject poverty. They are taught to strive for simplicity in daily living to counter attachments and to facilitate meditative stabilization, but "simplicity" is a relative concept, allowing a certain amount of latitude. To have fewer objects of desire around and fewer distractions in the material field helps in learning to concentrate the mind, while luxurious living can obviously be detrimental to the development of renunciation for beginning practitioners. The point is to steer a middle course, maintaining healthful living conditions adequate for mental cultivation and altruistic activity, while remembering that the greatest wealth is inner contentment.

Among Buddhist nuns, there are those who have a very difficult time with livelihood, those who have a very easy time, and those who manage somewhere in-between. Of those who have a difficult time, some benefit from the experience of adversity, some persevere despite adversity, and some give up. There are nuns who have an impossibly difficult time simply surviving, living in the most appalling conditions, who spend immense physical and mental energy gathering the materials for sustaining life and become extremely depressed. Others, in similar circumstances, rejoice in having only one mouth to feed, one body to clothe, and dwell contented with whatever comes their way. Obviously, many in the first category eventually give up their vows, while those in the latter tend to continue as nuns. Physical conditions are part of the equation, mental attitudes toward those conditions are another. Whatever the circumstances, inner fortitude is definitely advantageous in the ordained life.

Although the high standard of living and the generosity of donors allow nuns to live comfortably in Hong Kong and Taiwan today, most of them work very hard and conscientiously maintain a simple lifestyle. Ven. Shig Hiu Wan, a leading Chinese *bhikṣuṇī* master, trains disciples rigorously and teaches them contentment. She often tells them, "The life of a nun is a life of hardship; if you are not capable of accepting hardships, it is better not to become a nun." She reminds the nuns to practice purely and diligently to be worthy of the food they eat daily, this advice being one of the reflections regarding food that are customary among the Buddhist clergy. Work is an integral part of the daily program for every resident and vegetables are grown as a symbol of self-sufficiency, as was characteristic of public monasteries in China. The motto of her training institute to the north of Taipei is: "Sincere seekers of enlightenment welcome; others are advised to apply elsewhere."

In Korea, nunneries receive donations from the laity and may have income from property holdings as well. The resident nuns are provided with food, clothing, and necessities by their nunneries. In addition, they receive funds for medical treatment and for travel expenses whenever the need arises.

These benefits are contingent upon their adherence to a demanding schedule of work and practice. Much of the food is grown and prepared by the nuns themselves.

In the larger nunneries in Japan the nuns' requirements are met by donations and other income of the community. In the smaller temples, however, more individual responsibility for the functioning and financial management falls upon the single nun who is in charge. She performs religious ceremonies for the lay benefactors of the temple, and provides both for her own expenses and for the upkeep of the temple with the donations received. In general, nuns' temples tend to have fewer supporters and less income than monks' temples.

In the Theravāda countries, the living standard of the nuns seems distinctly linked with the fact that they are not fully ordained and hence are not considered members of the *Sangha*. In Burma, nuns who are not supported privately go for alms, but are not allowed to receive cooked foods like the monks do. They bear trays upon their heads upon which to collect donations of uncooked rice and other foods which they then carry back to their nunneries and cook for themselves. Usually one day each week is spent going from one household to another in the surrounding villages to gather supplies. Small groups of nuns then pool their supplies and cook together within the nunnery. It is rare that a whole nunnery has sufficient supplies to cook as a unit on a continuous basis.

In Sri Lanka, nuns are allowed to receive cooked food as alms and are also permitted to cook for themselves. Those who are educated and present a good appearance to the community manage quite well; others have quite a difficult time gathering their sustenance. As one government official puts it, "In Sri Lanka the upkeep of a nun will not be a problem provided her ways are good and acceptable. Knowledge of the *Dhamma* and the ability to perform religious rites will add to this qualification. In fact, looking after such nuns will be taken by the society as a great privilege rather than as a liability." The key to improving the living standards of the nuns, therefore, is upgrading their educational standards and thereby their image in the public eye.

Nuns in Thailand receive little public support and almost always must rely on savings or private support for their livelihood. Since they are only accorded the status of laywomen, they are generally required to pay room and board in the temples. Those with help from their families or other benefactors are able to stay continuously in a temple, engaging in religious practices. A few of these study and attend meditation courses. Many other nuns stay in a temple until their private savings are exhausted, then disrobe, get a job, and work to save up until they have enough money to get ordained and stay for another length of time in a temple. Thai custom permits them to disrobe and re-ordain like this, but having to repeatedly disrobe and go to work is decidedly disruptive to their spiritual life.

The circumstances of Western nuns vary. While staying in Chinese or Korean monasteries, their daily requirements are generally provided. In other situations, they must provide for themselves. Some of these nuns are regularly sponsored by their parents or friends, some live from occasional donations, while others must take up paying jobs to generate an income. There are very few monasteries in their home countries where they may live without having to pay. Nuns, and monks, are often charged for meditation courses and *Dharma* teachings in the West, a regrettable departure from Buddhist custom. A satisfactory solution to the problem of livelihood for Western *Sangha* has yet to be found.

Until now, wherever Buddhist culture has flourished, the ordained clergy have been provided with support by the laity. The nuns and monks, for their part, have been diligent in their practices and their monastic duties, providing whatever services were required by the lay donors. It remains to be seen whether this traditional system of mutual dependency will gain currency in Western countries with their cash economies and strong emphasis on the work ethic. It seems likely that Western Buddhist monastics will be forced to greater self-sufficiency, in accord with the Zen maxim: "A day of no working is a day of no eating."

THE ROLE OF THE *SANGHA*
by Abhaya Weerakoon

In Sri Lanka, the *Sangha* is looked after by all the laypeople, so there is no difficulty in obtaining their subsistence. At the same time, there are certain things that are expected of the *Sangha*.

The honor and respect which is showered upon the members of the *Sangha*, sometimes to the point of embarrassment, is a primary facet of Sri Lankan culture. *Sangha* members are greatly venerated and this veneration of the *Sangha* is an essential part of life. We refer to the three Gems: the Buddha, a venerable being; the *Dhamma*, the venerable doctrine which he set forth; and the *Sangha*, the venerable ordained community. To be worthy of veneration is a big responsibility that is placed upon the *Sangha*.

In Sri Lanka, this veneration for the *Sangha* is reflected in the language. We use special terms for referring to the actions of monks. For instance, when a layperson eats, it is "*kanawa*" and when a monk eats, it is "*valandinawa*." When we go, it is "*yanawa*," and when a monk goes, it is "*vadinawa*." When we sleep, it is "*nidagannawa*," but when a monk sleeps, it is "*satapenewa*." Thus there is a distinction in the words that we use for the same action performed by members of the lay and the ordained communities.

There is also a distinction in the meaning indicated by these terms. A layperson can eat standing, wherever, in whatever manner, but a member of the *Sangha* is expected to sit down very patiently, stay in that position, and mindfully take food. There is thus a big difference in this one action performed by two different kinds of people. It is the same regarding walking: a layperson can run, dance, or do anything, but a monk must walk about with a certain demeanor. People look up to him. There is something noble in the way he moves about. That is the role into which the *Sangha* is cast.

This tradition of regarding the *Sangha* with veneration has been carried down from generation to generation, and has a sublime quality to it. The outward behavior of the monks, as well as their being able to guide others with the wisdom they have collected from the *Tripitaka*, evokes immense respect and honor toward the *Sangha* from the laity. Therefore, looking after the *Sangha* is not a burden, not a responsibility; it is a pleasure. If we can give this message to laypeople—that it is a great privilege on their part to look after the noble *Sangha*—the *Sangha* will continue to exist. The *Sangha* will look after the laypeople and their requirements, and the laypeople will look after the *Sangha* in turn.

RIGHT LIVELIHOOD FOR MONKS AND NUNS

by Bhikṣuṇī Karma Lekshe Tsomo

A unique and historical process of transmission is currently underway as the Buddhist teachings are introduced into the twentieth-century Western world. These ancient teachings are being transmitted in a fascinating array of cultural vehicles, from whence they are being digested and adapted to suit the lifestyles and psychological inclinations of humanity today. In the process, an increasing number of people are being naturally drawn to follow the Buddha's injunctions to leave the household life, taking vows as monks and nuns. Monasticism, which is said to be an essential foundation for the proper establishment of the doctrine, is slowly evolving. Because conditions in the modern world are considerably different from those that prevailed during the time of Lord Buddha, however, many ordained *Sangha* members are facing problems in terms of material support. Since the establishment and maintenance of communities of male and female celibate practitioners have been integral elements of Buddhist life from the beginning, the question of livelihood for ordained *Sangha* in the present day is one that deserves careful consideration.

During the time of the Buddha, ordained monks and nuns led very simple lives and were willing to accept material hardships in the pursuit of their spiritual goals. In fact, the *niśrayas*, or resources of livelihood, are explained when taking higher ordination, and a candidate is asked whether or not he or she agrees to each one. For a *bhikṣu*, there are four *niśrayas*: wearing clothes made from rags, eating food obtained from begging, lodging under trees, and using cow urine for medicine. A *bhikṣuṇī* is exempt from the third of these—sleeping under trees—as it is considered unsafe for a woman to sleep in the open.

For example, the first *niśraya*, dealing with wearing apparel, is explained as follows at the time of full ordination as a nun: "O daughter of good family, listen! The Tathagata Arhat Samyaksambuddha, because of the desire to benefit all abundantly, has correctly explained and established the three resources for the group of *śrāvikas*. To the daughters of good family who patiently endure and are upright in their hearts, the *upasampadā* ordination shall be given. If they do not patiently endure, the *upasampadā* ordination shall not be given. What are the three *niśrayas*? (1) Clothes made of rags (*pamsukula*) are trifles, easy to obtain, fitting, and have nothing wrong with them, and thus should be used by the *bhikṣuṇīs*. One can become a *bhikṣuṇī* by using them, leaving home to enter the order, and receiving the *upasampadā* ordination. In this respect, therefore, can you patiently endure throughout your life, and use robes made from rags?"[1]

The other resources of livelihood are similarly explained, and the text reads similarly for *bhikṣus* and *bhikṣuṇīs*. From this it is clear that the Buddha meant for all to understand from the beginning that the life of an ordained being, far from being luxurious, is to be lived in simplicity and humility, with strength to endure whatever hardships may arise. The addendum to each resource, which is added after the candidate agrees to endure patiently such simple conditions of life, elucidates what is allowable above and beyond the minimum for subsistence. In the case of clothing, in addition to rags, one may accept robes of wool, cotton, silk, hemp, or linen, when they are offered. With regard to food, in addition to alms food, one may accept invitations and meals on special days when the occasion arises. In addition to cow urine for medicine, one may accept ghee, oil, molasses, butter, lard, etc. A *bhikṣu* is permitted to lodge for the night in *vihāras* and private homes upon invitation in addition to sleeping under trees. For *bhikṣuṇīs vihāras* and homes are the allowable options.

The essential point of this explanation seems to be that an ordained monk or nun should be ready to make do with the very poorest, minimal material conditions to free one's mind for spiritual pursuits and distance oneself from material attachments. Then if by chance one should happen to obtain something more or better than the minimal, fine. One may accept it.

The provision of the resources of livelihood, as set forth in the *Vinaya* texts, seems to be a skillful method of heading off attachment, greed, and avarice, and of engendering contentment in the minds of ordained practitioners. It also serves to limit the material burden of the lay community, upon whose generosity the ordained community relies. A logical corollary to this would be that if one is not willing to accept a simple, unencumbered existence which may at times entail difficulties, and is not able to make certain sacrifices on the material plane, it would be better not to seek ordination, but rather to continue practicing in the aspect of a layperson.

Subsequent to the Buddha's *parinirvāna*, as the numbers of Buddhist followers grew, lay supporters increasingly provided accommodations and other material requirements for the *Sangha*. As the Buddhist teachings spread to various countries throughout Asia, adaptations of this traditional support system evolved within each society. And in all Buddhist societies, in line with the Buddha's explication, the act of providing materially for monks and nuns was considered highly virtuous, a mode of accumulating merits by the laity.

The practice of generosity toward the *Sangha* assumed great popularity and is still very much in evidence in Buddhist countries and their overseas communities up to the present day. The devotion evidenced by laypeople as they offer donations of food and clothing in the traditional Buddhist countries is very inspiring. Furthermore, it engenders in the mind of the recipient an attitude of humility and acts as a spur to practice, in that one feels beholden to behave and practice in a way that would make one worthy of accepting such earnest offerings. In appreciation for generosity received, *Sangha* members offer teachings or prayers on behalf of the donors and their families.

Today, in most Buddhist countries, living conditions for monks and nuns are quite adequate,[2] providing a stable and conducive foundation for study and practice. In some countries the practice of going for alms has nearly disappeared due to the fact that sufficient food and necessities are provided by lay benefactors to monasteries and temples. The provisions thus donated are then distributed equitably to the residents. In addition to the basic necessities provided, special offerings and invitations may be received upon occasion.

It may also happen that an ordained practitioner lives independently, in isolation or retreat, supported by individuals or families. Occasionally, an affluent or well-supported monk or nun may offer donations to those who are less fortunate. Where material support is forthcoming from such sources, the case of an indigent ordained person is rare and the necessity of going to look for work is obviated. In fact, in most Buddhist countries the idea of a *Sangha* member engaging in business or working at an ordinary job would generally be frowned upon or prohibited. Where is the need for drawing a salary when all requirements are provided by the monastery?

Engaging in business dealings is specifically prohibited in the *Bhikṣu* and *Bhikṣuṇī Prāṭimokśa* precepts, and calls into question the legitimacy of paid employment by those who are fully ordained. There may be certain exceptions, such as the case of a monk or nun working as a teacher and receiving remuneration for this, but ordinarily the motivation of one wishing to work at a paying job would be considered questionable.

These days the *Buddhadharma* is rapidly spreading to countries which were not traditionally or not currently Buddhist. In such countries the custom of giving alms to *Sangha* members is not yet established. This has given rise to questions concerning how ordained beings are to maintain their livelihood. There are presently a large number of Buddhist monks and nuns living as refugees in foreign lands where they are experiencing difficulties obtaining food and necessities, and some have found it necessary to work at a gainful occupation. For example, there are more than 6,000 Tibetan monks and nuns living in exile in India, Nepal, Switzerland, and so on. There are also hundreds of Vietnamese, Cambodian, and Laotian monks and nuns living as refugees in France, Canada, and the United States. When donations received from the resettled, and often financially strapped, members of their particular communities are insufficient, they may be faced with a choice of either disrobing or working at a job to provide for their own needs.

Western Buddhist monks and nuns are another group who may be faced with this decision. Though hundreds of thousands of people in the West have embraced Buddhism, the general population in these countries is either Judaeo-Christian or non-religious. This results in a number of difficulties encountered by those who have taken ordination: women with shaved heads and men in skirts may occasionally incite hostility, while a person seeking alms might be courting arrest! Unless one is financially independent or is being supported by a benefactor, the question of livelihood is certain to arise.

Even though there are many thousands of Buddhist followers in Western countries, many are young or of subsistence-level income. In general, it seems that the necessity and importance of providing support to Western *Sangha* members has not yet been fully realized. In democratic and affluent countries, it is commonly felt that individuals should be responsible for their own livelihood, willing to make their own way, and that those who are ordained should be no exception. In fact, not working and relying on others is widely criticized as unseemly behavior. Western *Sangha* members are caught in a bind between their vows and their cultural context.

There is no truth, however, to the assertion that Westerners have no tradition of supporting monks and nuns. The Roman Catholic orders have for centuries fully provided necessities for their ordained clergy. Of course, it goes without saying that the members of these orders are expected to observe appropriate standards of behavior and to provide whatever service is required of them, but nonetheless, their living needs are definitely met. Amongst the Protestant denominations, too, a salary sufficient to cover the living expenses of the lay clergy and their families is provided in return for services rendered. Rabbis, who serve as spiritual leaders within the Judaic tradition, are also provided with housing and other necessities of life.

Thus, the procedures for Western and Eastern religious orders are seen to correlate to a large extent. In both, as long as members enjoy the facilities and support of the order, they are expected to observe certain rules and modes of conduct in addition to whatever vows they may have taken, and to fulfill any duties that may be required of them by their respective orders.

At present, a situation prevails in which the ordained Western members of various Buddhist orders often lack living facilities and support. As yet, there is a startling scarcity of monasteries and nunneries in Western countries. Even a person who is strongly inclined toward ordination would be wise to consider seriously the question of livelihood before deciding to take vows. Many people have taken vows prematurely, only to later discover how difficult it can be to find food and a place to live. Monasteries and plans for monasteries are slowly evolving, but many are still in the imagination stage and all unavoidably face financial uncertainties.

It is hoped that an awareness of the importance of a strong *Sangha* will grow in the minds of Western Buddhists and that this awareness will help generate a substantial material basis of support for the development of monasteries for both men and women in Western countries. Such monasteries are not only necessary as a foundation for the proper establishment of Buddhism in these countries, but should also serve as havens of refuge for the lay community by providing teaching, counseling, and retreat facilities.

In the meantime what are we to do? Perhaps my own experience will be of some interest. After having sought and been granted permission to take vows, I personally postponed ordination due to lack of funds. It seemed ridiculous to get ordained today and then put on a wig to go to work tomorrow. I resolved to work at a job conscientiously, save all the money, and go to study in India. The amount earned in six months covered the cost of my air ticket and my living expenses for a year in India after ordination.

The next year I got by on the money from my income tax

return and the sale of my guitar, but after that, things got more difficult. Living from occasional monetary donations from friends and from the food distributed at *pujas*, I was able to manage for two more years, but it was not particularly beneficial to health. I returned to Hawaii and served as translator at our local *Dharma* center, which provided room and board. For transportation and personal expenses, however, it was necessary to work part-time as an interpreter at a medical service. I felt that this work did not compromise my vows in any way; it even seemed to make me more conscious of my behavior and my identity as a nun. In addition, it was serving people, which is a fine way of developing compassion and actualizing Buddhist values.

After this, I accompanied one of my *lamas* on a teaching tour of the west coast for six months. Following this tour, I received permission from my teachers and decided to go to Taiwan to receive *bhikṣuṇī* ordination. A dear friend generously donated the air ticket and money for expenses. Along the way, I was able to visit monasteries and nunneries in various Buddhist countries and to observe firsthand how the living needs of monks and nuns are provided in Japan, Korea, Taiwan, Hong Kong, and Thailand. Currently, I continue to study in India, living from the donations received from friends and family.

From my experiences, I have drawn a number of tentative conclusions. First, it is essential for a person contemplating ordination to consider seriously the implications of livelihood before taking vows. To assume that support will necessarily be forthcoming as soon as one shaves one's head is to be overly idealistic and somewhat naive. It is more realistic to arrange support before taking vows, unless one happens to be independently wealthy.

One practical alternative is to work prior to ordination, saving to provide one's own support for some time. The first few years of ordained life require enough adjustments as it is without the additional strain of financial worries. These first years should be seen as a time of gaining stability in one's practice, as removed as possible from worldly activities. Since it requires very little to live simply as a monk or nun should, an aware person would take the responsible step of preparing for his or her own material support, rather than having to face indigence or the distractions of outside employment during this critical adjustment period. Another alternative is to save a substantial amount, invest prudently, and live from the dividends that accrue. In the eventuality that a friend, relative, or center expresses intentions of individual sponsorship, it is wise to clarify the nature and extent of the intentions beforehand, so as to avoid misunderstandings or disappointment. People's circumstances change and many a monk or nun has been left high and dry by a sponsor's shifting fortunes.

Secondly, after taking vows, one should live simply and be willing to accept a certain amount of material hardship in the course of one's spiritual endeavor. A person who becomes ordained without eliminating unnecessary worldly involvements and without abandoning undue acquisitiveness has obviously chosen the wrong vocation. The life of a renunciate requires determination, sincerity, and humility, and it is only by practicing with these values in mind that one can expect to elicit support from the lay community. If one feels a need for the latest design of sleeping bag or gourmet foods at every meal, one can scarcely hope to gain much support for these ambitions from the laity. Whatever donations are received should be used properly, frugally, and with appreciation. Since one of the chief responsibilities of an ordained practitioner is to serve as a model of virtuous behavior, more affluent monks and nuns should set an example for the practitioners by sharing their wealth with those who are poorer. By voluntarily working to reduce extreme disparities of fortune, Buddhists can contribute to human evolution positively by actualizing balance, harmony, and well-being within their respective societies.

Third, a *Sangha* member has an explicit obligation to maintain a high standard of conduct, to keep the vows as well as possible, and to refrain from any behavior that might discredit the *Sangha*. In addition, one has an implicit obligation to serve the spiritual needs of the lay community and to attend to the duties required within one's own living community. In short, one is expected to behave in a way that is worthy and will inspire donations from kind benefactors. This is not to say that one becomes a perfected being simply by shaving one's head and donning robes. Changing clothes does not automatically eliminate negativities inlaid upon the mindstream. Nevertheless, robes are a symbol of certain ideals and wearing them entails a responsibility to strive toward embodying the Buddha's teachings. Ordained *Sangha* members have a duty to conduct their lives in a manner that justifies material support and one would hope that their sincerity and diligent practice would spontaneously elicit such support.

Finally, I feel that one should be willing to accept work for remuneration only when absolutely necessary. To give up one's vows for lack of funds would be highly unfortunate, not only from the point of view of *karma* but also in terms of the proper spread of *Buddhadharma* to the West. Still, a paying job should be sought only when one is utterly destitute and there is truly no alternative, because in work situations monks and nuns are treated as laypeople and begin to lose regard for themselves as *Sangha* members. Since their lifestyle differs little from that of their colleagues, they begin to question their identity and rationale for being ordained and some lose their vows as a result. Some jobs entail social functions where one is under pressure to dance or drink and where sexual innuendos become unavoidable. Many times it is not possible to wear robes to work, and wearing lay clothes exposes monks and nuns to an intangible psychological vulnerability. This may sound prudish or bizarre, but recent developments within the Catholic orders warrant attention. It has been observed, for example, that nuns in make-up and short skirts may easily become caught up or confused by worldly involvements and often lose their professions as a consequence. Since the Buddhist orders in the West are so new, we can profit by learning from their experiences.

Before resorting to remunerative employment, there are certain other measures to generate income that can be explored. Living on little or nothing may in itself generate contributions without a word having to be spoken. After all, the Buddha is said to have vowed that no monk or nun genuinely practicing his teachings would ever die of starvation or cold. Demonstrating one's resoluteness and sincerity to engage in practice full-time despite poverty is likely to attract donations, bearing witness to the universal axiom that virtue brings its own rewards. Though skeptics may scoff, another valid method deserving of consideration is prayer. Notably, Jambhala is the deity whom Tibetan tradition regards as specifically apt to provide material resources when supplicated. I happened to place a small statue of Jambhala on my altar while doing prostrations as part of the preliminary practices, and unaccountably, four checks arrived within the week. Green Tara is also renowned of helping manifest the material needs of *Dharma* practitioners who petition her.

Many Western monks and nuns have diminished the dilemma of livelihood by taking up residence in India, where living costs are low, or in Buddhist countries where food and shelter are easily available to them. Though the discipline is strict and demanding, this alternative has the added advantage of providing excellent training as well as psychological support for those who are newly ordained. Still it is not a permanent solution to the problem which is, basically, how Western Buddhists are to provide for their *own* monks and nuns. It is hoped that teachers will instill in their students a sense of responsibility to support their own ordained *Sangha* and explain the benefits, both *karmic* and practical, that accrue from maintaining monks and nuns of their own nationality.

Another possibility for gaining support is to appeal directly to one's friends and relatives. Often they would be happy to contribute if they knew a need existed. It seems not to have occurred to many that material sustenance is required by those whose full-time (if unpaid) profession is being a monk or nun. Previously in Tibet a system was established whereby seven families shared the responsibility of supporting an individual monk or nun, all contributing equally to maintain their basic needs. The system still functions to the present day in many areas of Ladakh. Perhaps such a system can be developed to meet the needs of Western monks and nuns, providing them material security without overburdening particular donors. In an emergency, one should not be too proud to make one's need known. Of the two accumulations, generosity is important in the accumulation of merit and *Sangha* members serve a role as recipients of generosity. For the mendicant also, learning to receive with gratitude and dignity is fine training in the development of humility, but skill and discretion must be exercised when requesting help, whether directly or indirectly. Lacking proper motivation, manners, or scruples, the custom of requesting material aid is one that could easily be abused.

If one is indeed forced to work, it is important to choose the job carefully. Right livelihood, as part of the Noble Eightfold Path, is incumbent upon all Buddhists, ordained or lay. Therefore, any work which involves killing, falsification, misappropriation, intoxicants, or otherwise breaches any of the five basic Buddhist precepts is clearly unsuitable. If even laypeople are required to respect the five precepts, ordained people should obviously be far more careful in observing them. By extension, one should shun work which is involved with munitions or which takes advantage of others. Any position which requires one to distort the truth or jeopardizes one's vows is clearly inappropriate for any Buddhist, much less a monk or nun. For the sake of one's practice, it would be better to avoid situations which are extremely tense, irritating, or sensual, unless one has already gained a high level of realization. Naturally, bartending or related occupations where one is obliged to serve alcohol or wear revealing clothing are out of the question for those who are ordained.

In short, it would be best to seek work which is honest, low-stress, and of benefit to others. It is recommended that one work the minimum number of hours required to adequately provide for one's needs and that the job be terminated as soon as possible. Teaching, medical care, child care, and counseling are examples of occupations that seem compatible with ordained life, although this is by no means an exhaustive listing. Handicrafts and food production are two possibilities for monastic communities striving toward self-sufficiency.

Ultimately, it is one's motivation and mindfulness that are of utmost importance. In these pioneer stages of Western Buddhist development, much thought and care need be taken to discover means of livelihood that allow ordained *Sangha* to adapt to current conditions without sacrificing their vows and principles. May the day come soon when the *Buddhadharma* is firmly established on Western soil and all ordained beings are able to live closely by the monastic guidelines of Śakyamuni Buddha.

NOTES

1. A. Hirakawa, *Monastic Discipline for the Buddhist Nuns.* Patna, 1982, p. 66.

2. An exception to this are the eight- and ten-precept nuns of Thailand and Sri Lanka, where neither the *śrāmaṇerikā* nor *bhikṣuṇī* ordinations are available and where conditions for female practitioners are quite difficult.

10 *Living as a Nun in the West*

As the *Buddhadharma* goes to the West, it sometimes happens that Western people are inspired to lead celibate lives and receive ordination. The wish to become ordained may be a spontaneous impulse of the moment or it may be a reasoned decision based on practical considerations. In either case, there is usually a sincere commitment to the *Dharma* and a desire to devote more time to the practice. Almost all people receive precepts with the best of intentions, yet their lives following ordination take many different turns.

It is hard to visualize the effect that making such a serious commitment will have. Things are never exactly as we imagine. Ordination makes a deep impact upon the mind, often in ways that are inexpressible and imperceptible. Experiences differ, depending largely upon the extent to which we get caught up in judgments, labeling, and expectations. Nevertheless, we wake up the next day with a new perception of ourselves and our relationship to the world. We are faced with new feelings and practical realities that are complex in themselves, being further intensified by the responses of people around us. Even if nothing in particular changes, experiences register in new ways.

While the experience of living as a nun or monk within a

loving supportive community will certainly differ from getting ordained and immediately being left completely on one's own, in either case the first teaching of the ordained life is often that we are born alone and die alone. There is no longer anything or anyone to lean on. Essentially the ordained life means relying on the inner experience of the teachings without external props. In a sense, Western people who have been raised to function independently may find it easier to adjust to such a life. The sense of aloneness which persists even in ordained community life is much harder for Asian people to cope with, since they are generally accustomed to a closely interdependent family life. After embarking upon "the homeless life," the monastic community often becomes a surrogate family for them.

The problems encountered by Western people in ordained life more often relate to discipline, emotional conflicts, and physical circumstances. A high percentage return to lay life. If ordained life is so conducive to practice and the people who enter it are so committed to the *Dharma*, what accounts for the high drop-out rate? Clearly, this is a question that requires in-depth research and should not be over-generalized. It is a very personal and individual matter, but a few thoughts on the subject may be in order.

Logic tells us that a decision to give up the celibate life may relate to problems in maintaining celibacy. It has become something of an "in" joke in ordained circles that no one gives up their vows due to an overwhelming desire to eat after noon. Some frankly admit to "falling in love." Others become ordained without having satisfactorily explored the limits of relationship and later find curiosity gets the better of them. Some find abstinence restrictive after ordination, though it was never a problem before.

Another problem relates to discipline and culturally conditioned value systems. A valid *Prāṭimokśa* ordination is necessarily received in a particular *Vinaya* school, which at this point is transmitted through the medium of an Asian Buddhist tradition. The customs concomitant with the traditional lineage may complement individualistic Western lifestyles, but they may also conflict. The latter experience seems to be quite common.

While acknowledging and respecting the tremendous debt owed to Asian cultures, it is obvious that we Western Buddhists need time and space in which to find our own directions. We need to be strict, but not too rigid; to be open and flexible, but not sloppy. We need to learn from Asian Buddhist prototypes without being overwhelmed by Asian cultural components. We want to devise modes of practice which preserve the essence of the Buddha's teachings, yet are compatible with Western civilization. We should strive to preserve the most excellent values of East and West.

Accepting Buddhism does not mean forfeiting the positive aspects of our own religious and cultural heritages; however, becoming a nun or monk does imply adopting genuine Buddhist values authentically. One recommended method is to train closely with respected Asian exponents of monastic discipline during the first years of ordained life. Adjustments to Western cultural and social conditions can then be made on a solid foundation of understanding. Such training is an experience to be treasured. Similar to training in the martial arts, it requires humility and perseverance. While some people cite the hardships of traditional monastic training and the cultural adjustments it requires as reasons for giving up their vows, paradoxically, others cite the lack of such training as a reason. Certainly some experience of traditional training is important for nuns and monks, since they will be instrumental in the process of adapting traditional Buddhist institutions to the Western situation.

There is no doubt that Buddhism is a valuable spiritual path for large numbers of Western people, but is ordination a viable step when there are as yet very few monasteries in the West where they can stay and train? Is living on one's own a realistic alternative? What models should we look to in setting up monastic training centers and what problems can we expect to encounter in the process? Whose job is it to set up such centers and when are they going to get started?

There is a definite consensus on the need for centers where nuns and potential nuns can become accustomed to monastic life. Chaotic environments simply are not conducive to formal meditation practice and disciplined conduct. Living on one's own, isolated from a supportive *Sangha* and vulnerable to the onslaught of worldly values, can be quite unsettling, especially in the beginning years. Ordained women need monasteries where they can study and attempt to live by the *Vinaya*; laywomen need protective surroundings where they can prepare for ordination and can gain experience in monastic values before making a lifelong commitment.

In addition to an intense awareness of the need for training centers, there is a recognition that monasteries for Westerners will differ in some important respects from Asian Buddhist models. Along with this recognition, there is growing concern that meaningful time-honored traditions not be discarded simply on the basis of superficial impressions. Even if they may appear exotic, extraneous, or constraining in the beginning, some traditions have symbolic or psychological significance that can be of great value in the practice. Wisdom and mature judgement are required to discern what will ultimately benefit and what will impede our spiritual growth. Nuns, monks, and others who have undergone many years of formal training have a special responsibility to understand traditions and interpret them for others. They can serve as cultural bridges, helping to bring about a graceful transition from ancient to modern practice.

There are some traditional practices that seem especially apt to arouse resistance—for instance, bowing. It is the custom of bowing to *bhikṣus*, the first of the eight important rules for *bhikṣuṇīs*, that is most difficult for Western women to countenance. This is understandable; Western people normally have difficulty bowing to anything, especially another human being, whether female or male. The Buddhist custom of bowing to statues of enlightened beings has been widely misinterpreted as "idol worship," causing great misunderstanding since it contravenes one of the ten commandments of the Judaeo-Christian faith. Actually the custom of bowing is meant to demonstrate respect for the enlightenment potential within all living beings, including oneself, and is not a display of worship or subservience at all. Bowing is also used as a practice for engendering humility. In some Buddhist countries the custom of bowing to senior nuns and monks is still widely practiced; in others, it is normally reserved for paying reverence to learned or realized masters. It derives from the ancient Indian custom of showing respect to elders; even in contemporary Sri Lanka and India, well-mannered children bow to their parents every morning.

By contrast, Western people do not always naturally engender respect along the lines of seniority. Most are accustomed to making independent decisions, and may resist authority and structures altogether unless they lead to tangible rewards and punishments. The large measure of social, economic, and academic freedom current in Western cultures stimulates individual creativity, even genius, but does little to promote personal discipline. Discipline is frequently labeled suppressive, constrictive, or authoritarian. For those seriously interested in developing self-discipline, therefore, periods of monastic training in traditional Asian monasteries will prove greatly instructive. There are also some monasteries in the West, such as the City of Ten Thousand Buddhas near Ukiah, California, where people may go to train. Eventually, new and creative operational structures will need to be developed which are suitable to the capabilities and temperaments of the members of new monastic communities. Those who display resistance to discipline altogether and an unwillingness to accommodate may simply be unsuited to monastic life.

It is likely that Western Buddhist monasteries will evolve their own models of organization. They may not be run strictly along the lines of Asian monastic institutions, but compatible features can be incorporated from traditional models. The structure of existing meditative communities should be studied and experienced to ascertain which features of each seem most desirable. These can then be implemented on an experimental basis to see which are most workable in the new monastic situation. Some features of traditional structures will be suitable, others can be adapted, some will be rejected, and surely the process of synthesizing will be informative. It would also be good to take a look at the organization of the Christian monastic institutions that have evolved for Western people over many generations.

To my mind, the ideal Western Buddhist monastery should be a sensitive blend of Asian and Western elements that is comfortable for all and still conducive to intensive practice. For example, I would like to see an international, non-sectarian monastery for women grow up somewhere in North America where nuns and prospective nuns could receive training and learn to live by the *Vinaya*. A meditation hall patterned on the Chinese, Japanese, or Korean model, *Vinaya* discipline on the Theravāda model, and a study program on the Tibetan model, with Western-style private rooms and a vegetarian diet would be a good combination to try. Years of communal living lead me to favor a careful admissions policy and small beginnings. I would like to experiment with a community composed exclusively of women who accept the administrative guidelines set forth in the *Vinaya* texts, and then gradually try to adapt them to Western living conditions.

The concept of such a community would be to incorporate the worthwhile aspects of traditional structures, giving latitude for freedom of expression and a strong element of human warmth. Whether in matters of dress, practice, or monastic organization, there needs to be an adjustment period. Changes in Western societies occur so rapidly these days that expectations run high, both for ourselves and for others. Our push-button background inclines us to be in a great hurry for enlightenment, but achieving perfect awareness requires infinite patience. Taking the ancient guidelines as a basis and receiving commentary on them by great living masters, we can attempt to discover the original essence of the Buddhist teachings and integrate them in ways which are useful in transforming the minds of Western people.

This is definitely a time for women to explore new ways of doing things. At the same time, many people feel the need for preserving the purity of meaningful traditions. Experiencing the beauty of each of the Buddhist traditions helps us to appreciate the beauty of Buddhist culture as a whole. There seems to be a danger, particularly in America, of adapting and rejecting things before they have been sufficiently digested. In recommending a respectful stance toward these ancient cultures, we are not speaking merely from an anthropological point of view; there is something of great historical significance at stake in the transmission of the *Dharma* to the West. As the first generation of Western Buddhists, we need to conscientiously embody the complete, authentic teachings of each tradition before we can begin to accurately translate them into our own cultural experience. We hope spiritual communities of women will play a special role in this process of religious and cultural transformation.

CHINESE NUNS IN LOS ANGELES
by Bhikṣuṇī Shi I Han

My experience of living as a nun in the West has been in connection with Hsi Lai Temple, which is located in the Hacienda Heights area of Los Angeles, and is affiliated with Fo Kuang Shan in Taiwan. The official name of the temple is the International Buddhist Progress Society. The construction and all the activities of the temple are under the wise leadership of Venerable Shing Yun. The immediate responsibility for Hsi Lai temple falls to the *Sangha* members there under the guidance of Bhikṣuṇī Hsin Kuang. She and I were sent to Los Angeles in 1978 to begin a small Buddhist organization. Venerable Hsin Kuang is my master's most senior female disciple and is a capable administrator. She graduated from the Buddhist University in Japan and speaks fluent Japanese.

Our first task in Los Angeles was to search for a suitable site for a temple. After much perseverance, we found a Lutheran church in Gardena which could hold 300 people. Our master approved the purchase and we moved into the minister's house the next day. Ven. Hsin Kuang returned to Taiwan, so for the next six months I had the responsibility of caring for the temple. I went to adult school to study English, applied for permanent residency, and began all the legal work necessary for establishment of the new temple. There was much red tape involved.

After six months, Ven. Hsin Kuang returned with three more *bhikṣuṇīs*, and we launched into a full schedule of activities including lecturing, meditating, teaching *sūtras*, and doing ceremonies. But not all our duties were religious. We also had to do all the work of renovating and maintaining the temple grounds. Every week we had to mow 1800 square feet of grass, garden, clean, sweep, and paint. The compound was encircled by a black fence which the five us transformed by painting thirty Buddha images within four-foot golden circles. We began to gain the respect not only of the Chinese Buddhist community, but of the neighbors as well, for they could see that we five nuns did all the work ourselves. Our master returned in June of 1979 for the opening ceremony.

In 1980 we bought fifteen acres of hilly land in a suburb of Los Angeles called Hacienda Heights and converted an old building on the property into a temporary temple. We began drawing up plans for constructing a large monastery which would have separate living quarters for monks and nuns. Immediately, we ran into problems regarding our construction plans, The citizens of Hacienda Heights began raising strong objections, fearing that the proposed monastic complex covering fifteen acres of land was so big that it might attract many tourists, thus spoiling the special atmosphere of the area.

We sold the church in Gardena, bought a larger Christian church in Maywood, and brought three more *bhikṣuṇīs* to live there. At present four of us live in Hacienda Heights and four live in Maywood, where most of the religious activities are carried out. In the past six years, we have attended six public hearings and numerous conferences with building officials representing the county of Los Angeles and members of the home owners' association of Hacienda Heights. Last January we finally received our building permit for the construction of the proposed monastic complex.

Hsi Lai Temple will comprise a total area of fifteen acres. The buildings will cover an area of some 6,000 square feet. The architecture will be in traditional Chinese Buddhist monastic style, but we will use modern materials for the construction. The temple building will include the main shrine room, a meditation hall, a hall for the five great *bodhisattvas*, an auditorium, a library, classrooms, office space, living facilities, a kitchen, a museum and an exhibition hall, a memorial hall, and a conference hall with translation facilities for three languages (English, Mandarin, and Cantonese) simultaneously. There will be living quarters for both monks and nuns, as well as parking space for about 190 cars. The construction began last March and is scheduled to be completed by the end of this year.

We very much appreciate the government and the citizens

of the county of Los Angeles for granting us the permit to build our temple. It shows that the government of the United States is a truly democratic one and that the American people are truly accommodating and warm-hearted. Over the last six years countless numbers of people have either sent letters of support to the county or presented addresses on our behalf at the public hearings. We received the support of various members of the Southern California *Sangha* Council. Even strangers in supermarkets and shopping malls happily signed petitions to support our project, and our struggle has been fully reported in the pages of various newspapers and journals.

While Hsi Lai Temple is under construction, we are temporarily organizing Sunday ceremonies, meditation instruction, Buddhist seminars, instruction in Buddhist scriptures, Chinese language classes, Kung Fu classes, folk dance classes, weddings, funeral services, family counseling, and other community services. In addition, the nuns cook lunch for two to three hundred laypeople every Sunday. We have gained a reputation for serving delicious vegetarian food. All the nuns are also attending college classes to learn English. Even though our Abbess, Ven. Hsin Kuang, began studying English at the age of fifty and has innumerable other responsibilities, she has become proficient in the language in just two years. All our nuns are very proficient in practical matters, as well as *Dharma* and meditation. Being able to work with a quiet, calm mind is also a type of meditation.

It is our wish to establish positive relationships with our neighbors. Since Buddhism is one of the greatest religions in the world, stressing communal harmony as well as mental purity, we hope to be of benefit to the American people. All are cordially invited to visit our monastery at any time. Hsi Lai Temple means "monastery brought from East to West." The name refers to the fact that Buddhism spread from India to the Far East and is now spreading to the United States.

One outstanding feature of both Hsi Lai Temple and Fo Kuang Shan Temple in Taiwan is that they are largely comprised of nuns, most of whom are *bhikṣuṇīs*. These nuns receive the same training, responsibilities, and opportunities as the monks. Ven. Shing Yun always considers our abilities and attainments, not our gender. Therefore, nuns hold very important positions in the organization.

It is true that we monks and nuns have left our natural homes, but we have entered a religious family in which we are all brothers and sisters. As we grow in understanding and participate in various works of charity, we come to realize in a very tangible way that everyone we come into contact with is a member of this family—all elders are our parents and grandparents, all children are our children.

Whether we live in the East or the West, we should not shut ourselves up in a cave or a hut, or cut ourselves off from the concerns of the world. The key to fulfilling a religious career lies in engaging steadily in beneficial, worthwhile activities. All activities should be undertaken in the Buddhist spirit of altruistic giving and directed toward the welfare of others. We must seek the liberation of others before we seek our own liberation. We should help the young people, care for the sick, teach in the prisons, and even go to wild and barbarian places to share the teachings of the Buddha. It is important to establish orphanages and homes for the elderly, sacrificing ourselves for the goals of education, charity, and cultural development. It is through such altruistic activities that we will find happiness and spiritual fulfillment. We need to proceed from the theoretical to the practical, implementing Buddhism in a practical, humanistic way, causing the light of the Buddha to shine for all beings throughout the world. The water of *Dharma* will nurture all creatures and create a human Pure Land.

There are two other goals of our Buddhist life, namely, study and meditation. The academic study of Buddhism as well as the study of languages such as Sanskrit, Pāli, and Japanese are indispensable. Our master requires that we study at least four years at a Buddhist college, even after the B.A. degree, so we are continuing our Buddhist studies in the United States. We have daily chanting and meditation in our monastery, so that we remember the ultimate source of our religion.

We are living in an era of great change, and this change is most especially seen in the sphere of cultural change. The construction of Hsi Lai Temple is not only for the aims of our Buddhist monks and nuns, for reciting the Buddhist scriptures and for carrying on our traditional forms of Buddhist worship, but we also hope to be a significant cultural and religious center for the Southern California community as well as the world community.

We extend an open invitation to both individuals and groups to visit Hsi Lai Temple in Los Angeles to participate in our ceremonies and to share our life.

FINDING OUR WAY
by Sylvia Wetzel

The subject of Western women embracing Buddhism and living as nuns in the West is a provocative one. It concerns being a woman in what is still a fairly male-oriented society and a spiritual person in a very materialistic, non-religious, even anti-religious society. Living in the West means living in a materially developed country with a high standard of living, but there is also a deep understanding of individual freedom and appreciation for it.

Being a woman. At present we are all living in patriarchal societies. There does not seem to be any other type of society around these days. Thus our societies are oriented toward results and effectiveness, placing value on prestige, career, logic, rationalism, and worldly success. Such an orientation, if left untempered, can lead to the exploitation of resources and beings. When the more feminine values of caring and nurturing are neglected, we are faced with great social, economic, and ecological problems.

I am a Buddhist, which means I practice an Asian religion that at first sight is exotic and alien. It is definitely a challenge to live as a spiritual woman in a modern environment, but there has been some positive advancement for women in the last century. Women have gained access to general education and now learn and teach at universities. They have made their way into occupations that were previously considered inappropriate for them. Particularly in thc last two decades, women in the West have begun to enjoy incredible freedom, being able to enter almost any profession or vocation they wish. The process of advancement has been fraught with difficulties, but the achievements gained are very inspiring. The nurturing qualities that are seen as feminine are badly needed in society and now women are in an ideal position to begin implementing them.

Being a spiritual woman. I have talked with Catholic nuns in Bavaria, a very conservative area, who say that nobody understands why they have become nuns. They are asked, "If you are beautiful and intelligent, why become a nun?" People in the West often feel that being a nun must mean that you are trying to escape something or that you have some deep-seated problem. There is very little support for such a path, even for the Christian nuns. Therefore, there is very little encouragement or supportive understanding.

On the other hand, in recent years many people have been experiencing a crisis of meaning in their lives. They encounter irritations and a gnawing dissatisfaction that leads to religious questioning. In such an atmosphere where we meet people who are searching for meaning in their lives, to be a nun in the West can be something very beneficial.

I can never forget talking with a Catholic nun who said, "You are the first person who understands my reasons for being a nun." Even though I am a Buddhist nun, following an Asian religion, the Catholic nun and I felt ourselves acknowledged and supported by one another. Regardless of what denomination they follow, sincere practitioners have a deep appreciation for each other. As His Holiness often stresses, religious practitioners are all pulling the same rope; we have to pull together and support each other.

Being a Western Woman. Although Buddhist practitioners come from many different countries, such as Sri Lanka, Nepal, India, Taiwan, and Japan, we have many things in common. While acknowledging all the interests we share, I also recognize certain differences in our situations and experiences. It is important to be aware of the differences, too, to gain a deeper understanding of one another.

Some of these differences are superficial, but they reflect our varied conditions and orientation. For example, the behavior of the Western nuns may come as a surprise to our Asian sisters. We may often seem to lack discipline and respect for others. Our whole outlook on forms, rules, regulations, and conduct appears to be radically different. The root of this difference lies in the fact that we have undergone a long process of mental development centered around becoming more sensitive to our own needs, rather than just following an accepted set of rules. We have gained a deep appreciation of individuality. It is too simplistic to say that this process has resulted in a tremendous egotism that needs to be destroyed. Of course, there is the involvement of ego, which we must eliminate along with greed, hatred, and ignorance. There is a tremendous grasping at a solidly existing "self" or "I." Still there is something more subtle involved here than pure egotism, and it needs to be explored. I would describe this process as the first step of an intuitive awakening, of being able to listen to our inner wisdom and gain an understanding of our direction.

Finding our own way. From the first day, ten years ago, that I came into contact with Buddhism, I felt very strongly that I must be careful not to simply superimpose new patterns on my existing experience. I did not want to adopt some sort of set structure, but rather to incorporate Buddhist values in dialogue with my background as a Western person. It was never my intention to live my whole life in India or Nepal. The time I spent there was always seen as a time of learning in preparation for returning to my country and trying to adapt the wisdom I found there to my cultural environment in the West. This type of dialogue requires great courage, since we have as yet no indigenous role models.

Of course, we are very fortunate in having met with great spiritual masters in the East. Some of these wonderful teachers have much understanding and appreciation for our need to explore and to adjust the mode of practice to our own cultural milieu. My own teacher, Lama Thubten Yeshe, often said, "This I love with you Western students—you always question things. If I tell you something and you ask why, then I say, 'Because the Buddha said so,' or, 'Because Lama Tsongkhapa said so,' but you don't just accept it. You require, and request, an explanation. You want to know how it works." Lama Yeshe was very fond of this inquisitive attitude. We Westerners want to know how things work and how they function in our own minds. We cannot do *pujas*, meditations, prostrations, and offerings without questioning. We want to understand the practice and how it transforms our mind.

The Tibetan tradition is very, very supportive in this respect. The teachers give us incredible freedom to explore ourselves and to discover for ourselves how to best utilize the teachings. The amount of freedom they give us may explain why our discipline is not up to Asian Buddhist standards. I consider this as the growing pains of implementing the *Dharma* in the West. I request the patience and understanding of more traditional Buddhists in realizing that we do not mean to be impolite or impudent. We certainly cherish the precious gift of *Dharma* that we have received, but we must find our own way of making it meaningful in our lives.

It is not effective for Western students to follow set rules without really understanding how they operate and how they help us to grow. Lama Yeshe always stressed that if we do not understand something, the transformation it works is not as deep. Practice based on mere faith is useful, as it helps in creating less negative *karma*, but the transformation is much deeper if one's faith is based on reasoning and real understanding. It is wonderful to know the *sūtras*, to learn them by heart, to be able to quote them—but it is more important to truly understand them.

Practice in East and West. Asian people love to memorize the texts, but Westerners feel a need for more silent, contemplative meditation. This is the experience of many Western *Sangha* members living in *Dharma* communities. When discussing the daily monastic or center schedule, we realize that the traditional way would be to have an hour of *puja* in the morning and an hour of *puja* in the evening, but it just does not feel right to us. If I have to chant a *puja* for an hour in the morning, I do not feel clear, open, and sensitive during the day—I just feel full. Many of the ordained and lay sisters and brothers in the West feel that an hour of silent meditation in the morning is a better preparation for the day, helping to set the motivation for the day's activities in a peaceful and positive mode. We feel that a silent practice is more effective in opening and centering our minds. If recitation works for others, that is beautiful; but, with all due respect, it is not for everybody.

Another point is that, for instance, in the Gelug school of the Tibetan tradition, studies are very much emphasized. The students receive teachings sometimes six hours a day for months and years together. Tibetan students seem to thrive on these intensive teachings, but somehow Westerners have trouble digesting so many teachings at a time. We seem to need breaks between the teaching sessions to let the teachings sink in. Perhaps it is because we have already received so much intellectual training in our educational system. We have gone through so many years of schooling, being trained in grasping concepts without really digesting them, that we are on the point of gagging. Consequently, if we are put through more such training, without the benefit of meditation periods during which to integrate the material, we apply the same superficial approach to the Buddhist teachings and run into a dead end.

It is true that Germany especially is famous for scholarly Buddhism. Some people have vast knowledge and can quote the texts at length. Nevertheless, if it does not come from the heart, if it has not transformed the person's being, I question its value. Thus we need to experiment and to find a suitable balance between study, analytical contemplation, concentrative meditation, and time for understanding and digesting the teachings.

We have come to realize that many of the pragmatic methods of Buddhist psychology are ideally suited to the problems of Western people. These very practical methods of dealing with the basic delusions of greed, hatred, and ignorance, of explaining impermanence and so forth, are extremely useful in counseling. Although I am not specially trained in psychological counseling, my rudimentary experience with the fundamental meditations on death and impermanence, love and compassion, are very valuable in helping others deal with attachment, grief, hostility, and so on. There is still much work to be done in exploring parallels between Western methods and theories of psychotherapy and applied Buddhist psychology. There is a rich field of methods in the Western systems, but there are also simple Buddhist teachings that are applicable and easily understood by Western people in this kind of counseling situation.

To sum up, although it is difficult to live as a nun in the West without the support of a monastic environment, I am happy to have been a pioneer, and I want to investigate with others how we can best implement the Buddha's teachings in the West. I am confident that in time we will find suitable and effective ways of life in which lay and ordained practitioners in the West will inspire and support each other in new ways.

ESTABLISHING NUNNERIES FOR WESTERNERS

The following are questions and answers that arose in the course of an informal discussion on the topic of establishing nunneries for Westerners. Questions were directed primarily at two nuns who have gained experience as pioneers in the field: Sister Ayya Kehma, director of Parappuduwa Nuns' Island in Sri Lanka, and Bhikṣuṇī Pema Chodron, director of Gampo Abbey in Nova Scotia, Canada.

Q: Ayya Khema, could you tell us something about your experiences in setting up Buddhist practice centers for nuns?

Ayya Kehma: The first place I started was Wat Buddhadhamma outside of Sydney, Australia. It was intended as a place for both monks and nuns, but it did not work out to my satisfaction because the Thai tradition of monkhood leaves no room for nuns to express themselves. Although the place is flourishing and I am glad I started it, I did not want to stay there because I had no opportunity to do what I really wanted.

The next place I established was the International Buddhist Women's Center in Sri Lanka, which I handed over to Sri Lankan nuns to use as their study center. I provided a building with a large hall and rooms, as well as a library, for their use. This was very helpful for them, because previously they had had no place to meet and hold their teachings.

The third place I established was Parappuduwa Nuns' Island, which is specifically a nunnery. The idea behind it was to have a place in the East where Western women can practice and understand the teachings in their own language—English or German—and where the facilities are suitable for Westerners. Such a situation is not easy to find in the East. The Nuns's Island opened in July, 1984, and is open to Westerners for the rainy season retreat. About thirty people have participated in this three-month retreat.

I think that this is the first time there has been a nunnery in Sri Lanka which is strictly for women and run by women, but so far there has not been a great deal of interest in putting on the robes. Laypeople come for a minimum of three months and many stay as long as they like. Everyone in robes, of course, receives everything free of charge; the laypeople give a contribution.

Q: Could you elaborate a bit on what you envisioned when setting up the monastery in Australia, and why it fell short of your expectations?

AK: When I established Wat Buddhadhamma, I was not establishing a nunnery, but rather a monastery that was also open for nuns. That was the first great controversy that arose. It is a huge place, with 220 acres of land, so my idea was to have the nuns on one side and the monks on the other side. I had the idea that if I established the place and asked a monk to be the abbot, that I would also be able to put forth ideas as to the running of the place. That turned out to be totally naive. A situation in which all the authority rests with a male abbot turned out to be an unsuitable environment for myself as a nun.

Q: What was your vision in establishing Parappuduwa Nuns' Island?

AK: My idea in creating the Nun's Island was to provide a situation for Western women to practice *Dhamma*. Many Western women come to the East in search of a place where they can find instruction in spiritual disciplines, but find the conditions very difficult. I had the experience myself of roaming throughout the East trying to find a place where the food was palatable, the toilets were usable, and I could understand what was going on. Without knowing the languages, one is always at the mercy of translators. I had this experience both in Thailand and Sri Lanka. So I thought that it would be nice for Western women to have a place in the East where the teaching is done in English, where the food is acceptable, where the sanitation facilities are what they are used to. I thought that if they liked the place, they might eventually become nuns, but so far this has not happened.

Q: Do they come again and again to study there?

AK: In the beginning I let them come at any time, but the permanent residents complained that it was becoming like a hotel with people coming and going as they liked. So then I specified that they should come for the rainy retreat, which is July, August, and September. Many people come for that, and those who stay throughout the rest of the year are either nuns or are interested in becoming nuns, though they are very few. I thought that if people came for three months, they would see that it is a wonderful life and want to become nuns, but that has not happened even once. Perhaps they find it difficult, because we follow the discipline of a nunnery. We begin meditating at 4:00 in the morning, which people find a bit early. I may have to change this for people coming from the West, since they find it difficult to adhere to strict monastic discipline.

Q: What are the physical conditions like?

AK: The Nuns' Island is like a paradise. It is an island in a lake, an island of two-and-one-half acres that belongs entirely to the nunnery. It was given to me on a 99-year lease by the Sri Lankan government. The buildings are wonderful. Those who are nuns or want to become nuns have their own private kuti (cottage), which is one room with a bathroom and a little garden attached. There are three servants who do all the work. The place is fantastic, but still people complain. Either I have been too lenient or not lenient enough.

Q: Is it possible to stay there without taking part in the daily program, doing one's own practice?

AK: Absolutely. I leave it open for anyone to practice the way they want to—but it has to be practice! As long as people practice, they can stay in their *kuti* and even get their food delivered there.

Q: Have you had many problems with people going crazy? This is the experience of many centers, and I wonder if it happens as much in Asia as it does in the West.

AK: Yes, I have had many people with emotional and psychological problems. I am running the nunnery strictly for the benefit of others, but many of these people need professional help, and I am not a psychotherapist, a psychoanalyst, or a psychiatrist. I have absolutely no training in these areas. I am a meditation teacher and a *Dhamma* teacher. I have had thirteen years of experience, but I am not a psychiatrist, and it is simply beyond me to handle these sorts of cases.

Sometimes people appear totally normal when they first arrive and after a month or two they flip out completely. I often do not realize that they have serious problems. Some people have a long history of mental problems that recur again and again, and sometimes these problems really seem to be activated when a person is doing intensive practice.

In my own experience, it seems that the defilements come up in a rush during the first two years of intensive practice. This can cause terrible problems. The more you work on yourself, the more rubbish comes out. Eventually, as you clear out the rubbish, you can see light somewhere. However, Westerners from our push-button society are very impatient. They are used to things happening whenever they push a button, and suddenly there are no buttons!

Once Ven. Mahasi Sayadaw was giving a meditation course in Switzerland. Although he could understand English, he used a translator for the interviews. He gave interviews all afternoon, and when the interviews were finished, he turned to his translator and asked, "Tell me, young man, what is an emotional problem?" This points up the difference between East and West. People in Asia have problems but they do not talk about them. Western people talk about problems even when they do not have any.

Q: Westerners do have different things, more emotional things, that come up in their practice. I am probably not the only person who has gone to an Asian teacher with a problem and found that he just does not know what I am talking about. I think that this is one of the reasons why we need Western centers and Western nunneries, so that the practice can be adapted to suit our needs. We need to acknowledge where we stand as Westerners, with a lot of emotional problems, and learn how to deal with them somehow.

AK: I fully agree, and this was my reason for establishing the Nuns' Island, but I did not realize that it would be *me* who would have to deal with those emotional problems. I thought that by meditating and by learning the *Dhamma*, we could work these problems out for ourselves.

Q: Pema Chodron, what were your objectives in helping found Gampo Abbey?

Pema Chodron: There were many reasons or establishing Gampo Abbey, but the primary reason was that it seemed that the monastic *Sangha* needed a place where they could begin keeping *Vinaya* purely. We wanted to create a place where such energy could be pooled, which by the magnetic principle, would begin to attract more people to monastic life.

Q: How can Westerners find a practice and lifestyle that is suitable for them?

PC: There are many various Buddhist traditions available in the West these days, but there are dangers to be aware of in mixing them all together. American seem particularly prone to dabbling. It is generally felt that the various lineages and traditions need to be preserved, yet also adapted to the cultural context.

It is also recognized that we do not as yet have many Western teachers of the clarity and stature of the Asian teachers. Until we do, we need to trust and look for guidance to those Asian teachers who seem to have reached a certain level of mental development. For example, Trungpa Rinpoche recommended eating in the *oriyoki* style and brought in certain elements of Zen influence. His students trusted this recommendation because they trusted his clarity of mind and his wisdom. When the time comes that Western teachers develop in clarity and stature, they would be the ones with the wisdom to make changes.

Western people often seem to lack discipline and a willingness to develop it. The point in going into monasteries and taking up monastic discipline is that we know we need discipline. We should not complain later about the discipline; we should be aware of what is entailed in the monastic life from the start and be willing to do our best at it. We must accommodate ourselves to the monasteries, rather than expecting them to accommodate themselves to us. We should allow ourselves to be changed by the *Dharma*, rather than expecting the *Dharma* to change for us.

Conclusion

Since the time of the Enlightened One, in a dozen countries, Buddhist nuns have sought their spiritual objectives—the peace of *nirvāna*, the path of the *bodhisattva*, and the attainment of Buddhahood in one lifetime. Largely unacknowledged and unheralded, many among them achieved their goals. Although they have not figured as largely in the religious power structure as monks and have lacked many of the advantages enjoyed by their ordained brothers there are documents to show that great numbers of ordained women, both in India and beyond, attained spiritual heights. While some have achieved renown, far more have practiced quietly, persevering in their practice despite austere conditions and a lack of popular support.

Until this year, communications between the nuns of the world have been meager and sporadic, but now great changes have been set in motion which are of importance to future generations of women in Buddhism. In a time when dubious values are pervasive, Buddhist women came together for the International Conference on Buddhist Nuns to discuss how to help turn the tide. They asked what practical measures they can take to secure women's place in the sphere of religion and how their religious practice can best benefit humanity. To implement pragmatic solutions, they founded Sakyadhītā ("Daughters of the Buddha") to coordinate the efforts of Buddhist women internationally.

The world is witnessing heroic efforts to document women's performance in every field. We may question why it should be necessary to prove our capabilities and why we have doubted them in the first place, yet it is clear that women need to be encouraged due to the general devaluation of women that has gone before. In the field of spiritual endeavor especially, where women have been largely overlooked, we can help one another develop inner strength and awaken to our own abilities. Like young plants freshly awakening, our spiritual growth needs special care and nourishment to assure its best development.

The earnest devotion of women to religion is clearly visible in places of worship throughout the world. There have also been a large number of recognized female saints and mystics in history. Documenting women's spiritual abilities has been quite elusive, however, since inner realization is difficult to qualify. We may point out exemplary female spiritual masters and take them as our inspiration, but it is difficult or impossible to judge others' level of realization. Except as it provides impetus to our own spiritual work, such judgment is also somewhat irrelevant. Once we have gained confidence in our own capacity for realization, we need no further documentation. Once the message is across, we need simply to embody that potential. As long as we avoid the extremes of pride and self-denigration, if we apply ourselves fully to manifesting spiritual awareness, our lives will stand as testimony to our innate capacity.

Thus, the single most effective way to secure women's place in the field of religion is to actualize spiritual values and truly live the religious life. Nothing can be so convincing, both to ourselves and to others, as living up to our own spiritual potential. While this is as true for men as it is for women, the spotlight is now on women as never before.

Given the fact that women and men are deemed equally capable of spiritual attainments, it follows that women are fully capable of advising others on the path. We very much need women who can answer questions regarding Buddhist philosophy with precision, who can reliably guide students in the stages of meditation, and who can counsel them on the problems of daily life. There is every reason to believe that women will become fully qualified to take on the serious responsibility of guiding others in their spiritual development. We can look forward to the emergence of female role models and to a generation of women engendering respect and appreciation for one another as spiritual friends, teachers, and students.

This brings us to a topic which concerns all religious practitioners and has been surfacing regularly at women's Buddhist conferences—the choice of a teacher. In all existing Buddhist traditions, authorization to teach requires prolonged study as well as profound realization. To be able to teach effectively, it is important to have gained thorough competence in both the theory and practice of the tradition one represents.

Whether a teacher is female or male, it is very risky to begin teaching, much less adapting techniques, before we have fully mastered the fundamental Buddhist teachings and learned to put them into practice. Without sufficient preparation, there are dangers of misinterpreting the *Dharma* and of misguiding others in their spiritual development. These dangers are magnified in the case of transmitting *Dharma* in new lands and to fresh minds where there is little background against which to weigh and measure what is being presented.

In such a climate, both female and male students need to exercise maximum discretion in choosing a teacher. These days there are many concepts, practices, and styles of behavior being marketed under the label "Dharma" that have little or nothing whatsoever to do with *Dharma*. Even allowing for human error, there is a code of ethics involved in giving teachings. Likewise, there is a degree of individual responsibility incumbent upon those receiving teachings. Thoughtful people would do well to consider these matters and to be clear about what is involved in a choice of teachers, for their own psychological well-being as well as for the positive development of Buddhism in the West. There are times when it is wise and virtuous to suspend judgment and other times when it can be disastrous. It is therefore essential to allow ample opportunity for assessing a path and a teacher. Well-reasoned adaptation of the Buddhist teachings and traditions to Western situations will be of great benefit to Western people, but slipshod importation, gullible acceptance, baseless fabrication, and shoddy conduct can lead to an altogether mistaken amalgam which may do more harm than good.

One development in the West which cannot in good conscience go unmentioned is the trend of confusing, or even equating, spirituality and sexuality. On the basis of such a mistaken identification, some people, particularly women, have made themselves extremely vulnerable to manipulation. Regardless of the tradition, Buddhist or otherwise, it is important for individuals to exercise common sense and protect themselves from exploitation—sexual, financial, or otherwise. People are in such urgent need of spiritual guidance these days that, sad to say, they do not always take time to check the qualifications of teachers thoroughly enough beforehand. The lapse can have serious consequences.

Even when we go for medical treatment, we try to find the most effective treatment and the most reliable physician, often checking out several different possibilities before deciding under whose care to put ourselves. Health care merely concerns our physical well-being for one short lifetime; spiritual evolution and psychological health are far more critical concerns, the effects extending not only to this lifetime, but to innumerable lifetimes in the future. We should be ever so much more discerning when choosing a spiritual teacher, not judging by superficial matters such as attractive appearance, charisma, eloquence, or language proficiency.

Particularly in America these days, anybody can set up shop and teach practically anything. There is no way to certify the person's character, however, and no assurance of where the path may lead. Experimentation may prove harmless, but in the case of spiritual development, dabblers run the risk of creating much inner confusion. At this critical juncture, it is advisable to see beyond nationality and other external criteria, and to rely upon a qualified teacher with a traceable lineage that has been known to produce realized beings in the past. Confidence in the path and the guide are as important as confidence in oneself, and confidence should be based on sound judgment, remembering the fallibility of even that. Until full enlightenment is reached, we are liable to err in our perceptions of both self and others.

In all Buddhist traditions, perfect morality is the most fundamental of all qualifications for a teacher. It is the basis of all other accomplishments. For example, there are eight specific qualities required for *Vinaya* instructors,[1] ten qualities enumerated for a Mahāyāna *guru*,[2] and ten further qualities for a *guru* expounding *tantra*,[3] pure morality being prerequisite in all cases. To refrain from harming, misappropriation, sexual misconduct, untruthfulness, and intoxication are the precepts for ordinary lay Buddhists and are fairly elemental behavioral guidelines for all decent human beings. It goes without saying that those who claim to be spiritual teachers should be above such misbehavior. Since abuses of authority are unfortunately rampant these days, it behooves spiritual seekers to be judicious in their choice of guidance.

In the case of *tantra*, the matter is far more serious, since one is bound by certain commitments once the master/disciple link is formed. Even the receiving of a simple initiation puts one under these commitments, so great care must be taken to assess the qualities of a teacher before attending such ceremonies. One is allowed up to twelve years to observe the conduct and examine the qualities of a potential teacher before establishing a master/disciple relationship. It is my considered opinion that in these days of flagrant violations of personal trust, women in particular are well-advised to exercise caution and sound judgment. The value of keeping precepts is self-evident here. Happily, there have as yet been no reports of sexual opportunism concerning women teachers. Upright behavior on the part of female spiritual masters is to be applauded and encouraged.

As Buddhism goes to the West, it is our duty to weigh the teachings in accordance with new discoveries in physics, astronomy, neurology, psychology, and all available fields of knowledge. This will help us to verify the teachings and to gain insight into the true essence of the *Dharma*, which is beyond individual and cultural preconceptions. In a message especially important for Western Buddhists, His Holiness the Dalai Lama recently said, "We must evaluate the Buddhist teachings in light of observable facts. Where statements in the texts do not accord with actual reality, we may legitimately question the authenticity of those statements." This advice has particular relevance for Buddhist feminists when examining misogynistic statements by male Buddhist writers.

Among the enormous number of texts comprising Buddhist literature, there occur a few statements denying women's capacity to attain full Buddhahood, but nowhere has the Buddha denied the capability of women to attain liberation or enlightenment. On the contrary, he stated in no uncertain terms that women are fully capable of spiritual attainments. It is obvious that the Buddha in his all-seeing wisdom recognized the spiritual potentialities of women, clearly demonstrated by women who achieved *arhatship* and other stages of realization.

Feminist awareness in Western countries is progressing very rapidly, both in women and in men. This growth process is very positive, very painful, and very powerful. Certainly many important changes in religious institutions will result—changes which will provide hitherto unknown opportunities for Buddhist women's personal development and spiritual insight. Whole new cycles of evolution will begin and people may even begin to take their opportunities for granted. During this revolutionary process, I urge that Buddhist women remember their Asian sisters and actively generate compassion for those still struggling to gain their spiritual ground. Many women in developing countries are not yet even aware of the disadvantages under which they labor. Attitudes of self-denigration and delusions of incompetence that belong to bygone generations of women are still very much in evidence in large parts of the world and it will take time to loosen their grip.

Many nuns and other Buddhist women have very poor self-images and cling to preconceptions of inferior capability. In cultures where humility is a predominant social value, even the most aware among them are often intimidated and struggle to find their voices. Yet for *Dharma* to truly and fully benefit the women of Asia, these voices must be heard and heeded. In some countries, for example, the *bhikṣuṇī* issue has become politicized to the extent that many women dare not speak up for fear of character defamation and social alienation. The issue also tends to polarize the women themselves, creating an even larger chasm between the educated and the underprivileged.

The issue of emancipation for religious women is extremely complex and delicate, requiring informed awareness and skillful handling. It is a central purpose of this book to call attention to the need for a sensible resolution to this problem. The mind that wishes to benefit beings cannot overlook Asia's millions of Buddhist women and their dynamic spiritual energy that could be more effectively channeled for the good of the world.

The Buddhist path is only one of many, but it has proven to be of spiritual benefit to countless beings. It is therefore hoped that women can gain greater access to the Buddhist teachings and greater encouragement in their practice. When the good qualities of women are nurtured and made manifest, we can contribute positively toward improving the general quality of life for the world's peoples. It was in this spirit that the International Conference on Buddhist Nuns was convened. The intent was to provide a chance for Buddhist sisters to share their hopes and dreams. In the process, we realized that discussions alone are not enough to make these dreams come true—we must begin to actualize our aspirations in real, tangible ways. Despite our inexperience in international organizational matters, we founded Sakyadhītā to ensure an ongoing dialogue on questions related to women and *Dharma*.

The spiritual potential of women cannot be denied. On the contrary, the spiritual awakening of the world's women can be a powerful force for peace in the world. If we, ordained and lay practitioners alike, refuse to get bogged down in lesser pursuits and determine to use all our resourcefulness to relieve suffering wherever it exists, we will be able to effect real changes in the world. The transformation begins from within and gradually communicates to those around us. May the teachings lend solace to many and inspire the world's spiritually inclined women to align themselves with the forces of good to realize both inner and outer peace.

Sarvam mangalam!

NOTES

1. The eight qualities of a *Vinaya* instructor are given in I.B. Horner's translation, *The Book of the Discipline*, Vol. II, pp. 265-67: "I allow you, monks, to agree upon a monk endowed with eight qualities as exhorter of nuns: one who is virtuous, who is possessed of good behavior and lawful resort, who sees danger in the slightest faults, who undertaking, trains himself in the rules of training, who has become very learned, who knows the learning by heart, who is a store of learning. In addition, the monk selected must be a *bhikṣu* of at least twenty years' standing who has never committed a major transgression." "Lawful resort" (*gocara*) in this context seems to mean one who is suitable to be a field of merit.

2. In the *Guru Puja*, composed by the First Panchen Lama, Lobzang Chokyi Gyaltsen, we find a summary of the ten qualities requisite for a Mahāyāna master and the further qualities requisite for a Vajrayāna master. The ten qualities required in a Mahāyāna master derive from the *Sūtra-alankara* composed by Maitreya. They are: 1) well-tamed by pure morality; 2) calmed by meditative stabilization; 3) greatly calmed by wisdom, 4) having qualities and knowledge greater than the disciples'; 5) energetic in benefiting the disciples; 6) skilled in comprehension and transmission of the teachings; 7) having realization of emptiness; 8) wise in explaining the teachings;

9) having compassion and loving kindness; 10) willing to teach all disciples, without being discouraged by the duller ones.

3. The additional qualities required in a Vajrayāna master are described in the Fifty Verses of Guru Devotion by Asvaghosa. They are as follows: 1) well-controlled in body; 2) . . . in speech; 3) . . . in mind; 4) patient; 5) honest; 6) without deceit; 7) without pretense; 8) well-versed in both *mantra* and *tantra*; 9) having the twenty special *tantric* skills [ten outer and ten secret]; 10) skilled in drawing and teaching.

Contributors and Bibliography

Contributors

Bhikṣuṇī Pema Chodron is 50 years old and has two grown children. She was formerly an elementary school teacher. In 1973 she received *śrāmaṇerikā* ordination from H. H. Gyalma Karmapa in Scotland and in 1981 received *bhikṣuṇī* ordination in Hong Kong. Currently she is the director of Gampo Abbey, a monastery for Western monks and nuns in Nova Scotia, Canada.

Śrāmaṇerikā Lobsang Dechen was born to Tibetan refugee parents in Manali, India, in 1960. She was educated at the Tibetan Children's Village School in Dharamsala and received *śrāmaṇerikā* ordination from Ven. Lati Rinpoche in 1975. She earned a B.A. degree from St. Bede's College, Simla, in 1982, a B.Ed. from Chandigarh University in 1983, and has been teaching at the Tibetan Children's Village School in Dharamsala since 1984.

Ms. Kusuma Devendra attended the University of Indiana on scholarship and then studied Buddhism at the University of Sri Jayaradenapura in Sri Lanka, receiving degrees in Pāli, Buddhism, and English. Her M.A. is in Buddhist Studies, and she has recently submitted her Ph.D. thesis on the topic of Buddhist nuns in Sri Lanka. By profession, she was a teacher of science, and has also taught at the university level.

Anagārikā Dhammawati was born in 1934 in Patan, near Kathmandu, Nepal. She was educated in Burma, where she received the Sasana Dhaja Dhammacariya degree. After returning to Nepal, she founded the Dharmakirti Vihar in Kathmandu and currently serves as its head nun as well as chairperson of the Dharmakirti Buddhist Study Circle. She publishes a monthly Buddhist magazine and has written over twenty-five books in Newari language, many of which have been translated into Nepali.

Bhikṣuṇī Shih I Han was born in Taiwan in 1947. After receiving her diploma, she worked as a typist at the United States air base in Taiwan. Inspired by the teachings of the Buddha and encouraged by her mother, she gave up her career to study Buddhism at Fo Kuang Shan monastery. She received *śrāmaṇerikā* ordination from Venerable Shing Yun in 1973 and *bhikṣuṇī* ordination in 1976. After four years of study at Fo Kuang Shan Buddhist College, she was sent to the United States to establish a Buddhist organization in Los Angeles. She is currently majoring in psychology at California State University and serves as secretary of Hsi Lai Temple in Los Angeles.

Dr. Chatsumarn Kabilsingh studied at Visva Bharati (Santiniketan), at McMaster University in Canada, and took her Ph.D. from Magadha University in India. Since 1973 she has been teaching Asian philosophy and religion at Thammasat University in Bangkok. She has written a number of books on Buddhism in Thai and *A Comparative Study of Bhikkhuni Patimokkha* in English. Since 1984 she has been editor of NIBWA (Newsletter on International Buddhist Women's Activities).

Bhikṣuṇī Shih Yung Kai was born on the mainland of China and grew up in Hong Kong. She studied in Canada and received her B.S. degree from the University of Toronto. After graduation, she worked as a child-care worker with emotionally disturbed children for three years. In 1983 she went to study Buddhism at Fo Kuang Shan Temple in Taiwan and received ordination in 1984. She is currently Director of the International Department of Fo Kuang Shan.

Śrāmaṇerikā Sangye Khandro (Kathleen McDonald) was ordained in 1974 by Kyabje Song Rinpoche in Nepal. Since then she has trained under Ven. Thubten Yeshe and Ven. Thubten Zopa Rinpoche as part of the Foundation for the Preservation of the Mahayana Tradition (FPMT), based in Kathmandu, Nepal. She spent several years helping to establish Dorje Pamo Nunnery in France and taught for two years at Buddha House in Adelaide, Australia. She is the author of the popular book *How to Meditate*.

Reverend Tessho Kondo graduated from Japan Women's University in 1944. After graduation she received ordination as a Buddhist nun and studied and practiced at the Nuns' Training Center of the Pure Land (Jodo) school for two years. After ordination, she pursued studies in Buddhist philosophy at Otani University and received a master's degree in 1953. She is currently head priest of Shorinin Temple in Kyoto and director of the Nuns' Training Center (Jodoshu Niso Dojo) where she previously studied.

Śrāmaṇerikā Thubten Lhundrup (Hilary Clarke) was ordained as a nun by Ven. Thubten Zopa Rinpoche in 1986 at Kopan Monastery, Kathmandu, Nepal. She was previously an officer in the Royal Australian Air Force. Before becoming ordained, she worked as a massage therapist and receptionist at a medical clinic in Brisbane, Australia.

Venerable Nyanapoinika, a German *bhikkhu*, is considered to be the greatest Pāli authority today. He has translated numerous texts from Pāli into English and German. His own books in German and English are regarded as standard works on Theravāda practice. He is 86 years old and resides in Sri Lanka.

Daw Su Sein is a Buddhist laywoman who lives the life of a *yogi* among the nunneries in the Sagaing hills of Burma.

Heng-ching Shih was born in 1943 in Taiwan. She received a B.A. in foreign languages from Soochow University, and taught high school for three years before earning her M.A. in education from the University of Rhode Island. She was ordained as a *bhikṣuṇī* in San Francisco in 1975. She obtained a Ph.D. in Buddhist studies from the University of Wisconsin-Madison and is now an associate professor in the Department of Philosophy at National Taiwan University.

Bhikṣuṇī Jampa Tsedroen lives in Hamburg, West Germany, in the Tibetisches Zentrum. Since 1980, she has been under the guidance of the Tibetan master, Ven. Geshe Thubten Ngawang. She was ordained by him as a *śrāmaṇerikā* in 1981, and received full ordination as a *bhikṣuṇī* in Taiwan in 1985. Since 1981 she has been studying Buddhist philosophy in the traditional Tibetan system, with daily debates conducted in Tibetan language. This educational process requires at least fifteen years of study, with annual examinations, after which one receives a diploma as a teacher of *Dharma*.

Karma Lekshe Tsomo received an M.A. in Asian Studies from the University of Hawaii as an East West Center scholar. She received *śrāmaṇerikā* ordination from H. H. Gyalwa Karmapa in 1977 and *bhikṣuṇī* ordination in Korea and Taiwan in 1982. She studied with Ven. Geshe Ngawang Dhargyey for five years at the Library of Tibetan Works and Archives in Dharamsala and is currently studying Prajñāpāramitā at the Institute of Buddhist Dialectics, also in Dharamsala.

Bhikṣuṇī Shig Hiu Wan is the founder and director of the Institute for Sino-Indian Buddhist Studies (ISBS) in Taipei, Taiwan, as well as director of the Institute for the Study of Buddhist Culture. She is a member of the China Academy, a professor at the Chinese Cultural University, and a member of the International Association of Buddhist Studies (IABS). She specializes in T'ien-t' doctrine and meditation, Buddhist education, Ch'an meditation, and Ch'an painting. She has written numerous essays on Buddhist art and thought and five times has coordinated the International Conference on Buddhist Education (ICBE) in Taiwan. She is actively engaged in establishing a Buddhist college and in advocating enlightened Buddhist education.

Sylvia Wetzel was born in Germany. She has been teaching political science and languages since 1973. In 1977 she began a two-year study of Tibetan Buddhism in Dharamṣala, India, and at Kopan Monastery in Nepal. Since 1980 she has been director of Aryatara Institute, a Tibetan Buddhist meditation center in Germany, and has served as vice-president of the German Buddhist Union since 1984. She practiced as a nun for two years.

Bibliography

Allione, Tsultrim. *Women of Wisdom*, Routledge & Kegan Paul, London, 1984.

Amarasingham, Lorna Rhodes. "The Misery of the Embodied: Representations of Women in Sinhalese Myth" *Women in Ritual and Symbolic Roles*, Plenum Press, New York, 1978.

Araki, James. *The Roof Tile of Tempyo*. University of Hawaii Press, Honolulu, 1976.

Bapat, P. V. and V. V. Gokhale. *Vinaya-sūtra*, K. P. Jayaswal Research Institute, Patna, 1982.

Bapat, P. V. and A. Hirakawa (trans.). *Shan-Chien-P'i-P'o-Sha: A Chinese Version by Sanghabhadra of Samantapāsādikā*, Bhandarkar Oriental Research Institute, Poona, 1970.

Basnayake, Leila. "The Bhikkhuni Sangha: Modern Revival of an Ancient Order," *Ceylon Daily News*, Vesak Number, 1939, pp. 44-47.

Beal, Samuel. *A Catena of Buddhist Scriptures from the Chinese*, Trubner & Co., London, 1871.

Beal, S. and D. J. Gogerly. "Comparative Arrangement of Two Translations of the Buddhist Ritual for the Priesthood, known as the Prātimoksha, or Pātimokhan," *Journal of the Royal Asiatic Society*, Vol. 19, London, 1862.

Belenky, Mary Field, et al. *Women's Ways of Knowing*, Basic Books, Inc., New York, 1986.

Beyer, Stephan. *The Cult of Tara: Magic and Ritual in Tibet*, University of California Press, Berkely, 1973.

Bhagavat, D. N. *Early Buddhist Jurisprudence*, Oriental Book Agency, Poona, 1939.

Bloss, Lowell. "Theravada 'Nuns' of Sri Lanka: Themes of the Dasasilmattawa Movement," Paper presented to the National Meeting, Association of Asian Studies, Washington, D.C., March 23, 1984.

Bode, Mabel. "Women Leaders of the Buddhist Reformation," *Journal of the Royal Asian Society of Great Britain and Ireland*, 1893, pp. 517-566, 763-798.

Byles, Marie Beuyeville. *Footprints of Gautama the Buddha*, Theosophical Publishing House, Wheaton, Illinois, 1957.

Chang, Garma C. C. (ed.) *A Treasury of Mahāyāna Sūtras*, Pennsylvania State University Press, University Park and London, 1983.

Chau, Bhikkhu Thich Minh. *Milindapañha and Nāgasenabhikshu Sūtra*, Vietnamese Buddhist Institute, Nalanda, 1964.

Cissell, Kathryn A. "The Pi-ch'iu-ni Chuan: Biographies of Famous Chinese Nuns from 317-516 C.E." Unpublished dissertation, University Microfilms International, Ann Arbor, 1972.

Copleston, R. S. *Buddhism: Primitive and Present in Magadha and Ceylon*. Longmans, Green and Co., London, 1892.

Rhys Davids, C. *Psalms of the Sisters*, Pali Text Society, London, 1948.

Rhys Davids, T. W. and Hermann Oldenberg. *Vinaya Texts*, Part I, II, III, Motilal Banarsidass, Delhi, 1974.

Dhargyey, Geshe Ngawang. *Tibetan Tradition of Mental Development*, Library of Tibetan Works and Archives, Dharamsala, 1974.

Dhirasekera, Jothiya. "Women and the Religious Order of the Buddha," *Journal of the Mahabodhi Society*, No. 5-6, May-June, 1967, pp. 156-161.

Dowman, Keith. *Sky Dancer: The Secret Life and Songs of the*

Lady Yeshe Tsogyel, Routledge and Kegan Paul, London, 1984.

Duley, Margaret and Mary I. Edwards (ed.) *The Cross-cultural Study of Women*, City University Press, New York, 1986.

Dutt, Nalinaksha. *Gilgit Manuscripts*, Srinagar, 1939.

Dutt, Sukuman. *Early Buddhist Monachism*, Munshiram Manoharlal, New Delhi, 1984.

Edkins, Joseph. *Chinese Buddhism*, Kegan Paul, Trench, Trubner, and Co., London.

Falk, Nancy A. "An Image of Woman in Old Buddhist Literature: The Daughters of Mara," *Women and Religion*, Judith Plaskow and Joan Arnold Romero, eds., Scholars' Press for the American Academy of Religion, 1974, pp. 105-112.

Falk, Nancy A. and Rita Gross (eds.). *Unspoken Worlds: Women's Religious Lives in Non-western Cultures*, Harper and Row, New York, 1980.

Fernandez, Audrey McK. "Women in Buddhism: For 2500 Years a Persisting Force," *Women & Buddhism*, Zen Lotus Society, 1986, pp. 35-57.

Frauwallner, E. *The Earliest Vinaya and the Beginnings of Buddhist Literature*, Istituto Italiano Per Il Medio Ed Estremo Oriente, Rome, 1956.

Friedman, Lenore. *Meetings with Remarkable Women: Buddhist Teachers in America*, Shambala Publications, Inc., Boston, 1987.

Giles, H. A. *The Travels of Fa-hsien*, Routledge and Kegan Paul, London, 1923.

Godakumbra, Chandra. "Women in Early Sinhala Society," *New Lanka* 4, No. 2, 1953.

Goldberg, Ellen S. "Sri Lanka's Outcaste Nuns," *The Tampa Tribune*, January 26, 1985.

Gombrich, Richard. *Precept and Practice*, Clarendon Press, Oxford, 1971.

Goonatilake, Hema. "*Vinaya* Tradition in China is Theravada," *Sunday Observer*, Sri Lanka, May 14, 1986.

Gross, Rita M. "Buddhism and Feminism: Toward Their Mutual Transformation," *The Eastern Buddhist*, Vol. XIX, No. 2, 1986, pp. 62-74.

Hartel, Herbert. *Karmavācanā*, Akademie-Verlag, Berlin, 1956.
Hecker, Hellmuth. *Buddhist Women at the Time of the Buddha*, Buddhist Publication Society, Kandy, 1982.
Hirakawa, Akira. *Monastic Discipline for the Buddhist Nuns*, K. P. Jayaswal Research Institute, Patna, 1982.
Hopkins, Jeffrey. *Meditation on Emptiness*, Wisdom Publications, London, 1983.
Hopkinson, Deborah, et al. *Not Mixing Up Buddhism*, White Pine Press, Fredonia, New York, 1986.
Horner, I. B. *The Book of the Discipline*, Vol. I-VI, Routledge & Kegan Paul, Ltd., London, 1982.
________ *Women Under Primitive Buddhism*, Motilal Banarsidass, Delhi, 1975.
Hughes, James. "Buddhist Feminism," *Women & Buddhism*, Zen Lotus Society, 1986, pp. 58-79.
Kabilsingh, Chatsumarn. *A Comparative Study of Bhikkhuni Pāṭimokkha*, Chaukhambha Orientalia, Varanasi, 1984.
Kajiyama, Yuichi. "Women in Buddhism," *The Eastern Buddhist*, Kyoto, Fall 1982.
Keyes, Charles F. "Mother or Mistress but Never a Monk: Buddhist Notions of Female Gender in Rural Thailand," *American Ethanologist* 11.2, 1984, pp. 223-241.
Khantipalo, Bhikkhu. *Banner of the Arahants: Buddhist Monks and Nuns from the Buddha's Time Till Now*, Buddhist Publication Society, Kandy, 1979.
Ku, Cheng-Mei. "The Mahisasakas' View of Women," Paper read at a Buddhist Dialogue Conference in Chiang Mai, Thailand, August, 1986.
Law, Bimala C. *Women in Buddhist Literature*, Indological Book House, Varanasi, 1981.
Malalasekera, G. P. *Encyclopaedia of Buddhism*, Government of Ceylon, Colombo, 1971.
Miao, Shu-lien (trans.) *The Bhikṣuṇī Ordination Transmitted by a Joint Assembly of Bhikṣus and Bhikṣuṇīs*, Unpublished manuscript, Taipei, 1983.
________ *The Dharmagupta-Bhikṣuṇī-Karman*, Unpublished manuscript, Taipei, 1983.

________ *The Dharmagupta-Bhikṣuṇī-Prāṭimokśa*, Unpublished manuscript, Taipei, 1982.

________ *The Model Transmission of the Śrāmaṇerikā Ordination*, Unpublished manuscript, Taipei, 1983.

Norman, K. R. *The Elders' Verses II: Therīgāthā*, Pali Text Society, London, 1971.

Obeyesekere, Garanath. *Medusa's Hair*, University of Chicago Press, Chicago, 1981.

Oldenberg, Hermann and Richard Pischel. *The Therīgāthā*, Pali Text Society, London, 1966.

Pachow, W. *A Comparative Study of the Prāṭimokṣa*, the Sino-Indian Cultural Society, Santiniketan, 1955.

Pachow, W. and R. Mishra. *The Prāṭimokṣa-sūtra of the Mahasanghikas*, Ganganatha Jha Research Institute, Allahabad, 1956.

Pao Chang (trans., Li Jung-hsi). *Biographies of Buddhist Nuns*, Tohokai, Inc., Osaka, 1981.

Paul, Diana. *Portraits of the Feminine in Mahayana Buddhism*, University of California Press, Berkeley, 1979.

________ *Women in Buddhism*, University of California Press, Berkeley, 1979.

Prebish, Charles S. *Buddhist Monastic Discipline: The Sanskrit Prāṭimokśa Sūtras of the Mahāsaṃghikās and Mūlasarvāstivādins*, Pennsylvania State University Press, University Park and London, 1975.

Rahula, Walpola. *History of Buddhism in Ceylon*, M. D. Gunasena and Co., Colombo, 1956.

Rajavoramuni, Phra. "Re-thinking Women's Place in Buddhism," *Bangkok Post*, May 11, 1987.

________ "Reconciling the Differences of Men and Women," *Bangkok Post*, May 12, 1987.

Ratnapala, Nandasena. *The Katikāvatas: Laws of the Buddhist Order of Ceylon from the 12th Century to the 18th Century*, Münchener Studien Zur Sprachwissenschaft, Munich, 1971.

Richman, Paula. "The Portrayal of a Female Renouncer in a Tamil Buddhist Text," *Gender and Religion: On the Com-*

plexity of Symbols (ed. Carolyn Walker Bynum, et al), Beacon Press, Boston, 1986.

Rosen, Valentina. *Der Vinayavibhanga zum Bhikṣuprāṭimokṣa der Sarvāstivādins*, Akademie-Verlag, Berlin, 1959.

________ *Upāliparpṛcchāsūtra: Ein Text zur buddhistischen Ordensdisziplin*, Vandenhoeck & Ruprecht, Gottingen, 1984.

Roth, Gustav. *Bhikṣuṇī-Vinaya*, K. P. Jayaswal Research Institute, Patna, 1970.

Sangharakshita. *The Eternal Legacy: An Introduction to the Canonical Literature of Buddhism*, Tharpa Publications, London, 1985.

Seneviratne, Maureen. *Some Women of the Mahavamsa and Culavamsa*, H. W. Cave and Co., Colombo, 1969.

Sharma, Arvind. "How and Why Did the Women in Ancient India Become Buddhist Nuns?" *Sociological Analysis*, Vol. 38-39, Spring 1977—Winter 1978, pp. 239-251.

________ (ed.) *Women in World Religions*, State University of New York Press, New York, 1987.

Sherburne, Richard. *A Lamp for the Path and Commentary*, George Allen and Unwin, Ltd., London, 1983.

Sidor, Ellen S. (ed.). *A Gathering of Spirit*, Primary Point Press, Cumberland, R.I., 1987.

Sivaraksa, Sulak. "Buddhist Women, Past and Present," *Kahawai: A Journal of Women and Zen*, Vol. 6, No. 1 and 2, Winter—Spring, 1985, pp. 3-11.

Subhuti, Dharmachari. *Buddhism for Today: A Portrait of a New Buddhist Movement*, Element Books, Wiltshire, 1984.

Sunim, Ja Gwang. "Training in Songgwang-sa: A Korean Zen Monastery," *Spring Wind*, Vol. 3, No. 1, pp. 15-19 and Vol. 3, No. 2, pp. 35-40, Zen Lotus Society, Toronto, 1983.

Sunim, Samu. "Eunyeong Sunim and the Founding of Pomun-Jong, the First Independent Bhikshuni Order," *Women & Buddhism*, Zen Lotus Society, Toronto, 1986, pp. 129-162.

Talim, T. V. "Buddhist Nuns and Disciplinary Rules," *Journal of the University of Bombay*, Vol. 34, No. 2, September, 1965, pp. 98-137.

Thera, Nanamoli. *The Patimokkha: The 227 Fundamental Rules of a Bikkhu*, Wat Bovoranivas Vihara, Bangkok, 1966.

Thich, Thien-An. *Buddhism and Zen in Vietnam in Relation to the Development of Buddhism in Asia*, Charles E. Tuttle Co., Rutland, Vermont, 1975.

Thurman, Robert A. F. "Guidelines for Buddhist Social Activism Based on Nagarjuna's Jewel Garland of Royal Counsels," *The Eastern Buddhist*, Vol. XVI, No. 1, Spring, 1983, pp. 19-51.

Tsai, Kathryn A. "The Chinese Buddhist Order for Women: The First Two Centuries," *Women in China*, Historical Reflections, Youngstown, New York, 1981, pp. 1-20.

Tsering, Acharya Tashi, and Philippa Russell. "An Account of the Buddhist Ordination of Women," *Choyang*, Vol. 1, No. 1, Dharamsala, Spring 1986, pp. 21-30.

Tsomo, Karma Lekshe. "Tibetan Nuns and Nunneries," *Tibet Journal*, Dharamsala, Winter, 1987.

Tsong-ka-pa. *Tantra in Tibet: The Great Exposition of Secret Mantra* (trans. Jeffrey Hopkins), George Allen & Unwin, Boston, 1977.

Vajirananavarorasa, Phra Maha Samana Chao Krom Phraya. *The Entrance to the Vinaya: Vinayamukha* (Vol. I, II, III). King Maha Makuta's Academy, Bangkok, 1969.

________ *Ordination Procedure*, King Maha Makuta's Academy, Bangkok, 1973.

Waldschmidt, Ernst. *Bruchstücke des Bhikṣuṇī-Prāṭimokṣa der Sarvāstivādins*, Deutsche Morgenlandische Gesellschaft, Leipzig, 1926.

Warder, A. K. *Indian Buddhism*, Motilal Banarsidass, Delhi, 1970.

Warren, H. C. *Buddhism in Translations*, Atheneum, New York, 1972.

Watters, Thomas. *On Yuan Chwang's Travels in India*, Munshi Ram Manohar Lal, Delhi, 1961.

Weeraratne, Amarasiri. "The Bhikkhuni Order in Ceylon," *Journal of the Mahabodhi Society*, No. 10 and 11, 1970, pp. 333-337.

________ "A Welcome Move Towards Reviving Bhikkhuni Order," *The Island*, Colombo, June 4, 1987.

Welch, Holmes. *The Practice of Chinese Buddhism: 1900-1950*, Harvard University Press, Cambridge, 1967.

Willis, Janice. "Nuns and Benefactresses: The Role of Women in the Development of Buddhism," Paper presented at a South Asia Studies Colloquium at University of Virginia, Spring, 1985.

________ "Tibetan Anis: The Nun's Life in Tibet," *Tibet Journal*, Dharamsala, 1984, pp. 14-32.

Yuyama, Akira. *A Systematic Survey of Buddhist Sanskrit Literature, Part I: Vinaya Texts*, Franz Steiner Verlag, Wiesbaden, 1979.

14552
10^{00}